MELISSA STEEL

BOO
FOR WHO?

Previously, in Bae for Pay...

Sam is stuck in a dead-end job as the whipping girl of her boss, Sandra the CEO. She spends her Friday nights in local wine shop Divine Drinks, where she befriends shop assistant Dean. They bond over their desire to pursue different careers - Sam as a writer and Dean as an actor - and how they felt stuck in their current jobs. Sam's BFF from uni, Harriet, phones and invites her to a reunion in their student town of St Fillan's. Following a misunderstanding, Sam and Dean have to pretend to be a couple for the whole reunion weekend.

Sam's best friend, June, a Thai masseuse, puts them through their paces so they appear a convincing partnership. She also accompanies them to St Fillan's for moral support, and ends up getting involved with Sam's old lecturer, Professor P. We also meet Nicky, another alumna. She has always been prone to exaggeration and no one really trusts her. Throughout the day, she pays special attention to Dean.

Meanwhile, Harriet wants a baby with her husband, Allan. She has read some tips online, one of which is suggesting a threesome to your husband to make him realise how much he actually wants to commit to family life. She tries this, but it backfires when Allan tries to lure Dean into a threesome. Harriet is not pleased with the whole situation and is growing suspicious that Sam and Dean aren't actually a couple either - so she hounds them to their room. Only Paxton can distract her from her crusade.

Behind closed doors, Sam and Dean give into a real attraction they have started to feel to each other. However, Dean admits that he has conflicting feelings about the situation and goes for a walk. He doesn't come back that night.

Paxton wakes Sam up the next morning to relate his adventure the previous night - a threesome with Harriet and Allan. At breakfast, Sam sees Dean but Nicky leads him away to 'talk business'. June tells Sam that she is having a thing with Professor P, but Sam is distracted by the situation with Dean. She hears more about the night before from Harriet and how she feels it has repaired her relationship with Allan.

Nicky tells Sam that she has given Dean a business proposition - join her as an escort on her new app, Bae for Pay, that links women up with men willing to play their boyfriend at events like this. Dean confirms this and they part ways.

Sam skulks back to her life before the reunion. She finds out that Harriet and Allan are having a baby, June and Professor P are 'official' and that Paxton has retreated to an island with two beautiful women. Sam resolves to follow her own dreams to become a writer and pens a book about her experiences over the last few months.

Paxton hooks her up with a literary connection. They arrange a meeting at a fancy literary club, but Sam changes her mind and asks for a meeting at Divine Drinks instead. On the way there, she bumps into Dean with her boss, Sandra the CEO of all people, but walks away to start her new life.

CHARACTER KEY

Something for you to flick back to if you get confused about who's boo is who's...

Sam: She wrote a book about her adventures in Bae for Pay and the action picks up about a year and a half after the last book finishes.

Hatton: An actor who Sam is often paired with on Danish talk shows.

June: Sam's best friend. A Thai masseuse with aspirations of overthrowing capitalism, but she has to spend her days playing the 'exotic other' for her clients.

Harriet: Sam's BFF from her uni days. Used to be a party girl, but settled down and married her boring boyfriend Allan.

Allan: Harriet's unexciting husband.

Paxton: Sam's rich playboy friend from university. He ended up having a threesome with Harriet and Allan in Bae for Pay in an effort to spice up their marriage/misguided attempt to persuade Allan to want kids.

Dean: Wine shop assistant who volunteered to pretend to be Sam's boyfriend at the reunion in Bae for Pay.

Professor P: Sam's lothario former lecturer and June's current boyfriend - they met at the reunion.

James: A personal trainer working at the summer school.

Aubrey: Famous director - friend of Hatton and client of James - also working at the school.

Lorando: Long-suffering head waiter in Belkita.

Parthenope/Annie: Hatton's teenage daughter.

Jesus: Not Christ, one of Sam's students.

Koala: Uptight student of Sam's.

Melody: A bland student of Sam's.

CHAPTER

1

When you are approaching 30, there's nothing quite like watching teenagers prancing around in thongs on the beach to make you want to throw yourself into the sea.

At least that is the short version of how I ended up jumping in a canal in my underpants and causing a minor international incident.

The longer version, well, you would need a book to cover everything that happened before, during and after that was directly related to that event. Luckily, this is it.

It actually all started with one of those rare moments of clarity in life. The only issue was that it happened on a Danish TV show.

Culture Vulture was hosted by Maurice Markham, a once-popular stand-up comedian who had quietly left the UK five years ago after being sick on a minor member of the Royal Family at the Henley Regatta. He might not have had to leave in disgrace had it not been recorded and turned into a GIF, which was now commonly used in the UK to signal the hangover from hell.

He had a cult following in Denmark who welcomed him with open arms, though. The result was Culture Vulture, where he interviewed international celebrities from his studio in Copenhagen. Like him, they were often more popular in Denmark now than they were in their native countries. I was there because Bae for Pay had proved bizarrely popular with the Scandinavian market, for reasons I still don't understand.

I was standing backstage, waiting to be announced, gripping a glass of incredibly sugary sparkling wine because I needed a jolt of energy. I had decided to go it alone and self-publish Bae for Pay, which meant I was organising all this promotional stuff by myself, alongside still working for the dreaded Sandra the CEO. The situation was by turns awkward, horrifying and depressing, but until my fan-base expanded beyond Danes with dry senses of humour, I couldn't afford to leave it. Of course, she acted like using annual leave to do events like this was punishable by death. I was therefore on a quick turnaround, flying in on an inhumanely early flight before limping back to Edinburgh on a red-eye flight for work the next day.

All this swirled around my mind whilst a girlband, who seemed to be the result of a breeding experiment using puppies and Olympic gymnasts, rehearsed their dance moves beside me. They all had scarily similar saucer-like eyes, bouncing hair and limbs flying about at all angles as they gyrated against each other. It looked like a number from Kama Sutra: The Musical, and my ire only grew when one's bubble butt nudged my glass and sent the last of my prosecco flying, the flute smashing on the floor.

I was just about ready to puncture her arse with a shard of glass when I realised Maurice was about to call me on. He was doing a bit on this week in the news and just wrapping up a heartwarming tale of a little girl in Rungstedlund who had taught a squirrel to do backflips. "What a fantastic story. Talking of fantastic stories, next up we have a novelist who is sure to have some great tales for us. She's my bae, but not for pay, it's Sam Chambers!"

I walked out into the hot studio lights, smiling warmly at the anonymous audience. Maurice wrapped me in one of his signature, effusive hugs as the audience applauded. It sounded like a hundred turbo hand dryers taking flight. I stiffened in his embrace; I am absolutely terrified of the noise those hand dryers make and avoid them whenever possible, instead choosing to shake my hands like they are two spaniels straight out a river. I had been feeling guilty about this of late though because a new virus was in the news and we were all being encouraged by politicians to improve our hygiene habits, but it was so vague that I only periodically remembered to feel ashamed of myself.

Anyway, Maurice continued the love-in by plonking two massive kisses in the vicinity of my cheeks. Perhaps he was health-conscious because he completely missed any skin contact, but more likely he was just a luvvie with the emotional depth of a sink.

"It's been too long, my darling!" he said, despite the fact we had never met before. I could only just hear him above the crowd, but it was his shimmering neon suit that was the loudest thing in the room.

I dodged another volley of air kisses and made my way over to the studio's sofa, which is obligatory on a talk show, but this one was quite atypical; it was fuchsia and shaped like a seated camel. I knew from flicking through Maurice's Instagram while bored at the airport that he had recently hosted a travel programme about Morocco. If his social media was in any way reflective of his experience, he had spent most of it clinging to an unfortunate local young guide called Ahmed on the back of an unwilling camel. Having noticed this unique nod to North Africa, I couldn't help spotting various other things around the studio, an ornate coloured-glass lamp on Maurice's desk, a grand and intricate Berber rug on the floor and a Fez on the dromedary's head.

As I scrambled into the low camel 'seat'. The first guest out, I was at least spared the indignity of humiliating myself in front of someone semi-famous, even if I suspected the audience had got a flash of my butt crack as I mounted the camel. At least I had worn trousers, I thought, a pair of Mom jeans I had found in a vintage shop last time I was in Copenhagen. In one sense, it was highly ironic because I don't have a maternal bone in my body, but, as people kept reminding me lately, I was almost 30 and did you know that so-and-so just turned 30 and they have two kids now?! It was as if it was expected your uterus turned into a gestational factory line when you hit the big 3-0.

The applause and some titters at what I presumed was my builder's bum faded to a hum and then to silence. I tried to smile naturally, but feared the more that I tried, the more I looked like an imposter robot. I had done a few similar shows by now, but I could never shake the strange feeling of being under a very large, communal Scandinavian microscope. Even if the audience laughed at all my jokes, I still felt like I was being examined in forensic detail on a national scale. Flicking through my Instagram comments after a show, I would always find that one that said 'I would shag her but why is one of her boobs bigger than the other?' or 'her laugh sounds like an injured donkey'. Sometimes I would reply 'Why don't you ask your wife?' (the boob questions always came from guys with loved-up profile pics and bios proclaiming they were a 'loving husband) or' 'ee aw'. However, you never get a reprieve in the court of public opinion.

Maurice settled on his own chair, which I now noticed was some sort of Moorish knock-off throne, its wooden frame covered in carefully whittled lattices. However, he obviously hadn't embraced the Muslim religion of his new obsession because he produced a chilled bottle of sparkling wine from the well-stocked fridge beside his desk.

"It's not I'm Sorry Rosé," he said with a wink, which made his perma-tanned face scrunch up like an old leather jacket. "But we thought you would still appreciate it."

"Well, it certainly makes up for the one that was knocked out of my hand backstage," I said. The girl band member with the errant arse stared at me icily from the wings.

"What happened?" asked Maurice, sensing a good 'talk show story', though he also looked a bit confused. Normally these anecdotes are given in advance and are meant to be funny, if they weren't so painfully rehearsed. He flicked through his cards to find mine, but it wasn't in the stable of banal wine-related stories I had submitted.

"Oh, I think it was just a casualty of a last-minute rehearsal of...what's the girl band's name?"

"Daddy's Little Girls!" said Maurice with a grin.

"Well, that's something. It's not often you associate Freud with popular music," I said, taking a sly sip of my drink.

Sensing danger, or even worse, an honest opinion, Maurice interjected with, "So, it has been quite a year for you, Sam! This time 12 months ago you were working in an office and dreaming of writing a book. Now here you are, a published author on the second most popular talk show in Denmark after 10.30pm!"

I think I was supposed to say "Oh yes! My life has completely changed! All my problems have been solved and I spend my downtime being served vintage champagne by muscled men wearing only strategic body glitter." That's not how life works, though. An awkward silence crept out from me and began to consume the room as I considered my response. Beads of sweat rose on Maurice's dyed mahogany hair.

"Well," I said eventually. "My life has changed, but not a lot. After this interview, I'll still go back to work in that same office tomorrow morning. I'm a barely successful self-published author, not an Instagram sugar baby with a sideline in selling leggings and protein shakes to my followers," I shrugged.

The audience laughed - nervously. Maurice threw his head back and laughed too, at what, I don't think he was sure, it was sort of an automatic response to fill time and make the show move along more nicely.

"You're one funny lady, Sam!"

"That's one way of putting it, yes."

Maurice turned to the camera in front of his desk. "Join us after the break where we will be hearing more from my BFF Sam and our next guest, action man Hatton Finch!" Maurice waved at the camera before picking up his own glass up with a flourish and draining every last drop. He then made his way unsteadily offstage, brushing off a couple of interns who had come to his aid.

The audience clapped with renewed enthusiasm - Hatton Finch was clearly a favourite here. I remembered he had been in some cult classic teen drama a few years ago and was married to Electra Lawson-Finch, an intimidatingly beautiful actress turned wellness expert. More recently, he had become more famous for his ability to keep a straight face while uttering ridiculous lines in action films that apparently did very well in Denmark. Even if the audience liked him, they were by now all preoccupied with their phones, so I took the opportunity to sneak out of the limelight for a few minutes. I extricated myself from the camel with all the grace of Jabba the Hutt and made my escape.

"Hey! Stick to the script! That's how we get the magic of live TV!" a stern producer informed me straightening the camel's fez informed me. I smiled tightly, as if I was barely concealing a middle finger between my lips.

In the wings, I found Maurice air-kissing another man, who I presumed was Hatton Finch. He looked about 40 and was dressed in 'I just threw this on' jeans and leather jacket that a stylist had no doubt spent many hours deliberating over. If Maurice looked like he was being pickled in middle age, this guy looked like he had been cryogenically frozen at peak silver fox. There were a few lines on his face, but only enough to capture the mum market, and his full head of hair was attracting the vengeful gaze of a much younger but much balder runner. His hair was freshly cut too, I noticed a peppering across his leather jacket as I loitered, waiting for Maurice to introduce us. Growing increasingly bored, I couldn't decide whether his hair was blonde or brown, it couldn't seem to make up its mind and neither could I.

"Ah Gary!" said Maurice, his eyes finally focussing on me. "Gary, we are almost blood brothers. I can't believe I have not introduced you to this wonderful woman before. This is my other guest this evening, er..." He trailed off, clearly at a loss without his cue cards.

"Sam Chambers," I reminded him.

"Ugh, I would have got it eventually!" Maurice spluttered. Gary chuckled and gave me a sympathetic look.

"Anyway, I need another gin, Gary. I will leave you and.."

"Sam," I said, more to annoy him than anything else.

"*Sam* to chat." Maurice stuck turned away. We watched him stick his nose in the air and clop off like an affronted Shetland pony.

"My name's not Gary, by the way," he said as we watched Maurice trying to attract the attention of a young muscular barman. "I'm Hatton, I'll be on with you after the break."

"I thought that might be the case," I said, turning back to him.

"Don't take it too much to heart that he didn't remember your name," said Hatton, grabbing us a couple of glasses of fizz from a passing waiter.

"You have to stick up for him, since you're best friends and all," I said as he handed me a glass.

"Ha! I've only ever spoken to him on this show."

"How many times have you been on?"

"Oh, maybe 10 times. I'm not really sure, to be honest. I can tell you though that you should buckle up and prepare for him to greet you like a long-lost relative every time he sees you from now on."

Maurice was now making his way back to us with a G&T. "My darlings! My lovelies! You beautiful..." Maurice looked me up and down before settling his eyes on Hatton, "you beautiful man. Let's step out into the limelight once more!"

"When you said like a long-lost relative, did you mean red-headed stepchild?" I whispered to Hatton as we followed Maurice out.

"I don't know what he's talking about," said Hatton with mock-horror. "You're much prettier than those girl band members over there. At least you don't look like your face would melt if you got too close to Maurice's Moroccan lamp."

"Please, I'll blush!" I said sarcastically, but I did suddenly feel quite hot. Must be the studio lights, I thought.

I walked out and lowered myself back onto the camel, making sure to back in like a dump truck to at least avoid any bum exposure this time. Hatton waited just offstage to be called and Maurice was settling back into his throne. We were counted back in and the show began again.

"Welcome back to Culture Vulture with me, Maurice Markham. The fabulous author Sam Chambers has joined me tonight, and now I am delighted to welcome our second guest, Hatton Finch!"

Applause rang out as Hatton strode onstage with a confidence I couldn't even begin to think about faking, before flopping casually onto his side of the camel.

"It's glorious to see you again, my old man!" declared Maurice.

"Thank you, Maurice."

"How are you?"

"I'm good, thanks, I always enjoy being back in Denmark," said Hatton with a soppy smile to the audience. I heard a sound I couldn't quite place, maybe it was ovaries popping.

"You're back here to promote your new role in Morgenstern Murders, yes?" asked Maurice.

"Yes, I'm very excited about it," Hatton replied, sounding about as excited as Anne Boleyn on the way to the chopping block. "It's my first 'web' TV series."

"Yes, yes, how thrilling. What about your daughter, Pomegranate? What's she up to?"

"She's actually called Parthenope."

"That's what I said," bluffed Maurice. "Parthe-Parthe-negranate is the hottest thing on Instagram. Rumour is that bikini picture she put up the other day netted her a modelling deal with a fast fashion label that advertising law prevents me from naming." Maurice turned to the camera and mimed a hammy 'boohoo' crying face. "Aren't you a proud father?"

However good an actor Hatton might have been, his limits were obviously being tested. He crossed his legs and rolled his eyes. "I'm proud of Parthenope, but not necessarily because of how many likes she gets for posting photos of herself in a bikini. She's only just 18. Anyway, let's move on, there's something unseemly about grown men sitting about talking about one of their daughters in a swimsuit." He finished with a firm but good-natured laugh.

Maurice laughed along too, but his lips curled up as he began to formulate a retort. I mean, how dare Hatton not want to talk about his daughter making borderline child pornography!

"You know, the pressure to be a certain way on social media is immense, isn't it?" I interjected. "I think I'll spare the public any pictures of me in a bikini though, I get enough harassment on it for daring to exist when I'm fully clothed!"

A few appreciative claps came from the audience. Maurice chuckled like canned laughter. "Ah, Sam, yes, I did have a couple of questions for you I didn't get to in the first half!"

My tactic had worked, Maurice had moved on. Momentarily distracted, his goldfish-like faculties had reset, avoiding a scene with Hatton. Maurice looked down at his cards, beginning to read aloud robotically, like a 5-year-old in a nativity play: "Sam...What-is-it-like-to-be-a-writer-is-it-as-lonely-as-they-say-it-is."

"It's not especially lonely. I mean, I can feel as lonely in the office as I do writing."

What I imagine were five or six millennials in the grips of a spirited quarterlife crisis cackled supportively from the dark of the audience.

This did not quite compute with Maurice, who sought refuge in his cards, searching for his next prompt.

"That's actually quite a good point," said Hatton. "Parthenope might have an incredible following on Instagram but her real best friend is probably a stuffed elephant we gave her when we brought her home from the hospital."

Now I became the interviewer. "Sorry, but do you want your daughter to never speak to you again?"

"That suggests she speaks to me at the moment. Maurice, can we get some more bubbly?"

"Yes! As if you have to ask," said Maurice, who was obviously very quick to forgive and forget, flashing a flirtatious smile at poor Hatton as he passed him the bottle.

I took a sip of mine after Hatton poured.

"Maurice! I know you have a handsome man in front of you, but didn't you say you had some questions to ask *me*?" I asked, or was it the sparkling wine?

"You're an only child, aren't you?" asked Hatton.

"Yes, why?" I asked. Wasn't it Maurice who was at least supposed to be pretending to interview me?

"Just a hunch," shrugged Hatton with a pantomime wink at the audience, who burst into laughter.

"Oh, yes, yes," I said, warming up for a speech I had made so many times that I should probably draft a PowerPoint presentation to complete the production. Everyone at St Fillan's had heard it before and knew not to ask, but talk shows were new territory.

"All only children are solipsistic narcissists. They are obsessed with themselves and think they are the centre of the universe," I said, rattling off my introduction. "Oh, or maybe I'm getting confused, Hatton, isn't that actors?"

Applause and hoots emanated from the audience.

Hatton smiled at me. "I wouldn't know, I am far too self-obsessed for introspection."

"Moving on," said Maurice, realising the attention had not been on him for a good 30 seconds. Gripping his cards, he asked, "Sam, the question everyone is asking...why didn't Sam and Dean get together in the book?"

The audience murmured approvingly, but I was vibrating with irritation. I had a moment of realisation: if one more person asked me why Sam didn't end up with Dean in Bae for Pay, I was going to push them into the path of oncoming traffic. This was a pedestrianised area of Copenhagen though, so there were no immediately available massive lorries to crush them under. Besides, the Danes love cycling, so HGVs are in short supply anyway.

It was the one thing everyone wanted to know. At first, I didn't mind explaining it to readers who asked at book signings, or journalists in interviews. To me, it always seemed quite clear why Dean and Sam didn't end up together, but I was happy to clarify. However, I had now been asked it so much that I never wanted to hear it again, and couldn't understand why my explanations hadn't sunk in.

"Oh God, Maurice, why does everyone ask that?" I sighed.

Maurice looked at me blankly.

"I genuinely want to know!"

Maurice puzzled on this for a few seconds. "Erm...I'm sorry Sam, I just read what's on the cards."

I rubbed my forehead. A headache was coming on. Maurice looked at Hatton for back-up, but he simply reclined on the camel and left him to his fate.

Maurice touched a finger to his ear, no doubt desperately trying to keep up with the instructions he was getting from the gallery on how to disarm me.

"We only ask what the audience want to know, Sam," he said through a gritted smile.

"It's just that I wonder if no one noticed that Dean was actually a bit of an idiot whose one true love was actually himself?" I asked on the edge of my camel seat, opening up my interrogation to the audience.

Next to me, Hatton nodded. "That's a pretty good point. I read it and he was pretty self-obsessed. And that's coming from an actor!"

"And an only child!" I said. We turned to each other, glasses in hand. We raised them to each other and clinked, it seemed like the natural thing to do.

"Haha, you're both such cards," Maurice said to the camera, in a tone that said 'I wish I was back in Morocco being slathered in sun lotion by Ahmed'. "But I'm afraid that's all we have got time for tonight. Please give it up for Daddy's Little Girls, who will play us out with their new single, 'I Need a New Daddy,"

The lights faded on us as the act went on.

CHAPTER

2

Deciding to jump before I was pushed, I quickly gathered my things from the dressing room after the show. I had visions of that producer who had been straightening the camels fez finding an inventive way to kill me with it. The audience had enjoyed our banter and I was already getting tagged in lots of comments with Hatton about how good we had been, but the production team had given us stony glares as we made our way offstage.

We had lost track of each other as we were hurried off by runners. I considered messaging him on Instagram later. Would that count as sliding into his DMs though? What even was my life?

I poked my head round my door and breathed a sigh of relief, no angry producers were about. I shuffled at speed down the corridor.

"Oi!"

I froze. Was I about to be strangled with a fez tassel? I turned and let out a sigh of relief, it was only Hatton.

"That was a lot more fun than these things normally are," he said, jogging up to me. He was carrying a complimentary Culture Vulture tote bag on his shoulder. He pulled it down to reveal a bottle of booze.

"I swiped this from Maurice's fridge on the way out, fancy a drink?"

"Yes, let's celebrate being the adult equivalent of those two naughty children at the back of the class!"

"Excellent," said Hatton, taking my arm and moving at speed down the corridor. He looked behind us as he opened the door.

"Just checking. Think one of the producers might kill us," he said.

"Was it the one loitering by the fez?"

"Yeah! He had a Demon Headmaster glare going on, didn't he?"

We clipped down some stairs and out a fire escape, which led us to the waterway behind the studio. The city was purring softly, a mix of distant traffic, lapping water and idle boat engines filling the air. I took a deep, calming breath, filling my lungs with air that was hot and salty.

"My agent is going to kill me. I don't think I said anything about the TV show," laughed Hatton, unwrapping the foil at the top of the bottle. He walked over to the water's edge, a stone embankment used for canal tours during the day, or, as it had been amusingly amended to by vandals, 'Anal Tours'.

"At least I don't have that problem," I said, walking over to join him. "There's no one around to kill me, apart from myself, obviously, but I am determined to not give into those people on Instagram who keep telling me to do it."

"Oh, you get them too?" he said, still fumbling with the bottle. "One said I should commit seppuku because they didn't like my CBeebies Bedtime Story."

"That's one angry toddler." I looked about, half-expecting Maurice or an irate producer to burst through the fire exit. "Will we be ok here? They won't come out looking for us?"

"Ha! Don't think so. Maurice is usually enough of a handful after a show after he starts on his edibles." At least that's what I think he said, I was finding it hard to focus because he was making such a hash out of trying to open the bloody bottle.

"Give it here," I sighed, pulling the bottle off of him. I felt the pressure on the cork from inside the bottle. It was going to explode, no matter what I did. "What did you do? Strap this to a pneumatic drill?"

"I have a very bouncy gait when I run, OK? It's a proper condition and I have to do Pilates twice a week because of it. It's a very difficult subject for me," he said.

"Wow, surprised you're not in the Paralympics," I said as dryly as I could, but I was concentrating on the task at hand. The cork was about to pop, I couldn't avoid it any longer. "Better out than in," I said with a flick of the wrist, which sent the cork into the water, along with the fizzing contents of the bottle.

Hatton produced a couple of plastic cups from the tote bag and I poured the wine. "Skål, as they say here," said Hatton, raising his glass.

"Get it down ye, as we say in Scotland," I said, the plastic cups crackling as we pushed them together. As we sipped the wine on the canal bank, I became aware of a group of teenagers coming down some steps to the water. They were carrying cheap cans of supermarket beer and engaged in loud flirtations and screeches of gossip, like a flock of hormonal seagulls. However, all that soon died down when they caught sight of us; the noise was replaced with silent, pitying looks.

"Maybe they recognise us?" shrugged Hatton once they had passed by.

"Come on," I smirked. "They're not exactly our target audiences."

"Who are our target audiences?"

"Well, disaffected Danes, obviously," I said. "For God knows what reason. We actually have two very distinct audiences, though. Me, people in their late 20s and early 30s who consider olives from Lidl a luxury. You, over-40s who would die if their farmer's market ran out of £20 jars of olives."

"And can you segment our audiences any further? My manager is also going on about segmenting my audience like it's a damn satsuma," said Hatton.

I took a contemplative sip of fizz. "Well, ok, let me see. Me: Quarter-life crisis, you: Mid-life crisis. Me: people Googling why their backs hurt for the first time. You: people who know why their backs hurt because they can afford an expensive chiropractor. Me: women who dislike me but their weird friend is making them read my novel. You: men who hate you but want to know how to avoid Dad bod." I paused because Hatton's laugh was becoming distracting.

"Wow, you know your stuff."

"What can I say, I work in marketing."

"Yeah, I heard you mention you still have another job."

"We're not all so fortunate to be ourselves full-time professionally," I said, pouring more wine, of course.

"You should try it. I think it could be a brilliant career," he said, looking at me the way he looked at Halle Berry when she shot a pterodactyl out the sky in Dinosaur Danger in nothing but a ragged shirt; the memory of hate-watching it at an Edinburgh multiplex aged 15 came flooding back. Why was he looking at me like that, and why had that slightly awe-struck yet aroused look been filed away in my mind so long?

I didn't have much time to think about it because I could feel the teenagers' eyes flitting back and forth at us, as painful as lash whips. They would look, but only for a moment. It was like looking at the sun, the embarrassment they felt was so intense that they could only stand it for a few seconds.

"I think we might be an unwanted presence," I said, nodding my head towards them.

"You're right, we are clearly cramping their style. In the 'Anal Canal', of all places" sniggered Hatton, turning his eyes to the water, in case he earned more burning mortification by looking directly at the teenagers. It was clear that the waterfront was a hang-out for underagers. I wouldn't have been surprised if they normally carded people and refused entry to anyone over 18.

The teenagers gave us another collective glare before beginning to undress.

"What's going on? Have we got caught in some sort of paedophile entrapment?" asked Hatton, trying to look anywhere but the underage flesh.

"Ha, no, I think it's some sort of graduation celebration." The kids were discarding the white sailor-style caps all Danes who graduate high school wear with pride. One or two even had oversized Danish flags - not that that was unusual. The Danes loved their red and white flag - it streamed from the boats going past us and the buildings above us.

One of the boys downed his can of beer and leapt into the water in his boxers, spraying Hatton and I with canal juice; it was as hot as the evening air when it hit our faces and a bit of what I hoped was turgid seaweed clung to my face. I flicked it away quickly so I didn't think about it too much.

We both laughed at the grossness, even though the dive bomber's message was clear: go away, you decrepit dinosaurs.

A girl stepped closer to the water. She was so tiny that she almost didn't exist, but she made up for her lack of physical presence with pure bad bitch energy that only the most popular girls possess. She began to wiggle out of a pair of equally tiny denim shorts to reveal thong underwear; they had a sporty style, made of jersey with athletic tape around the waist, but there was no way anyone could do any sort of exercise in those, apart from bracing your butt cheeks against a wedgie.

"How can 15-year-olds dress like that?" I said, prodding Hatton to look at the underage bodies while he kept his gaze firmly on the water. "When I was 15, my best underwear had the Care Bears on them. I still have them, actually, and they are probably one of the most erotic undergarments I own."

"You know, when I graduated from RADA, I never suspected my career would end being banned of going within 100m of children because I had a drink on a canal in Copenhagen with you," he said, knocking back his glass.

The girl whisked her crop top off to reveal a lace bralette. She looked back at the lesser mortals in the main group, the girls who once ate chocolate or actually had periods. The look on her face was the same one Elizabeth I probably gave courtiers whose necks she had grown tired of. She beckoned forward an unlucky winner, a girl, although

26

blessed with a large set of boobs, could never compete in the bralette stakes; her chest looked like two freshly caught octopi attempting to escape the material. It was then that I noticed that all the girls were wearing the exact same bralette and thong combo. I had flashbacks to the popular girls of my own spotty youth, who all had the same 'school' bag, a satchel too small for any textbook, made by a brand called Koolux. The girls' verve for pettiness and persecution earned them the name the Koolux Klan, and it seemed like I was being faced with their nearly-naked successors.

"Individuality truly is dead," I said to Hatton. "Look at the identikit underwear."

"I would rather not," said Hatton, balling up the foil from around the bottleneck and popping it into the water. "Plus, I'm a married man, but you probably already knew that." I rolled my eyes. Just because he was famous, he presumed I would be obsessed with his life. I mean, of course I knew he was married to Electra Lawson-Finch, the top model of 2003 and ageless nymph with her own health and beauty brand, but that was really besides the point.

"Married for 20 years. It's a long time. But a good time. Believe me, still have plenty of good times, if you know what I mean."

"Ew, unfortunately I do. Pro tip: Don't say that in interviews. Celebrities only ever mention how much sex they are having right before they get divorced. Everyone will think you're overcompensating."

"Really?" he asked, looking a bit lost.

"Oh yeah, it's definitely a thing."

The foil was now bobbing hopelessly out to sea to fulfil its destiny as part of a garbage island floating off of Indonesia. Hatton crumpled his empty cup and made to throw it in the water.

"Don't do it!" shouted one of the boys. "Think of the environment!"

Hatton put the plastic down like he was surrendering a gun in a stand-off with the police.

I gave him a theatrical dirty look for the benefit of the teenagers. "Don't you know that plastic waste is the new infanticide?!"

"Of course I do, I just wasn't thinking. I'm an Ambassador for Plastic-Free Planet, for Christ's sake," he muttered back.

The queen bee was now emerging like a small designer-breed seal. She slipped up the embankment towards us, ready to do battle, even if a penetrating stare and her soaking underwear were her only armour.

"You two disgust me," she said, the words dripping from her lips like polluted water.

"Is this about the cup?" asked Hatton sheepishly, looking at it instead of the jailbait parading in front of us.

"The cup is bad enough," she said without a shiver, even though there was now a definite chill in the air. "But you're both way too old to be hanging out round here drinking." Her tone was the perfect mesh of embarrassed teenager and disapproving schoolmarm.

"Hey, I'm only almost 30!" I said, half-joking, half-mortally affronted.

"Only?" she asked. Her group had slowly approached during the exchange and now cackled like well-trained hyenas.

"One day you will be 30 too," piped up Hatton. "Unless they Logan's Run all of you, but chance would be a fine thing."

"What's a Logan's Run?" came a confused voice from the back.

"God, I feel old," said Hatton into his hands.

"Hey," I said to the girl. "Do you think just because you are young that you have a monopoly on making a spectacle of yourself?" I stood up, my double-digit BMI making me an imposing figure above the Queen Bee. Her squad's eyes lit up and so did their phones as they scrambled to record the moment, but I didn't care.

The Queen Bee folded her arms over her soggy bralette and didn't actually say anything, but made a sort of soundscape of embarrassed teenager noises.

"I've been stripping off and jumping into questionable bodies of water for as long as you have been alive. I went to St Fillan's, bitch," I said, unthreading my belt from my jeans like they were a dressing gown and this was a bathroom, not a dockside thoroughfare in one of the largest cities in Northern Europe.

"Wh...what are you doing?" asked Hatton as I threw my jeans on the ground.

"I'm going in. I used to do this all the time at uni. Jumping into the North Sea was a rite of passage," I said, striding past the teens who were playing paparazzi with their cameras. Hatton scrambled to his feet and pushed through the crowd.

Now the teens were shouting what was (probably?) encouragement in Danish. A wave of nausea came over me as I peered down at the water below, which suddenly seemed very far away, dark and deep.

I was committed now though, just as I had committed to jumping in the North Sea one freezing February day after seven pints with Paxton 10 years ago. I had followed through then and I would follow through now, I vowed. Nervously, I adjusted my bra and pants, even though I knew they would be totally displaced when I hit the water. It was only then that it dawned on me that I was parading about in a brown bra that had been battered by the washing machine one too many times. Oh, and that my left boob was always on an escape mission from it, for some reason.

I could see Hatton appearing out of the corner of my eye. My first thought wasn't 'What is he doing?' but, 'Oh my God, Hatton Finch has seen me in my ill-fitting underwear and I have just remembered that I had a massive panini for lunch and consequently have the stomach of a pregnant donkey.'

Why did that matter? I asked myself. I didn't have time to answer though because I had, at least outwardly, committed to being a champion of ageing disgracefully and body positivity. Once again, I had started something, so I would finish it, even if I felt like a cumbersome aquatic mule in the process.

"You've not come to talk me down?" I asked, suppressing a shiver, even though it was a warm night.

"No," said Hatton, throwing his jacket on the ground. "I have come to join you."

"Really?" I asked as he fumbled with his shirt buttons. "Yes," he said definitively as he got the hang of it and got his shirt off. I looked back at our audience; the kids were filming it all while the Queen Bee made a face of pure revulsion, like a Roman emperor watching a plucky Christian outwit a lion.

I turned back to see Hatton standing next to me in a pair of budgie smuggling underpants. I raised an eyebrow, I didn't think anyone wore these out of 1970s catalogues occasionally resurrected for comedy value on Buzzfeed. They were so old school that they almost distracted from his complete lack of Dad Bod. He had a sort of wiry but not entirely unattractive body, a bit like a hot fisherman in a romance novel. My mind was clearly wandering when Hatton said, "Don't look at me like that. They were the only things not in the wash when I left the house," a protective hand covering the offending underpants.

"You read my mind," I said, trying to focus on the underpants and not the man inside them.

"Shall we?" he asked, taking my hand as if we were going to hot-foot it around a Regency dancehall, not throw ourselves into a Danish waterway in our worst underwear.

"Yes, we shall," I said, stepping forward, pulling Hatton with me. The key was not to hesitate on the ledge, I thought in the long seconds we whooshed towards the water below. I had learnt that on St Fillan's cliffs; the longer you lingered, the worse it seemed, the more you thought about breaking your back and having to go through life as a plucky paraplegic, completing challenges most able-bodied people would find horrific to raise money for charity. It was better just to jump in and embrace your fate.

We hit the water with a crash, our hands flying apart. The water was cold, but not as bad as the North Sea in February. Spiralling back to the surface, I managed to rearrange my inevitably displaced bra. What a professional, I thought, smiling up at the aghast teens. I looked around but couldn't see Hatton. I was swivelling and shouting his name when I felt a sharp tug on my hair. I was dragged out the water and found myself on a tough synthetic surface, like being thrown onto a tent. There was shouting in Danish and bright lights. I could make out Hatton in glinting tinfoil as the water cleared from my eyes. I saw a man in bright orange shorts holding a floatation device and deduced he must be a lifeguard.

"Are you both OK?" he asked loudly.

"Yes. I mean, apart from our swim being so rudely interrupted," said Hatton. We both laughed shuddering giggles and the lifeboat crew looked at us like disappointed parents who have picked up their vomiting adolescent from their first party.

"Bunch of timewasters," muttered the lifeguard. "Don't they know there is a virus going about? We don't need this crap."

"Hey, no one asked you to pluck us out the water! We were just minding our own business!" I argued.

"Not you," said the man. "The people who called for us to rescue you. They said that two elderly infirm people had fallen in."

"Did they?" I said, my eyes rising to the group of cackling teenagers on the deck above us. "I wonder who would do such a thing."

"Twats," said Hatton.

"Yeah. Sure. Whatever. Anyway, we will give you a ride to the next dock while you warm up. Not much else to do tonight," said the lifeguard, signalling to the guy manning the wheel to restart the engine. The boat lurched back to life and we pulled away from our tormentors.

"Elderly and infirm," I muttered.

"Cheeky tits," said Hatton.

"I'm not even 30!! I have got plenty of time left to fritter away my youth."

"And I'm only 40!"

I gave him a glare.

"OK, 41...and 18 months."

"Measuring your age in months...what are you? The world's oldest baby?"

"Wow, being lectured by *you* about acting my age!"

"It's not very becoming for a lady novelist to take the piss on a talk show, get a bit drunk and verbally abuse some youths and jump semi-naked in a canal, is it?" I said, crumpling a bit of tinfoil to hide behind coyly in the absence of a fan.

"No, but why not, when you look that good doing it?" he said, our tinfoil wraps crackling against each other. "God, that sounded pervy, I didn't mean it like that. I just meant, you pull it off. Whatever the hell you're doing."

"I'll let you know if I ever work it out," I said, swaying as the boat passed by our adolescent audience.

CHAPTER

3

We had the last laugh though. The kids might have called the authorities on us for being old and filmed the humiliation too, but the footage was a hit online. Millennials and Gen Xers found the way *we* had embarrassed the kids hilarious and kind of empowering, or so the comments and messages I got on Instagram kept telling me. Coupled with our double act performance on Maurice's show, producers and executives started requesting we appear together on their programmes, usually taking on some challenge equally as hairbrained as jumping in a Danish canal.

Next time we met, it was in the bar of a hotel off of the town hall square. I was becoming a bit of a bigger deal so the TV channel was even paying for the room here for me. I had stayed here a few times now and liked it because the whole thing felt like one giant comfortable apartment that I could never afford, filled with random stuff like a life-size glow-in-the-dark unicorn and oddly engrossing coffee table books about Zoot suits and funeral practices in Amish country.

I made myself comfortable on a long sofa that looked out onto Copenhagen's city hall on the Rådhuspladsen, a grand building bigger than Holyrood Palace back home in Edinburgh. You had to admire mainland Europe for their flare when it came to municipal buildings.

In the UK, most city council offices are decaying grey buildings covered in suspicious stains.

That's not the reason I chose this table, though. It had become our 'usual', the one Hatton and I would meet at before whatever show we were going on. I had found him sitting at it about six weeks beforehand because it was also right in front of the TV and there was a news report on about something people were calling the Baby Botch, that new virus the lifeguard mentioned when he pulled us out the water. It had started out going through an entire high school in Detroit and was now spreading throughout North America and, at the very least, infecting international media too.

The symptoms of the virus itself were fever/chills, inflamed skin, poor impulse control and irritability, most of which I thought were just symptoms of being a teenager. Hatton didn't appreciate it when I said that though, pointing out he was worried about his daughter Parthenope, who was at school in the US.

She was also at a posh, girls-only boarding school in Massachusetts, a far cry from the sink school in Detroit where the outbreak had happened. The way it was depicted in news bulletins, you would think the virus was so discriminating that it only targeted kids below the breadline who weren't white. Since then, there had not been any more large-scale outbreaks, at least not in any fancy fee-paying schools with gates, so Hatton relaxed about the whole thing, with only periodic bursts of absent father guilt. It all felt very far away from our citadel overlooking clean and orderly Copenhagen.

Anyway, I was the first to arrive that day. Memories of that news report were already fizzling out like the bubbles in the two glasses of prosecco I had just ordered; it had become 'our drink' since we were pulled out of the canal. Through the windows, you got a panoramic view of Rådhuspladsen, which always had a steady drip of people crossing it. I wondered if I would see Hatton making his way here; his agent always had him in a fancy AirBnB which he said had 'all the soul of Margaret Thatcher turning her hand to Danish design'.

I couldn't pick him out, but I could see a couple strolling across the square. I was a few storeys above them, but there was no mistaking that they were a couple. They moved almost as one, with only the occasional patch of light appearing between their two shadows. The shadows split as they drifted around a bike rack, but were still held together by the silhouette of their hands. It was all quite sickening.

"What are you looking at?" Hatton had snuck in while I was judging the love of random strangers I would never see again.

"Just a couple in the square who are disgustingly in love," I said, still watching them as he sat down next to me. I automatically handed him his glass as I felt him hit the chair. Soon I felt the familiar weight of him leaning slightly against me; it was a massive sofa, but we always seemed to roll into the middle.

"Urgh, those two over there?" he asked, pointing with his glass. I nodded. "I saw them on the way across here. They had their tongues down each other's throats. In the middle of the street. Vomit-inducing."

"I was just thinking that," I said, leaning back on the sofa, watching them as if they were a TV show.

"I wonder if they know," said Hatton, stretching out beside me.

"That they are making people almost physically sick with their slobbering?"

"You have such a way with words, you should write a book," he said, poking a finger in my side. I poked him back, I wasn't sure why, a witty retort was really more me. "Oi! I *was* going to say how obvious it is that they love each other, actually," he said. I tensed, waiting for another dig in the ribs, but he kept his hands to himself.

"I mean, they must do. It's obvious to everyone around them," I argued.

The waitress who had given me our drinks appeared in our line of vision and disrupted the show.

"Oh hey!! I'm really sorry, I forgot to get a note of which room the two of you are staying in!" she said, apologetically twisting her notebook. We smiled awkwardly at each other and her eyes brightened. "Silly me! Look at you two! It must be the honeymoon suite!"

"Oh! We are not together!" I said as if she had accused us of murdering babies for kicks. I could feel my cheeks going red. I took a slug of prosecco; for once, it would come in handy having the ruddy complexion of a North Sea fisherman.

"I have lots of sex with my wife who is not her!" blurted Hatton.

"You need to stop saying that! It sounds so suspicious!" I hissed.

"I am so sorry," spluttered the waitress, placing her notebook over her mouth. "It's really none of my business. If I can just get a room number, I will leave you alone. I will just go behind the bar and die of embarrassment."

"It's 365, isn't it?" Hatton asked me. "That's the one you always stay in."

I considered throwing my prosecco over him, but it was too good to waste. Now she would definitely think there was something going on.

"Yes, that's right. And there isn't anything going on here," I said through a thin smile

"Thanks," she said, making a note, presumably of the room number, not our relationship.

Then, I could feel a burst of offense go off in my chest, I couldn't help myself. "But you shouldn't make assumptions about people. You were totally mistaken. You're lucky we haven't asked to speak to your manager."

"I know. I am sorry that I got it wrong," she said, but her eyes said I was the one who had made a mistake. I remembered having to deal with entitled customers when I was a waitress many moons ago and a wash of shame came over me.

"No, I'm sorry," I said, pressing my hands together. "I was out of line, I don't know why I said that"

The waitress pulled her notebook away from her face to reveal a relieved smile. "Maybe it was…" she started, "but no." She giggled to herself, scribbling in the notebook

"Go on," I said, with a forced good-natured chuckle. "What were you going to say?"

"Well, I saw on the news that there is this virus going about and one of the first symptoms is you get more irritable. But…it only affects young people, so…" she shrugged her shoulders. "At least you guys won't get ill!"

"Rejoice," said Hatton.

Suitably sheepish, we walked over to the TV studio, but the conversation wasn't as easy as it usually was. I think we were both experiencing residual embarrassment from the encounter with the waitress. I say this because we had stilted conversations about what felt like anything else, including how cloudy it was, how nice it was Danish people cycled so much, again how cloudy the sky was getting and the possibility of it raining later.

As we neared the tall glass building we would be filming in, following about 90 seconds of silence after discussing the likelihood of rain, Hatton said, "How do I stop telling people I have lots of sex with my wife? I think it's becoming a compulsion."

I laughed, relieved that he had taken a swing at the tension with an ice pick.

"What about me?! I am so mortified I even brought up speaking to her manager. I am becoming a Karen! Urgh, it's literally my middle name, as well. Maybe it was always inevitable."

"Next you will be getting a fringe!" he said, entering the revolving door in front of me.

"Oh, shut up," I said, giving the door a push so he stumbled into the studio lobby. "Now you're just being ridiculous."

"Actually, *she* was being ridiculous. You had a point, Karen!"

"I know, it *was* a pretty ridiculous assumption to make," I said as Hatton signed us in at the foyer. He handed the form he filled in back to the receptionist and began to turn away.

"Sorry, new Botch rules," said the receptionist offhandedly as he passed the form back to Hatton. In fact, everything about him was offhand, from his askew glasses to the crumpled shirt that had clearly been pulled out the back of a cupboard only hours before. "I will need you to add the address you two live at".

"We're not together!" we both shouted.

"We live at very separate addresses. In different countries," I clarified.

"It's really none of my business," said the receptionist with a seen-it-all sigh as Hatton passed the form to me.

"Don't make me speak to your manager," I said, making sure to fill out my very different address in all caps. "Hatton, why don't you tell him how much sex you have with your wife while I write out my postcode?"

CHAPTER

4

"Well, that was a bit weird, wasn't it?" Hatton said the next day as we sat in Copenhagen Airport. We were waiting for our flights back home, or into exile, it felt more like.

"What was?" I said.

"What the waitress said about us yesterday."

The question hung in the air; it's an unusual airport with the tranquil feel of a hushed library, everything is muted as if your ears are yet to pop after a flight. That in itself is strange when you are used to being greeted by stag parties shouting about boobs and beer at 6am in the airport Wetherspoons, but it was a different ball game across the Channel. Even the quite clearly terse conversation Hatton had had with his agent about today had been conducted by video call so that they could both lipread instead of raising their voices.

We were sitting watching planes slide silently into the airfield. I was flying back to Edinburgh in just under an hour, and Hatton was going back to London soon after. He was originally from there but you would never guess, his accent seemed to be caught mid-Atlantic after too many trips to the States.

"Do you think we give off a...vibe?" asked Hatton. He posed the question as if he was asking if an unflattering caricature really looked like him.

I considered it and a flame of self-righteousness began to flicker.

"I blame the patriarchy."

"You do?" Hatton turned his attention away from the planes.

"Oh yes. It's classic. A man and a woman can't just work together, or have a drink, or be friends. They *must* be involved because marriage, because babies." Even as I said it, I thought I had a point, but I wasn't sure that everyone who had presumed we were a couple didn't have a point either.

"Yeah. 100%. Bloody patriarchy," said Hatton, relaxing into his uncomfortable airport chair, relieved.

"Plus you love your wife and have lots of sex with her." Hatton rolled his eyes. "Hey, joking aside, haters gonna hate, right? We shouldn't let them affect our relationship as business associates!"

"Hell yeah!" said Hatton, banging on his armrest. Other occupants of the airport-library shot us disapproving looks.

"All passengers on the CheepCheep Airlines flight to Edinburgh..." began an announcement that even had an apologetic note to it for disturbing the peace. I didn't have to listen to the rest, I knew the drill by now. I pulled out my passport and hoisted my bag over my shoulder, ready to join the border patrol queue.

"When are you next in town?" he asked, standing up with me.

"On the 14th. There's a book festival down in Kolding that weekend."

"Right, well, I am here for most of February, we should get lunch. My agent will have calmed down by then, get us booked to do a few more things."

"Ok, yeah. Great," I said. Goodbyes always looked so much more impressive in train stations, people pulling away in train carriages with bittersweet expressions, waving as they turn into a blur pulling away from the platform. Here I was just shifting from foot to foot like I needed a pee while 'EDINBURGH: LAST CALL' flashed on a screen above us. "I better go," I said, motioning to the queue.

"Yeah, ok, well, safe journey. See you in February!"

"See you," I said, walking away.

I was a few steps away when I heard him say, "Hey, one sec!" I turned around, irrationally worrying I had dropped my passport, even though I had it in my hand.

Before I knew it, I had been spun into a hug and my nose was smooshed into his collarbone. "What's that for?" I mumbled into his shirt, apparently trapped. I mean, I wasn't *struggling* to get away, but he did have a good grip.

He loosened his arm and I came up for air. "Um. Don't know. Isn't it how people say goodbye in airports?"

"There's usually fewer broken bones," I said, rubbing my nose. "It's fine, we can try again next time," I smiled. He head bobbed a nod but he kept his arms firmly at his sides, in case he did more damage. I made my way up the way to the now empty concourse to the border patrol booth and handed my passport over to the woman behind the plexiglass.

She picked up my passport and flicked it open. "That was a very cute goodbye," she said, but in the same officious voice she probably used when informing someone she would soon be searching their rectum for cocaine.

I sighed, I was tired of arguing, also I didn't want a date with her in the rectum room. Plus, like the rest of them, she wasn't entirely wrong, so I smiled.

"It kind of was, wasn't it?"

CHAPTER

5

It was chilly when I got off the airport bus a few hours later, so I did a speedy penguin shuffle down my dark Beath street. I was also eager to get home, not just to see my cat, Lily, but a new addition to my single pet parent family.

I put my key in the lock and could already hear paws scurrying about as they prepared the welcome party. Pushing the door open, I saw Lily on her usual winter perch, the radiator., and my new pup Brutus scurrying between my legs like an animated brush.

I had spunked most of the money I had made from Bae for Pay on Brutus, a mini-husky. I had spent many hours awwing over videos of them on YouTube on Friday afternoons at work, so when I realised that I could finally afford one, I messaged a breeder I had been following for ages on Instagram. The rest was very hyperactive history.

Nigel, who used to manage my regular haunt, Divine Drinks, appeared in the hallway too. When June, Dean and I had gone to St Fillan's, he looked after June's dog, Leni. It turned out dogs naturally gravitated to him due to their shared love of biscuits, farting and enthusiastic attention from young women. He had soon handed in his notice and taken up dog-sitting full-time. While Lily was quite independent and could probably run the flat better than I could, Brutus was a different matter. His favourite hobbies were attempting to hump Lily, women's legs and other dogs. He was so small that he, mercifully, never got past the attempt stage. Oh, and he revelled in stealing my dirty underpants when there was nothing around to hump. As such, he needed other sources of stimulation to distract him from this intense schedule. Nigel was more than happy to take him on long walks around Beath when I was away; young women would go into Elvis-like hysteria at Brutus' stuffed toy cuteness and Nigel could bask in his reflected glory. He even got the odd date out of it with women who would normally not only be in a different league from him, but a different planet.

"They have been as a good as gold," he told me. He was covered in muddy pawprints and there was a Zorro-like scratch across his forehead.

"Did Lily get you again?" I asked, squinting sympathetically at his cut.

"Oh this?" he said, delicately touching the gash. "It was just an accident. She didn't mean to do it. It was my fault, really. I shouldn't have come up behind her while she was eating her dinner."

"Nigel, you sound like a domestic abuse victim," I said as Lily sweetly slinked into my arms.

"It's nothing, really," he said, pulling on his jacket. I scooped up Brutus with my free arm and the pup proceeded to try and stick his tongue down my throat to show me just how much he had missed me. "How was your trip? You were filming that cooking show, right?"

"Yeah, it was...interesting," I said. A rogue dog tongue hit a tonsil and I spluttered. As I struggled for breath, I realised Brutus' latest assault was a great diversion from discussing whatever the hell had actually happened in Denmark. I coughed a bit too dramatically. "Brutus! Behave!" I said as he began to eye up Lily with a worrying lust in his beady eyes.

"Well, I look forward to seeing it. You and that Hatton fella are always so funny together. Are you two...how do I put this delicately...doing what Brutus likes to do with that Yorkshire Terrier in the park?"

"Nigel! Out!" I said, pointing him towards the door. "And no, we're not. Why does everyone think that," I muttered as he made his way out.

"You would make a nice couple, that is all. He's miles better than that Dean who used to work for me. God knows what you saw in him. He had all these pretensions about being an actor. I used to say, well, act like you work in a bloody wine shop then and price some stock. Jesus wept."

"Yes, yes, thank you Nigel for that panorama of my past mistakes," I said, beginning to close the door.

"Goodbye, my little booboos!" he cooed to the nonplussed Lily and the panting Brutus. "See if your mummy can make that nice man on the TV your new daddy!" I heard Nigel chuckle to himself through the now slammed door as I walked my pets through to the bedroom.

I flopped down on the bed and was immediately smothered in kisses by Brutus that had a degree of intimacy with my tonsils no lover had ever known. I knew Lily had missed me too because she offered her highest declaration of love, a blink of recognition while looking down imperiously from a shelf.

I was wrapped in a warm blanket of zoological love, but I couldn't help notice how lumpy and bumpy my bed was compared to the hotel bed in Copenhagen. I missed having the room cleaned every day too;

I noticed a yoghurt pot I had left in my haste to catch the flight which probably had its own ecosystem by now.

Hatton was probably in some wanktastic London penthouse right now being greeted by Electra, rolling out of a carpet Cleopatra-style. She was like every sex symbol through the ages into one; Marilyn Monroe's head on Jennifer Lopez's body with Elizabeth Taylor's eyes chucked in. It was as if a graverobber with a refined aesthetic had created his own bride of Frankenstein.

Meanwhile, I rolled over onto my stomach and indulged in some unhealthy screentime before bed. June had posted a photo of her looking wet on the beach at St Fillan's with #wildswimming. I shivered, the sea looked a cold, glassy blue. She was up in St Fillan's visiting my old lecturer Professor P (yes, that was still going on). I had almost got over the ick factor of their relationship, then they would do something disgusting like tongue kiss in the supermarket and I would try not to vomit into the nearest ready meal freezer.

Further down my feed, I noticed Harriet with her and Allan's baby, Caspar, who was born a few months ago. Nine months to be exact, or so read the bright blue sign in the picture. She posted things like this for every conceivable occasion, including baby's first bath, baby's first mashed up sweet potato, baby's first time waking at 3am, baby's eighth bath, etc. Caspar might not even be able to say his first word yet but he had certainly mastered the same withering side-eye as Harriet, as was evidenced by one picture at a mother and baby group when he was forced to play with a child in a mini tracksuit. It was funny though, I couldn't really see any of Allan in the kid, but maybe that was because I had only seen Caspar online. Harriet hadn't really spoken to me since the book came out. She would never be so déclassé as to actually confront me about any problems she had with me chronicling her and Allan's threesome with Paxton at the reunion, but I could still feel her steely disapproval every time she didn't like a post or reply to a message.

Her occasional likes of my posts had in fact completely dried up after she had a few too many gins one evening and took to Twitter after a fan @ed her asking if she was the Harriet in the book. She had declared, in very colourful terms, that she most certainly was not, which, of course, made the entire world decide it was completely based on her. I had messaged her to ask her if she was ok afterwards, but, in her words, this was 'most inopportune', which was the same phrase she had used when she accidentally swallowed her engagement ring on her Hen Night. If it was going to be as messy as that, I knew it wasn't worth pressing her on it.

However, I did give the Caspar pic a sympathy like to maintain some sort of relationship.

I tapped on my new notifications, a lot of likes of a picture I posted of our glasses of prosecco in the bar. There were comments too, which had taken an awkward turn of late: someone tagging a friend along with "See I told you they are definitely boning", "Sam and Hatton are my OTP [one true pairing - fandom phrase meaning they wanted us to be a couple]" and "I ship Samon", a combination of our names that, I cringed, you could search the hashtag on Instagram and find photos where we did appear to be looking at each other rather adoringly during interviews.

It was close to midnight and I really should have gone to sleep so I was refreshed for work in the morning, but I had been there in body alone for months while my mind wandered, usually back to Denmark and Hatton. I knew I was heading for a full-blown inappropriate crush, but it spiced up the increasingly pointless drudgery of office life, which in turn paid most of my bills. I was too tired to think through it all though. I could feel my eyes drooping shut when I realised that my phone battery was dangerously low but I was too exhausted to fish my charger out of my bag. It was in the hallway, but might as well have been back in Denmark. I decided to set my alarm and put my faith in the Gods that the battery would last through the night.

Before I had published the book, before my hybrid set-up as office drone by day and novelist by night, I would have been experiencing anxiety gags at the thought of sleeping in and rocking up late to work. Sandra the CEO would send an URGENT!!! email for every minute that I was late. All the requests were not time-sensitive, but there would be demands to rewrite the employee handbook by 10.30am or tell her another word for 'feckless' because she wanted some variety when she wrote my performance review.

While I still didn't have the courage to actually resign, I had realised that I could get away with a lot more when Sandra the CEO didn't actually fire me for the loosely fictionalised portrayal of her in Bae for Pay. My colleague Patience told me that she had 'accidentally' logged into the HR email and seen that Sandra had been advised that she would have to give me a big severance cheque to avoid bad press. This was compounded by the fact that the company was now working on a big government-funded project which came with a large dose of bureaucracy; it was literally in our contracts now that we had to set something on fire in order to be fired.

Patience also told me that Sandra had expressed a desire to wait until I committed 'suicide by cop' and make such a hash of things that she could legitimately fire me. However, I had yet to bring anything highly flammable to work, so the joke was on her.

That was the energy I strolled into the office with at 9.26am the next morning. My phone had lasted through the night, but then I had pressed snooze seven times. I made my morning porridge in the office kitchen and finally settled down at my desk about 10am. I was just summoning up the will to open my email inbox when Patience tapped me on the shoulder.

"Sandra wants to see you in her office," she whispered.

I sighed heavily and pushed out my chair. I wondered what it would be this time. Since I had seen her with Dean after he started working as a male escort, Sandra was almost a little afraid of me. It didn't stop her dishing out her usual humiliation and probably fuelled it a bit, but there was a dartiness to her eyes that told me she was scared I might reveal all, except I wouldn't because I needed to earn enough money to keep a roof over Brutus and Lily's furry heads.

As I walked to Sandra's glass cube office (always great for public humiliation) I noticed that Patience was following me. "What are you doing?" I asked.

"Sandra the CEO has asked me to sit in on the meeting," she said in hushed tones.

"Oh," I said. It appeared that it wouldn't be enough to humiliate me in her corporate thunderdome cube for all the office to see, she needed someone inside to record it.

Luckily I was perfecting the art of being dead inside from 9am-5pm, Monday-Friday, so I only felt twinges of the terror that this was supposed to strike into my heart. I casually swung open the door and slumped into the chair like I was Judd Nelson in the Breakfast Club. In fact, I wasn't dressed much differently; I saved all my good clothes for author appearances, so an old shirt and a pair of leggings that I was kidding myself looked like jeggings were the order of the day.

Sandra the CEO sat in front of me in a low-cut wrap dress and a giant pendant necklace that pointed directly at her cleavage. I wondered why she didn't just invest in a neon sign that said "LOOK AT MY BOOBS" to prevent any last shreds of ambiguity. Patience sat down beside her, buttoning up her cardigan in the chilly room.

"Sam," smiled Sandra, but the atmosphere just seemed to get icier. "Thank you for coming in this morning. Not just to my office, but to work, and only half-an-hour late."

"It's no problem at all," I sighed heavily, eager to get whatever it was over and done with.

"Yes. Well, the reason I wanted to meet with you this morning was to discuss your future at the company."

"Oh really?" I said, sitting up. A masochistic thrill ran through me. Was she really going to do it? Was she really going to fire me? I was too chicken to take the leap and quit, but one of my major, bordering on sexual, fantasies was being fired with maybe a bit of gardening leave thrown in. If Sandra wanted to drop-kick me out of this hellhole, who was I to refuse?

"The government programme we are working on has a new funding stream coming in related to the arts. They want to host a mini festival in Edinburgh next summer celebrating self-publishing. As a successful self-published author, they want you to head up the new department," she said, sounding far too pleased about it. I was simultaneously disappointed yet excited; I wasn't being axed, but working in the arts was something I had always wanted to do. It might even give me more platforms as an author. Maybe I could get Hatton over to host a panel or something, but I was getting ahead of myself.

"Oh really?" I said, trying to keep a poker face.

"Yes. Unfortunately, this would mean that you no longer report to me, but Malcy MacAskill from the Scottish Commission for Creativity," Sandra said, pantomiming sadness.

"Oh, that's a shame," I said, trying to suppress the urge to shout "FREEEDDOOOOM!" Malcy MacAskill's team were known in the industry for having all the best Christmas parties, 'research trips' abroad to anywhere sunny with a festival going on and even a bar in their actual office.

"Yes, it will be a wrench for me too," said Sandra, absentmindedly flicking through what I presumed was my new contract in front of her. "Of course, this comes with an increase in salary to reflect your increased responsibility. It is the Arts though, so it's not a huge amount."

"Yes, perfectly understandable," I said. Normally I would feel a rant building about how the creative industries are undervalued, but I would have been happy with the new arrangement if my salary was a packet of crisps and an expired carton of apple juice.

"So it's only an extra £20,000 a year," Sandra said casually. Patience looked at me like, 'You jammy bastard. Take me with you.'

"Oh. Oh well," I said, blood thumping in my ears, dollar signs threatening to appear in my eyes. "I'm sure I could get by."

"So you are interested in the role?"

"Yes!" I blurted.

"Excellent. Malcy will be pleased," Sandra said, passing the documents in front of her to Patience. "Take these and have HR prepare the transfer paperwork." Patience nodded solemnly and went to take the papers, but Sandra stopped suddenly, as if she had noticed a dead fly on them. "Oh! There is one more thing I forgot to mention."

What could it be? This had all been a ruse to buy enough time to gather every copy of Bae for Pay for a team-building book burning at lunch?

"Malcy and I were talking, and I pointed out that there are possible conflicts of interest with your own writing and running the festival. So, after some discussion, we added this clause to the contract of page 28," she said, flicking through the paperwork. "Just a small thing...Oh yes, here it is. The employee will not write, publish or promote any of their own intellectual property during their tenure in post. "

"Excuse me?" I said, my blood pressure now climbing to previously unknown heights.

"Like I said, just a teeny amendment."

"That I can't write?"

"Exactly, I told Malcy you would understand."

"I'm not sure I do. There must be other ways to maintain fairness. Lots of artists are involved in running festivals," I scrambled.

"Sam, that might be the way other people do things, but I'm running the show," she said, handing the documents to Patience while twisting a smile at me.

"Well, in that case, I would need to think about it before I signed anything."

"Of course," she said magnanimously. "Malcy expects an answer by the end of the month."

"I will get the transfer forms drawn up, but it's only the 1st now, so you have plenty of time to think about it dear," said Patience, shuffling the papers. "I mean, what is there to think about, 20 grand," she muttered to herself as she left the room.

The door shut behind her and Sandra smiled at me, the way Disney villains do when they are watching their evil plan come to life.

"You want to stop me writing. You're handcuffing me, you know that? It's so cheap," I said, my head shaking in anger.

"It's not cheap, it's 20 grand. Those handcuffs are golden."

CHAPTER

6

Sam: June, it's really not romantic, trust me.

I looked around the dark and deserted restaurant, which was almost entirely furnished with animal products; the bar stools were in the shape of mini-bulls you could sit astride (and made of real leather, of course). Along the thick wooden walls, deceased beasts were displayed in various states of post mortem; a stuffed buffalo head, longhorn bull skull and what I presumed was the skin of a particularly large raccoon. Opposite me, an anatomical model of a pig wearing a cowboy hat was displayed. I took a photo of it and sent it to June.

June: Visual allusions to porking?! Stop denying it!

I was rolling my eyes like a baseball pitcher winds his arm. I prepared to write a scathing reply, but I was interrupted when I caught sight of Hatton entering the bar. He looked more casual than when we were on the chat shows, it was always the same desert jacket, flannel shirt and jeans when he was off duty.

He looked around the room and gave me a wave. I raised my hand in return but a Stetson-wearing waiter thrust a menu into it. I decided to look at the food on offer because everyone had to leave their details at the front desk when they dined in a restaurant or cafe in Denmark now; it seemed like a good way to kill a few minutes while Hatton gave his, plus I was getting hungry.

Everyone back home thought it was a bit ridiculous, but it was a public health measure to track down Botch cases. Not that there would be many here, the average clientele age was probably about 65, I thought, spying two old codgers in a corner. And yes, that was with me bringing the average down by a good 30 years.

The menu was helpfully illustrated with pictures; rubbery-looking steaks, baked potatoes filled with what I hoped was unfortunate-looking chilli and something that appeared to be pork after a housefire. It was called 'Stegt Flæsk'. A little sticker with a Danish flag on it told me this was a national dish.

I looked up and the waiter had recognised Hatton, by the looks of things. He was cosying up to him with his arm outstretched for a selfie. The waiter examined the image but it didn't meet with his approval, he mussed his hair, pouted and tried again. And again. Then began fixing Hatton's hair.

I could tell this was going to take a while, so I snapped a pic of the menu and sent it to June.

Sam: It's like culinary contraception.

June: It's still Valentine's Day...

The operative word was 'day'. It was an early bird lunch in a 24-hour cowboy restaurant. The only Valentine motif they had bothered with were some peeling paper hearts tacked up on the windows. The restaurant was on a busy corner; box-like buses chugging along, people breezing by on their bikes, somehow carefree but still with purpose. I didn't think I had ever been that carefree, or even had that much purpose. I was also crap at riding a bike.

Maybe there was something romantic about the wide boulevard though; the streetlights suspended on wires between colourful but tasteful buildings of imposing stone. They were the sort I imagine ambassadors live in. Perhaps the French ambassador lived here; after all, the street, Værnedamsvej, was known as Little Paris due to its similarities with the French capital.

The city of love. But no, June was still definitely wrong about this one.

There were plenty more Parisian nooks in the street more suitable for a liaison dangereuse; Bistros with doll-like tables and chairs outside to watch the world go by with a glass of wine or an espresso, for example. There was even a bloody wine shop that specialised in French vintages. If anyone with a clue was trying to seduce me, they could have gotten a bottle of wine from there and retired to the little park at the end of the street, which was a quiet leafy island in the middle of a busy thoroughfare.

But no, we were having burnt bits of pig flesh in what looked like a Spaghetti Western retirement home. June was definitely barking up the wrong cactus.

Hatton sat down at the table. "Sorry I kept you waiting," he said, jerking his head at the waiter, who was standing at the bar flicking through his man selfies. "There was that. And I was running late anyway. I overdid it in the gym this morning and I've been shitting like one of those bulls up there on the wall ever since."

The waiter handed him a laminated menu and told us they were out of the 'Crispy Cow Bits' starter. What a shame. He also gave Hatton directions to the nearest toilet.

Hatton coughed self-consciously while he examined the menu, I took the opportunity to send a sneaky text to June.

Sam: He basically just told me he was late because he has been shitting out his innards all AM. SEE! NOT ROMANTIC!!

"What are you thinking?" I asked as he flipped over the menu to see the full breadth of bovine on offer.

"I don't know. I have had a lot on my mind. That's why I went to the gym. Helps me think." He turned the menu upside down, as if trying to make sense of a map.

"I meant, what are you thinking of eating?"

"Oh."

"But I also could have asked, what were you thinking when you chose this restaurant?"

"It's pretty crazy, isn't it?" He gestured to an alarmed-looking staghead. "But the food is great, even if the menu makes it look like the aftermath of a fire at an abattoir."

"You're right. Very powerful imagery," I nodded as I reviewed the card. "You can practically smell the smoke coming off it."

Hatton put his menu down on the table like it was a good hand in poker. "I'm going to have the stegt flæsk. It's really good, very Danish. And a beer. A very big beer. Why don't we make it a pitcher?"

"OK," I said warily. Hatton was more of a spirit man than a beer bro, he was always mumbling about the empty calories. I would say, how empty can they be when you attach so much meaning to them? Maybe he was finally taking my advice.

"I think I will have the st..the steg...what you're having too," I said, putting my menu down.

"Good choice. I have been meaning to bring you here for a while. I'm glad we managed to do it." He sounded genuinely happy for the first time today. I did a double take but disguised it by pretending to check the menu. It sounded more like something you would say to your wife or girlfriend, not some random you work with sometimes. Was this his version of romance? Oh God, maybe it was! I mean, his ultimate indulgence probably was fatty meats and lager.

He signalled to the waiter. While he was telling him our order, I quickly typed out my theory to June. She sent back a GIF of two pigs humping, which was very constructive and supportive of her.

I clicked the conversation shut as the waiter walked away. "Sorry," I said, "Some...ongoing consultancy. I'll put my phone away now."

"Oh, don't worry. I'm used to it. I don't think I have seen my daughter without her phone since about 2013."

"Wouldn't she have been about 9 then?"

"Yeah," confirmed Hatton in a 'don't ask' tone. I had heard many tales of Parthenope, who he had represented as a teenager 'on steroids', except she would never actually take steroids because she was obsessed with '90s heroin chic, which was now 'vintage'. Urgh.

Hatton grabbed the pitcher and poured himself a large foamy glass.

"Sorry," he said. "I probably should have poured yours first. It would have been a bit 1950s of me, but polite if you put gender aside. God, why is everything so complicated? I will just let you pour your own bloody beer next time."

What a state to get yourself in over pouring a drink, I thought.

"I suppose I should take advantage of your misplaced chivalry, then." I clinked my glass to his, which was still sitting on the table. He reluctantly picked it up, but took a long sip. "I might not be back next month."

"What do you mean?" he asked, wiping a foam moustache off with his expensive shirt sleeve. Oh, to be so rich that you would sully such costly but hilariously undurable material, I thought as the white material went a questionable shade of brown. Then I remembered that he had had a real moustache last year for Movember and how much I had mocked him for looking like a toilet brush while we were on a gameshow, when I really thought he looked like a hot World War I army officer.

"What's that look supposed to mean?" he asked and I blinked any residual dreaminess away.

"Anyway, don't keep me in suspense, why won't you be back next month?"

"I have been made a job offer. One that I cannot refuse."

"Oh Jesus," he grimaced. "It's not from that demented witch, Sandra?"

"The CEO, yes."

He mumbled something about dunking her to see if she floats.

"She has offered me 20 grand more a year. The only catch is that I can't write anymore."

"And you're actually considering it?!" He had gone gammon, the exact same shade as the photo of the ham on the menu and everything. At least his outrage wasn't about immigrants, I thought.

"Look, I know that to you 20 grand is just endorsing some brand of aftershave on Instagram-"

"Hey, I stand by my collaboration with Musky Men!"

"Just don't stand too close to them, OK? Anyway, 20k a year is a lot of money for a peasant like me. More than I would ever make from writing." I watched some sad bubbles peter out on the surface of my beer.

"Come on, you can't put a price on writing!"

"I think I can. It's about 20k more than my current salary. That's holidays, vet bills, maybe some plastic surgery so people on Instagram stop pointing out that I have wonky boobs…"

"Oh come on, you don't need plastic surgery. Your boobs are completely normal!" declared Hatton as the waiter returned with our food.

The waiter looked at me as if appraising Hatton's statement. We both glared at him - he quickly unloaded a mound of pork cuts and a heaving side dish of potatoes onto the table and backed away.

What an endorsement, I thought. Hatton Finch told me my boobs were normal. If I ever reactivated my ill-fated Tinder account, I would definitely have to put that in my bio.

"All I'm saying is that it's tempting," I told him as I dished up some food onto my plate. He was right, it was better than it looked on the menu, juicy and tender.

"What could tempt you away, then?" he said, already ploughing into the meat like it was a demolition project.

"I don't know," I said, but I knew. Financial security, creative freedom, Hatton, freshly divorced, covered in oil and sent to my bedchamber.

"Yes, you do," he said, the meat, not immune to his charms, almost dissolving on his lips. "What is it?"

"Stop deflecting," I improvised, opting for a crispy roast potato, which sank into my cutlery almost too easily. I took my time chewing the surprisingly delicious spud. He sniffed haughtily, but it was too impatient to be at me alone. I pieced it together with the epic binge he was embarking on and caught him in my crosshairs. "What's up with you, anyway?"

"Oh, I suppose I couldn't hide it from you, after all these odd but nonetheless enjoyable occasions we have been in together."

I didn't say anything, but drove my fork into some pig on my plate.

He flinched. "I have just had a video call with Electra."

"That's nice?" It was a question because I was now completely lost. We were swerving between platonic friends and possible flirtation so quickly that I thought I would need a seatbelt.

"Ha!" he said, taking another slug of beer. "Nice'. Well, I don't know. Is 'nice' how you would describe your wife of 17 years telling you she wants an open marriage on Valentine's Day?"

Our waiter, who had been approaching the table, began to reverse backwards. I was surprised he didn't start beeping, to be honest.

My mind now began whirring as I tried to put a positive spin on things. It reminded me of the time Sandra the CEO tasked me with writing a good news story about how she had only faced three unfair dismissal lawsuits that year instead of the usual 10.

"Um, well, I suppose some men would think it was nice?" was what I finally arrived on. "A free pass to do whatever you want, with whoever you want?" Suddenly my throat felt very dry so I took a long sip of beer.

"But what if all you want to do is be married to your wife?"

Well, that cleared up a lot. Thanks, Hatton.

"I mean, everyone has thoughts...feelings...the occasional vivid dream when you have been married as long as us, but that doesn't mean that it's something you act on. Or maybe it does. She just got the call asking her to be on the next series of Hello and Cheerio."

"The celebrity cheerleading competition?"

"Yes," said Hatton grimly. It was notorious for the celebrities copping off with their professional coaches who guided them through the process. "She said that she wanted to be free to experience everything the show had to offer."

That was not good news for his marriage. I mean, I was a little perversely pleased, but I still felt bad for him, I'm not a psychopath.

"Her exact words were," Hatton leaned back and assumed an arched pose, as if modelling a designer bra, "Just wanted to run something by you. Shall we give an open marriage a whirl? As if she was suggesting we switch laundry detergents!"

"Wow," I said, in the absence of anything constructive to offer. "What did you say?"

"I asked why, and do you know what she said?"

"What?"

"It's good for the skin. Like it's a new wellness fad on her blog."

"I mean, her skin already glows like she is a baby alien, how much better can it get?!"

"I know, right? I told her that. I mean, I didn't call her an alien, but her mind seemed set. I can't stop her doing anything, you know?" He looked sad and confused, in a way you can only ever really feel and never mimic, even if you are an actor. "Anyway," he said, snapping back to the restaurant. "Enough of my sob story. You can't give up writing!"

"Why?"

"Well, for one, apart from being very good at it, I will miss you, that's why!"

"I would miss you too!" I found myself saying. We looked at each other a bit too long over the pitcher of beer and I quickly glanced back down at my plate. It seemed we were swerving back into Flirtsville. On Valentine's Day. On perhaps the last day we would see each other. When he had just been given permission to sleep around by his wife. The stars were aligning but I wasn't sure that we should become star-crossed lovers. At least, not yet. It was all so complicated right now and I didn't want to enter into another odd romantic entanglement after the situation with Dean, they didn't seem to work out well for me.

"Look, it's not that I don't want to..." the sentence drifted off. I could insert so much: Quit my job, be a writer, take you roughly on one of those weird bull seats at the bar. "I'm just...scared of not knowing what happens next. I just don't think I'm ready." I realised my face was wet, I had started crying.

"Hey hey hey," cooed Hatton as he got up and joined me on my side of the table. He pulled me into the crook of his arm. I realised that I was going to leave snot marks on his expensive desert jacket, which just made me cry harder.

"Wow, if you don't think you are ready to become a full-time writer, then I'm definitely not ready to become a geriatric shagger! Now who is up Shit Creek without a paddle?" I lifted my head and we both laughed. A thought crossed my mind; it wouldn't be half bad to sit here like this with him if I wasn't such a mucussy mess.

A waiter appeared at our side. "Is it the pig?" he asked.

We looked at each other, then him, in confusion. He pointed to the anatomical model in a cowboy hat in front of us. "It has that effect on people..." he said as he took our empty plates away.

CHAPTER

7

June nimbly leapt into the sand, clearing the broken bottles and bonfire remnants with ease.

She had dragged me to Industry Bay as part of her latest obsession - wild swimming. I had my reservations, partly because the only thing that seemed industrial about it was the amount of faeces rumoured to float in the water. Beath Sewage Plant, whose pipes entered the sea a mile or two away, denied having anything to do with it, however.

"Isn't wild swimming just a middle-class euphemism for swimming in sewage?" I grumbled. A shard of glass from a pile of smashed Buckfast and Bat Brew glasses had got stuck in the sole of my trainer. I bent down to pick it out but June whipped round quickly, surely made more aerodynamic by her top-of-line wetsuit.

"Don't use me and 'middle-class' in the same sentence ever again. I'm a class warrior!" She fiddled with some big-name goggles, but she had scratched off the logo as an act of 'class warfare'.

Despite June's protestations, I was still sceptical about wild swimming. The only people I knew who did it in Beath had enough disposable income to buy all the gear, or at least a husband who did. It was part of a 'wellness routine' which featured body scrubs, paying muscle-bound ex-squaddies to shout at them at boot camps in the park and weekly massages. In fact, it was one of June's regulars who had turned her on to it.

Wild swimming felt a far cry from whoever had had their bonfire here the night before. The bargain booze and graffiti, 'Big Al woz here' and 'BLT AAF'. 'BLT' stood for 'Beath Liberation Team', a local gang made up mostly of 15 year-olds from the tower blocks with a shared interest in setting fire to bins.

"STOP!" June commanded as I was about to jump over the debris. "I need to film this."

June had set up a YouTube channel called 'The Televised Revolution' last year, where she explained the history of capitalism using a Barbie, Russian Doll and a toy tank. She now had tens of thousands of subscribers, ranging from desperate 16 year olds cramming for exams to respected military historians. As she would often remind me - we were both famous now.

"Why do you need to film this?" I moaned.

"Hold the camera," she said, passing it to me from her bag.

"June, I'm not your Instagram husband," I grumbled, but I was already zooming in for a better angle.

"Hit play and I'll tell you why we need to film this!" she said, flicking hair out her face.

I dutifully hit the button and June snapped into action. "Hey comrades! I was just out for a wild swim with my friend Sam because I'm not going to pay some health club £60 a month to swim in a pool full of warm baby pee! Here we are at Industry Bay in Beath and we've just come across some really cool graffiti." June gave me a nod and I zoomed in on 'BLT AAF' and 'Big Al'. This wasn't my first time at this particular rodeo - June was always roping me in to film segments she couldn't quite communicate fully with Barbie and a Babushka.

"This 'Big Al' was Alastair McTaggart, the first leader of the Beath Liberation Team, a fraternity of factory workers and ABSOLUTE LEGENDS who took part in the Great Strike of '79 in my neighbourhood of Beath."

I turned the camera to June - I didn't know this! Now I was interested.

"Police officers would use any excuse to break up their gatherings in the pubs of Beath, so they would meet under the cover of darkness on these beaches, part of their industrial wasteland at the time, to arrange strikes and protests. I personally saw Big Al scrawl this on a rock last summer after we shared a bottle of delightful local wine, Buckfast, at his 80th birthday party. Nice one, Al! And cut, Sam!"

I pressed 'stop' and handed her the camera. "Wow, I didn't know that was the story behind BLT. Big Al must be disappointed that all those NEDs are running about sullying the name."

June sighed. "Sam, I love you, but you have no idea about class struggle. Setting fire to a bin is an act of radical activism against local government administration!" she lectured. "Especially when you have an incompetent Mayor like ours..."

I nodded along and picked my way through the ash and broken bottles. June was now walking ahead of me continuing her rant, so I jogged through the sand to catch up, dodging an assortment of washed-up seaweed, wood, more bottles and even the odd melted tyre. Ahead, the waves were somehow an unappealing brown with an icy glint. June turned to see me making a distinctly unimpressed face.

"Come on, Sam! I would have thought this was right up your street after skinny dipping in Denmark!"

June had now abandoned her towel on a rock and was striding into the murky water. I laid my towel down next to hers and reluctantly shedded the puffa jacket I practically lived in all winter. When people say that, it's usually hyperbole, but I had been known to sleep in it because it was cosier than the old duvet I kept meaning to replace.

A blast of cold sea air as I denuded myself of my jacket-duvet hybrid. Underneath, I was wearing an old pair of branded leggings and a t-shirt that Sandra the CEO had kitted us out with for a 'fun' run a few years ago. I say 'fun', because what is amusing about being told your probation will be extended if you don't come in the top 15% of runners? Of course I didn't and of course my probation was extended. In fact, I wasn't actually sure my probation had ever ended...

I hugged my arms close and began to follow June. Water that felt like the inside of a supermarket freezer hit my feet and I gritted my teeth, focussing on June. She was now doing a vigorous front crawl through the waves, so determined, like a wind-up swimmer toy.

I could be that determined too. Maybe. Maybe not. My resolve came and went with the cold waves that were steadily climbing my body.

"Come on!" shouted June, heading back towards me. "It's very invigorating!"

"What's invigorating about putting your vagina on ice?!" I squealed as a wave hit my nether regions. "Is it a cheap way to freeze your eggs?"

"It's not that bad once you are fully submerged," said June, paddling wildly around me. "You don't feel the cold after a while."

"You feel numb?"

"Yeah, sort of. Very zen."

Even though I didn't believe her, I lowered my waist into the water - it felt even colder. I decided to keep going though. I would take zen, even just numb with the cold, just anything that wasn't lurching between the dread of staying at my job and anxiety about pursuing writing. All I wanted to do was accept my fate, whatever that was.

So I sped down into the water like one of those buildings neatly demolished in a single column like dynamite.

The February water was so cold, it felt like all my organs had been put on ice for rich Americans wanting new kidneys and corneas. I surfaced with a gasp and began doggy paddling frantically.

"That's it! Just keep moving!" June said with an encouraging smile as she glided along, a rubber-clad swan to my clumsy dog.

"You, you make it s-s-sound like sharks. They d-d-d-ie if they s-s-top m-m-moving," I chittered. A slunge of brown water hit me in the mouth. I thought about retching but didn't want to risk more getting in.

"Well, why did you think I told you to just keep moving? Jack would have survived in Titanic if he had just followed that advice," said June, but she was distracted by something out at sea. "Looks like some bigger waves are coming in. Make sure you face them so you don't get smacked in the back of the head by one."

We watched the sea, doing some amateur version of aqua aerobics below the water line to keep ourselves 'warm'.

"What's that?" I asked, spying something long and brown surfing the waves. I hoped it was seaweed, but feared it was something else.

June pulled down her goggles for a better look. "Oh God," she said. "Swim, swim out of its way!!" She pulled me towards the shore, but I still managed to catch sight of what I can only describe as a corpulent jobby on the crest of a wave. It was coming straight for us. We paddled furiously towards some rocks and held on, crouching down for extra protection.

We saw the beast swirl past us. I know it's impossible, but I swear it had a sadistic smile. We waited for a few cold seconds, partly because the water might suck it back out again, partly in case it was sentient and came back for us.

The coast was clear. Safely out of the poo's path, we laughed giddily, though that might have been the hypothermia setting in.

"I don't think the temperatures are the only thing that can kill you here..." I chittered.

"That thing was a monster!" gasped June. "We should probably follow it back to shore. If you stay in too long, you can get nerve damage."

"Sorry, remind me, what are the health benefits of this, again?"

"You will feel them later!" called back June, who was now strutting out the water like a Bond Girl. I slipped on some rocks and crawled ashore like an injured seal.

"What will I feel? Circulation returning to my extremities?" I said, hobbling on to the dry land with feet feeling like cement. They were the only part of my body that felt numb, though. The rest of me was pumping with blood. I wouldn't tell June, but maybe there were health benefits after all. I might have looked like a red raw oversized chicken, but I felt invincible. I knew the decision I had to make - tell Sandra to shove her golden handcuffs up her arse, in addition to the usual stick that resided therein.

"You said you would tell me what happened at your cowboy lunch!" said June, waving her towel above her head as an improvised lasso. I filed away my newfound confidence for later.

"Oh," I said, shimmying out of my wet leggings. I say shimmying, it was more like a walrus trying to free itself from a tyre. "It was not about romance, that's for sure."

"Are you *really* sure?" June had a wicked yet forensic glint in her eye.

"Yes," I said, concentrating on freeing a numb foot from my leggings. "He told me that his wife wants an open marriage and ate his own weight in pig meat. What's romantic about that?" I could tell June these things without fear of her selling a story because she considered that behaviour one of the many ways of exploiting the poor invented by Late Capitalism.

"Ha! You know why he told you that, right?" said June, unzipping her wet suit and slinking into her towel, only a hint of skin ever visible in her aquatic fan dance. Meanwhile, I had half a butt cheek stuck in my leggings and I feared I was going to have to call the fire brigade to free me.

"Why?" I asked.

"Why bring it up unless he wanted you to do something about it? I bet it was his way of seeing if you were interested. And I have already explained the porking allusions of his meal choice."

"June, I can't believe I am having to tell you of all people this, but human relations aren't all just cold exchanges of information to get something from the other person," I said, even though I would have given her anything to get me out of these trousers. "It's very capitalist of you!" I said with a gasp, which was half-mocking, half-relief as I finally slithered free of my leggings. Defeated, they lay in a pathetic sandy pile, but so did I.

"He's a celebrity, of course he is capitalist swine!" said June, deftly slipping into a dry pair of Thai harem pants - she had a massage client back at her parlour in half an hour.

"And what does that make me? I'm a sort of celebrity. In Denmark." I said, pulling a hoodie over my shivering upper body.

"Exactly! You're a sort of celebrity. In Denmark. One of the most Socialist countries in the world. I'm so proud," said June. "Now come on, we need to get going. You can explain whatever convoluted reason you're not shagging him to me on the way back to the car."

"It's not convoluted," I said, following June back across the glass graveyard of Buckfast and Bat Brew bottles. "It's just that he might be in an open marriage but he is still married. And I just don't really see the point because I like him, which makes me think, why would I sleep with him then? Because he will still be married at the end of it and I will just like him even more probably. And he will go back to his hot wife and I will end up writing another book and everyone will ask me why Hatton and Sam didn't get together in the last chapter and my life will be stuck in some sort of purgatorial Groundhog Day of romantic despair. I have learnt my lesson after Dean. No more weird and wonderful dating-but-not-dating situations. Besides, I bet he doesn't even actually like me anyway so none of this really matters."

We were now standing at June's car and she was staring at me. "You do know it's not normal to overthink everything that much? How do you even get dressed in the morning?" She unlocked the door and we stepped in.

"It can be a struggle. Sometimes I worry one top will get jealous if I've not worn it for a while. So I feel sorry for it, put it on and end up not dressing weather appropriately."

"Oh, so that's what that is," nodded June. "So, the TL;DR version is that you're worried about getting hurt again?"

"Pretty much, yeah," I said as June drove us out of the carpark and back towards Beath.

"Makes sense," she replied. We sat in silence for a little while as she drove by the offending sewage plant. "Would make a good book, though..."

CHAPTER

8

About 20 minutes' later, June's car came to a stop outside her shop. As I undid my seatbelt, I realised that I hadn't inquired after Professor P the whole trip. I didn't really want to, but I felt I should.

"Oh, I meant to ask! How's Professor P?" I said, clicking open the car door.

As I stepped out, I heard a howl and I jumped, thinking that maybe June's precious dog Leni had bounded out of the shop and been run over. I was wrong though, the noise had come from within the car. I bent down to see June banging her head off the top of her steering wheel.

"Was it something I said?" I cautiously manoeuvred myself back into the car and shut the door for privacy.

June took a deep, cleansing breath, the sort she makes her clients take at the start of a massage. "Oh, Sam, it was awful. I've never felt so disrespected. And one time a drunk man on Beath Walk groped me and blamed me for Pearl Harbour, then vomited on me, all in about 30 seconds."

I nodded with a sympathetic smile. Although I could never understand that level of wildly off-base discrimination, I could guess where this conversation was going. A new semester had just begun, and Professor

P's eye had probably been caught by a willowy Teaching Assistant or a girl going for her Masters in being a Manic Pixie Dream Girl. I brushed a stray hair off my shoulder, preparing it for June to cry on.

"What's he done?" I said, as if the fiftysomething professor was a naughty schoolboy.

"You'll never believe it. Honestly, he's disgusting." June wiped her cheeks, her head shaking like a pot lid about to boil over.

"Try me!" I said, mentally running through my 'He's a complete pig and you're far too good for him anyway' speech that I had been saving up for over a year now.

"He wants us to move in together!" Hot tears exploded from June's eyes as she collapsed on my shoulder.

"The filthy pervert!" I gasped sarcastically, although I *was* a little surprised.

"Don't make fun of me!" June said, throwing her head up for air.

"Hey, I'm sorry," I cooed, patting her head against my shoulder. "It's just...such a normal thing. There are discarded 23-year-olds who would kill to be in your position."

"Well," said June, rising from my shoulder with a satisfied hair flick. "I'm not a 23-year-old basic bitch with daddy issues."

"Thank God for that...I still don't understand why it's so upsetting, though?" I asked, wiping down a damp patch on my shoulder.

"Patrick always said-"

"Patrick?!" I shouted. He had always been known as Professor P to everyone, or 'P' if they were on 'biblical' terms with him.

"Yeah, that's his name," shrugged June. "Anyway, Patrick always said this was just a bit of fun. Some company on research trips. Tantric sex on a tugboat in New Orleans, licking saffron off each other in Bhutan, you know?"

"Oh, who doesn't? I don't leave the house without licking expensive spices off someone," I said with an extra dose of sarcasm.

"OK, so we need to maroon you on a desert island with a vat of coconut oil and a proper lover at some point, but this is about me right now," replied June.

"Sorry, tell me more," I said, but I was a bit distracted by the coconut oil comment. I was mainly thinking about how I could use it to cook on the desert island and moisturise my skin, then my mind wandered to what if Hatton and I got stranded on an island because our plane crashed on the way to some event and did he have dry skin? But I didn't want to tell June any of that.

"I just don't understand why he has got so serious all of a sudden! Why ruin a perfectly good shagathon by moving in together?" June retched on the last words like a vegan at the Brazilian barbeque.

"Maybe it's because you've both had, er...such a good time with the tugboats and the saffron?" I said, instinctively making my exit from the car, in case June strangled me at the mere notion of evolving emotional intimacy.

"How can you even say that?" June gasped, following me out. "You sound just like him! I thought you would be on my side."

"I am!" I called as she stormed towards her shop.

"Ugh, whatever," she said, taking keys out of her bag and unlocking the shop. "I have a new client coming in 10 minutes, I don't need this right now. I have to go into Happy Thai Lady mode."

She walked into the shop, leaving me in the street. I decided not to follow her, she would be in an even worse mood now that she was going to have to do her 'act'. June was convinced that if she presented as the bilingual, highly-educated woman she was, it would ruin the mystique of the massage, so she had been pretending not to speak English or hold grudges about the racist and colonial comments from her clients for years now. It had been starting to get to her for a few months now, cursing out the worst customers in Thai, and even getting a one-star review on Facebook when it turned out one guy had a Thai wife and spoke the language fluently, as well as just being a bit of a wanker who talked down to her.

I waved meekly at June, who was throwing a traditional Thai top on over her Dead Kennedys t-shirt. She smiled reluctantly, but her face quickly dropped as she peered behind me. June threw her hands up in the air and marched to the back of the parlour.

"Hello, Sam," said Professor P nervously as he appeared at my side. "I think I'm in the doghouse."

Leni appeared in the shop window, his beady eyes laser-focussed on Professor P, his jaw clamped tight like a bear trap.

"For daring to suggest a conventional relationship with June!" I said, scandalised.

"I only suggested moving in together! It's living in sin, isn't that unconventional enough for her?"

"This isn't the 1860s, so probably not."

"I should talk to her," said Professor P.

"No, you really shouldn't. I'm her best friend and I amn't even going to talk to her when she is like this."

"No, no, no. It will be fine. I will just explain and I am sure she will see sense," Professor P said, his moustache bristling at my intrusion.

"June is seeing red. Brilliant, Communist red. It's best to let her take it out on some poor bugger with a torture massage and come back later. Come on, we'll go to the pub and pop back in an hour or two," I said, nodding my head towards a bar down the street in a last-ditch attempt to coax him away with alcohol. "My treat. I will even buy you that fancy vermouth you like."

He was already striding towards the shop door though. Leni was barking angrily, dragging a line of drool along the window as he bounded towards the door. I groaned with resignation and stomped after the professor. Annoyingly, my conscience wouldn't let him be mauled to death.

"I'll go first," I said under my breath, shoving him aside and opening the door. Leni liked me, but was annoyed he was having to give me kisses instead of killing his main rival for June's affections. "What's this?!" I exclaimed with the excitement of a children's TV presenter, producing a rawhide dog treat from behind the counter.

Leni howled in approval and ran over to me, Professor P sneaking through to the backroom on his ill-fated mission. Leni had only just settled on the sofa with his treat when I heard, "I told you to get out, I have a new client coming in five minutes!" coming down the corridor.

June speed-walked over to her speakers, jabbed some buttons on her phone and plugged it in. Her eyelid twitched as the stereotypical tinkly muzak began to play.

"Don't worry about it," Professor P said, attempting, unsuccessfully, to grab her hand. "I'm the client, I booked online under a pseudonym because I knew you wouldn't see me otherwise." He smiled, pleased at his ruse. June silently made her way through every swear word she knew, too taken aback to give voice to them.

"You poor, foolish man," I muttered, distracting Leni with a squeaky toy, now that he had demolished his treat.

"Are you kidding me? You have lost me money!" raged June, slamming her massage room door shut.

"Come on, it's not like you enjoy doing this anymore," said Professor P. He had a point. This was just totally the wrong time to make it. "Plus, when did you become so concerned about money? Not very Marxist, is it?"

"Er, sorry to interrupt," I piped up. They both turned, looking almost as angrily at me as they did at each other now. "But do you want to live, Prof? This is a suicidal line of questioning. Let's let June get on with her day and go to the pub, like I said."

"Yeah, go off to the pub with one of your floozies!" shouted June, opening the door for us.

"I told you, that's all over now!"

"Patrick," said June, leaning her head on the door, exhausted from the fight, which she had been battling against the tide of relentlessly for so long now. "I *want* you to go to the pub with floozies. I want to slide into the DMs of punk band lead singers again. This has all got way too serious."

"*You* can't be serious," said Professor P, moving closer to June. "We are so good together." He leaned his head on the door too now. "I don't even think about other women." June, swayed by the romance of the moment, looked up at him hopefully. The Professor smiled. "I mean, Angelica Goldsworthy has been trying it on for weeks and I amn't even interested."

"Who's Angelica Goldsworthy?" asked June, moving away from the door, her tongue sticking out as if she had been fed something foul.

"The hottest girl in the Art History Society," I said, feeling like I should occasionally chip in if they insisted on having an argument in front of me.

"How do you know?" said June, rubbing her head wearily.

"Oh, there's always an Angelica Goldsworthy," I said, a smile creeping across my face, but it was stopped in its tracks by a venomous glare from Professor P.

"Samantha Chambers, you are not helping me right now!"

"Hey, I meant it as a compliment," I slunk onto the sofa to avoid the crossfire. Leni threw himself across me like a bodyguard and began to lick my face furiously. "Angelica Goldsworthys have the personality of spinach and ricotta tortellini." June let out a guffaw. "But June, you're more of a sexy satay, delicious but nutty."

"Sam, you know I hate Thai food. How would you like it if I compared you to a haggis? Lumpy and hard to stomach?"

"Sorry, point taken. Look, you two need to sort...whatever this is...out. I am going to take Leni a walk, pick up Brutus too. I will be back in a couple of hours."

"Fine," sniffed June. "She's probably right, we need to talk."

Professor P nodded solemnly. I too bowed my head and headed for the door.

"June, you're really overreacting. I mean, it's not like I can have sex with Angelica, even if I wanted to. The Dean says all teaching will probably be online soon if this virus thing keeps going. It's not like I can shag her if we're not in the same room as each other!"

I almost felt sorry for him. So close, yet so far.

CHAPTER

9

I came back about an hour and a half later, having taken Brutus and Leni for a promenade around Beath Community Park, reclaimed scrubland that had everything from a skatepark to a vegetable garden in it, as well as, allegedly, the best smack dealers in all of Edinburgh operating under its flickering streetlights. I was used to getting a lot of attention when out with Brutus due to both his smallness and his cuteness, which seemed to be amplified with the hulking Leni next to him. It always added a good ten minutes to the walk answering the same questions from fascinated dog fans. By now I knew the questions before they did and had my answers ready: "Yes, he's a real dog. A mini-husky. Yes, he's fully grown. No, your screaming child can't touch him if they want to keep their fingers."

As we neared June's shop, I could see her sitting alone on the sofa, no sign of Professor P. It was hard to tell if she was sad, she looked like she was concentrating on a magazine that she had in her hands. Cautiously, I pushed open the door and sent in the dogs because June loved animals and this was bound to lift her spirits if she was down in the dumps.

"Come here, boys!" she called as Leni loyally cuddled into one leg. Brutus humped the other manically. I sighed. I really couldn't take him anywhere without him causing some sort of scene. June was used to it though and even giggled playfully. Brutus had this effect on women, and some men. I would be trying to wrench the randy hound off their leg or arm and they would say 'it's no trouble at all!' when it clearly was and probably broke some laws of nature, if not actual UK law. Luckily, Brutus had a short attention span and was soon off picking a fight with Leni, who I am pretty sure had done a poo that weighed more than Brutus in the park.

"Sorry about that," I said. Brutus turned and, I swear, *winked* at June.

"Oh, it's OK. Brutus and Leni are the only men I need!" she said, throwing the magazine on the coffee table. 'Visit Belkita' it read, alongside a disturbingly caucasian nuclear family frolicking in the sparkling surf. A holiday would be nice, I mused.

I snapped back into concerned friend mode, a little ashamed at getting distracted. "Is it over, then?"

"Yeah," said June, resting her head on my shoulder as Brutus licked a tear off her face. "You know he said he wanted to get married and have kids?"

"Really?" I said. Professor P refused to get a gym membership because it was too much commitment.

"Yeah. And I just don't want those things. I want to take over the world, you know?" June said matter-of-factly, like she had declared her intention to do the dishes when she got home.

"Of course," I said.

"He said he was OK with that too, but I knew he wasn't. He needs someone who wants what he wants, and I need someone who won't reveal my plans to overthrow Capitalism under interrogation. Actually, I don't need anyone, but you catch my drift." June handed me the brochure she had been reading.

"Take a look at this. I think we both need a break," she said as I flicked through the pages.

"Why Belkita? Isn't that a tiny island in the Med?"

"That's it! Paxton recommended it to me."

"Paxton?" I bristled, sitting upright. What was doing June talking to my old university buddy? Sure, they had met at the St Fillan's reunion last year, but this felt like very different, very separate worlds of mine colliding; June was a committed communist, Paxton committed to wasting his vast inheritance.

"Yes, Paxton. We sometimes message. Don't look so shocked!" said June, giving me an elbow in the side.

"Hey! It's just not something I imagined. I'm glad you two get on though," I said diplomatically, turning my attention back to the magazine. I tried to concentrate on the pretty pictures and enthusiastic descriptions of sun-drenched shores, but I was starting to feel guilty about always being off in Denmark, it felt like I was missing out on all these connections and conversations while I was pissing about on TV shows and developing a crush so large I would probably have to get a doctor to lance or remove it one day.

"Well, he said he has just bought a retreat in Belkita as part of a tax write-off," said June. I smiled to myself. This was typical Paxton. When the IRS began to look into his family finances, he promptly held a charity bash to raise awareness for the three-legged hedgehog. They definitely needed the publicity, as no one had heard of them and also they didn't exist. Half of St Fillan's was invited and he piled thousands of pounds into the open bar to avoid a big tax bill.

"He said you and I should go out there for the summer and relax. For free!" June said, now jiggling with excitement. "And you know there is nothing I love more than exploiting the rich."

"June, I think you're forgetting that, unlike Paxton, we need to work," I slammed the brochure shut to avoid further temptation. "We can't go for a whole summer. What about a week or two?"

"He says it's three months and there are no exceptions. I can leave the shop with Alejandro for the summer, no problem," said June, picking up the brochure and opening it at a dog-eared page that showed two women drinking wine on a terrace as the sun went down. "That could be us!" she said, stabbing the picture with her index finger.

She did have a point. Alejandro was a great masseuse and a hit with the customers since June had taken him on last October. "That's fine for you, but there is no way I can go," I said.

"Why not? I can tell that you are going to quit that shitty job once and for all."

She did have another good point. It was only a matter of time before I was out of there. I searched for a good enough reason for June to drop it. It would be great to galavant in the Mediterranean for the summer, but Paxton always got me into drama. Even if it was fun, it wasn't something I needed right now.

"Aha! The pets! Who will take care of Lily and Brutus? I'm not leaving them with Nigel for three months."

"Oh, Paxton says we can take them with us. He will pay for them to be flown over," said June, now pointing at a bronzed, shirtless Belkitan man on a speedboat.

"Really?" I said, imagining Lily lounging on a sunny balcony, Brutus doggy paddling after women in bikinis.

"Yes! And if all the locals look like this, it will be a great distraction from married men..." said June, fanning herself with speedboat man.

She did have a point. If all the men looked like that, I would probably struggle to remember my own name, never mind Hatton Finch.

"When do we leave?" I asked, watching June's eyes light up.

"Yesssss! Ladettes on Tour!" she cried. "And in three weeks. Just enough time to hand in your notice and get the hell out of Dodge."

"I will hand in my notice first thing tomorrow," I said, gulping at the thought. Financial insecurity, here I come. It was just too good an opportunity to pass up though, I resolved. I was sure I would have plenty of time to plot my next move while touring the island on a speedboat driven by a muscular Belkitan.

CHAPTER

10

The next morning I arrived (late) at work with 'come at me' energy. It had been brewing on my walk to the office; a meandering cyclist on a JustEat bike was trundling down one of the narrow pedestrian walkways hastily erected to accommodate the construction of a vanity project for the council; a cablecar transport system. They hadn't predicted it would be a PR move to have all the rich people who lived outside the city literally looking down on their poorer counterparts on their way home. Anyway, I had told the unfortunate cyclist that if he didn't get out my way, I would throw him in one of the plague pits that had been uncovered during the roadworks.

The genuine fear in his eyes pleased me. It was refreshing telling the bastards what you really thought, taking a satisfying sip of Pepsi Max from my Keep Cup (I hate tea and coffee but liked to pretend I was a proper adult, though that illusion might have been spoiled by the customised cup with Lily and Brutus on it).

When I walked through the office lobby, I was a little disappointed there was no one there to feel my wrath. Walking to my desk, I fished out the tub of porridge I had brought in for my breakfast and put it in the microwave, even though it never really heated the food properly, made strange noises and you felt sick if you stood too near it while it was on.

Sitting down at my desk, I opened my laptop and was immediately greeted by a diary notification - 'Digital Metrics Workshop' at Dynamic Earth, a weird hybrid of natural history museum and conference venue shaped like an armadillo. With all the book stuff, I had been getting worse at tracking my work schedule, but not actually bad enough to be fired, much to Sandra the CEO's chagrin. Not that any of that mattered anymore.

Then the reason why I was being dispatched to the conference popped up in another notification: the 'Empowered Employee' assessment was today. As a very much disengaged employee that Sandra was trying to manacle to a life of professional unfulfillment, she wanted me nowhere near the event.

The Empowered Employee Awards are supposed to be an industry benchmark of how well you treat your staff, but it's actually just an excuse for CEOs to have a circle jerk. A running joke at the company had been how our results seemed to get better the lower morale actually got. A classification was achieved by 'randomly' selecting all the quietest and/or most scared colleagues to be interviewed by the Engaged Employee Assessor, who mysteriously never found any issues.

Problem employees were sent away for the day to avoid anything as awful as the truth being revealed. It reminded me of school when the inspector came and all the delinquents just happened to be packed off to a remote playing field for the day with a sacrificial P.E. teacher. Only now I was one of the bad kids, instead of the one selected to present an extracurricular project I had willingly done (why?) on the Industrial Revolution to the inspector.

I smiled at how horrified my teachers would be to learn that I had developed some sort of late-onset delinquency as I googled 'best quitting your job stories' to stoke the fire of rebellion. I had only just pressed 'search' though when I saw a woman leaning curiously over the welcome desk in the lobby. She looked like the result of a middle management breeding experiment, with her streaky highlighted hair, botoxed forehead and scratchy-looking black blazer.

I craned round my laptop out of curiosity, which attracted her attention.

"Oh, hello! Do you work here?" she called.

"Allegedly," I muttered to myself as I went over to see what she wanted.

"I'm Nicola Short," she volunteered. "I'm the Empowered Employee Assessor. I will be telling you whether you are empowered or not. I am supposed to meet your CEO here at 11 but I am afraid I am a bit early."

Then I remembered where everyone else was. Sandra took all the employees being assessed out for a slap-up bribery breakfast with a side of vague threats about job security before the interviews.

"I'm sure they will be back soon," I said, gesturing for her to follow me into the office.

"Back from where? I don't suppose you could let me into Conference Room B? It would be good to get set up for the day," she said, fluttering fake eyelashes like a dying but fashion conscious deer. It didn't work on me, but I wasn't bothered about the rules anymore. Hell, if she had asked me for the logins for all the company's social media accounts, I probably would have given them to her and told her to do her worst.

"It's just through here," I said, leading her through the office. She walked as if this was where she came to work every day, casually hanging up her jacket on the coat rack and heading over to the kettle to make herself a cup of tea. I supposed that she was at home in any office, spending every day in a variation of the same faceless flatpack furniture workspace.

Once she was situating herself in Conference Room B, I made my excuses and headed back to my desk.

"Not so fast," she said. "Are you not supposed to be interviewed today?" She stirred a cup of tea cosily.

"No," I said with a hearty laugh. "I am 'officially' at a conference today."

"Oh, are you one of the naughty kids?" she giggled. "They think we don't know about that trick. I bet she has taken them all out for breakfast too?"

"Something like that," I said, leaning in the doorway with the energy of a 14-year-old bad bitch caught graffiti-ing her desk. If only those Danish kids could see me now, I thought.

"Why don't we have a sneaky interview before they come back? Confidentially, of course. I want to know what it is really like to work here. If I have to hear one more person tell me how grateful they are for the opportunity to be sent on an Excel training course, I will throw myself out of their high-rise office window." She fluttered her eyelashes again, this time with a conspiratorial flick.

"Go on then," I said, feeling a weird throb of impulsiveness that didn't even seem to be coming from me. If I was a conspiracy theorist, I would have blamed it on 5G.

Nicola beckoned me in like a cool girl encouraging you to bunk off school and go shopping with her.

I felt the magnetic pull and sat down on the far side of the conference table, giving me a panoramic view of the empty office while Nicola finished arranging her papers for the day opposite me. It was like watching Brutus turn around over and over on the same spot before going to bed, the way she ritually shuffled and stacked her sheets of A4. I got the feeling that her naughty streak didn't run very deep, that her idea of true subversion would be saying you didn't own a television. I could feel my own newfound bad streak beginning to burn though, like those hot coals people run over for charity and their ego.

"So, I need to start by telling you that all responses are anonymous and totally confidential," smiled Nicola, just about managing not to laugh.

"Of course, apart from the list of employees passed to the CEO and the transcription of interviews available upon request," I said, not even trying not to laugh.

"That's all true, yes. But duty binds me to emphasise how important confidentiality is to our organisation," explained Nicola, clicking 'record' on her phone and adding my name to the top of a list of interviewees in front of her.

"Oh yes, I completely understand," I said, leaning back in my chair with the air of the coolest boy in Primary 7. It was Year 6 of this nonsense and I think it had just broken my bullshit-o-meter. Six years of being stuck in this MDF iron maiden, I thought, looking at a stain on the ceiling I had originally noticed during my interview.

Nicola was too busy leafing through her murdered rainforest to notice.

"So, Sam, let's start off with a nice easy question. What's your job title?"

"Digital Officer."

"And what does a Digital Officer do?" she asked, typing my response.

"I'm not sure," I shrugged. Was I really going to throw Sandra under the bus? It seemed so.

"You're not sure?" said Nicola, a plucked eyebrow quivering in concern. "How long have you worked here?"

"Six years."

"And you still don't know what your job is?"

"Well, I just know that it's not whatever I have been doing because the highest praise I have ever received is it would be 'an HR nightmare to get rid of me.'" Apparently I was out to prove that, while the old song says that you cannae shove yer Granny off a bus, you can most certainly push your demonic boss under one.

"Really?" asked Nicola, typing furiously.

"Yeah, I wrote a book and Sandra the CEO didn't enjoy it. But she isn't prejudiced against artists. She's always hated me."

"Wait," said Nicola, ceasing to type. "You're *that* Sam Chambers? And *she* is your boss?" Her jaw almost hit her keyboard.

"Yes. Although, all characters were a product of my imagination, which Sandra has described as 'decrepit' on many an occasion."

"Wow, that's a lot to process. Let's come back to that...the next question is, 'What is the most life-changing thing this job has given you?'"

"A scalp condition."

"A scalp condition?" Nicola said flatly.

"Yeah, I got stress eczema last summer organising a conference. It has been pretty life-changing, I still need to use a special shampoo," I said, automatically checking my shoulders for dandruff.

"Right..." said Nicola, clinically typing my words like a concerned nurse. "Let's move on to the next question: What's your favourite thing about working here?"

"Home-time."

Nicola's forehead made a Herculean effort to overpower the botox and pinch in a frown. This clearly wasn't the cheeky chat she had expected. I couldn't concentrate on her disapproval very long though because I spied Sandra the CEO leading her band of empowered employees back into the office, each carrying a takeaway coffee and an obscenely large pretzel. I waved and smiled sweetly, watching Sandra's face twitch from a grin into a snarl.

"Now, I'm all for a bit of fun, Sam, but I don't think you're taking this very seriously," said Nicola, shaking her head, her perfect bob swinging like an unmoored lampshade. "Let's wrap this up for now. I am contractually obligated to finish the interview with one last question, which is...oh dear... What one thing would improve your office?"

"If it was on fire," I said as Sandra began to claw manically at the conference room window, a human honey badger in a Size 4 skirt suit out for the kill. Nicola turned with a start to view the spectacle. I reckoned I had about 10 seconds before Sandra regained some of her sense and scrambled towards the door to throw herself into the room, so I braced for impact.

However, she abruptly stopped pounding on the glass and hurried out of sight towards the kitchen. A blast of smoke came from the direction she had just gone in. Nicola and I stood up and headed for the door, half-evacuating, half-intrigued by the source of the smoke. Poking our heads out, we could see flames flickering in a mass of smoke. Eddie from Maintenance ran past with a fire extinguisher and blasted the thing.

Once the smoke and spluttering had died down, the culprit was revealed:

My porridge.

I must have set the timer for something ridiculous like 30 minutes instead of 3 minutes and forgotten about it.

"Woops. My bad," I said, craning my head out into the corridor. Sandra, who I could now see was covered in a lumpy film of exploded porridge, swivelled towards me.

"Sam, this is the last straw," she said, her intimidating stride interrupted by some errant porridge on the floor.

"I think the last straw was actually when you made me that insulting golden handcuffs offer," I said, folding my arms, mostly so I too didn't explode with the nervous energy now buzzing through me. I felt like I was watching someone else, someone braver, flame out in front of the be-porridged CEO. "Besides," I pressed on, or whatever that was inhabiting me did, at least. "You can consider this mess my avant-garde, performance art resignation. I'm out of here."

I turned to leave triumphantly, the vibe slightly impaired by having to pick through the smouldering porridge.

"Ha! You can't resign when you're already terminated. The HR handbook says that if anyone *does* set the building on fire, they are fired with immediate effect. So you're a few minutes too late, isn't that right, Patience?" said Sandra, folding her arms with satisfaction, like a war criminal admiring the work of someone who has just dug their own grave.

"Yes," confirmed Patience reluctantly, wiping a lump of porridge off her pretzel.

"Ugh," I lamented. "And just when I was starting to feel like an empowered employee," I said to Nicola, who was watching the whole thing with the same terrified look people have at the Edinburgh Fringe when they stumble into a show about abortion and bananas but are too polite to leave.

She shook her head as if awakening from a nightmare. "Sam! Wait a minute. I just...I have to know, why didn't you get together with Dean at the end?"

Sensing another explosion, Eddie the Maintenance Man grabbed my arm and began to escort me out. I turned to see Patience give me a timid thumbs up behind Sandra, who was too busy imagining murdering me to notice.

I smiled back because I was already far away, mentally sipping cocktails with June on our island retreat.

CHAPTER

11

"What are you doing?" I asked June as she wrote 'L.O.S.C' on the calendar on the wall.

"Marking today as the Liberation of Sam Chambers so that we can celebrate the national holiday in years to come!"

A few hours had passed since the porridge debacle, and we were sitting on my living room floor, drinking whatever we happened to find in the cupboard. I hadn't done my weekly shop yet, so June had made do and concocted a powerful cocktail of tequila, off-brand Irn Bru and flat prosecco. It was remarkably passable, especially after the first couple of glasses when all your tastebuds fell into a coma.

"I just hope I don't end up like one of those criminals who re-offends because they miss prison. If you see me applying for another job looking for a 'self-starter' who 'likes working under pressure', shoot me."

June poured more tequila into my glass before swiftly pulling it away - Brutus was trying to drink it like it was a water fountain.

"You know what you should do, you should write another book," instructed June.

"What about? I would need something interesting to happen."

"You don't think the porridge thing could be described as interesting?"

"Yeah," I said, making a face at my glass, the fumes it was giving off nipping at my eyes. I drank it anyway. "I mean, it's the start of a story, though. Or at least I hope it is. I don't want that to be the end of it."

"You're going to do so many great things!" said June, planting a kiss on my forehead. "Or at least you will be around to see me do them and ghost write my autobiography." Now she was draining the last of the prosecco into her glass. The sound of running liquid made me realise how much I needed to pee.

"I will be back in a minute. My bladder is bursting with tequila," I mumbled, trying to use the sofa as some sort of lever to stand up. It took a couple of goes, but I was so proud as I Bambi-legged my way to the bathroom.

Mid-flow in the bathroom, looking at the same worrying crack in the ceiling I always do, I heard June talking. But to who? Not Brutus or Lily, she wasn't using the cutesy voice she put on for animals, but there was something excited in her tone. In a feat of pelvic prowess, I halted my pee instantly so I could hear.

"Not at all Hatton, she will be back in a minute. She needed a massive pee because I have been plying her with tequila, you see."

I have never pulled up my pyjama bottoms so quickly, even when trying to look semi-presentable for a delivery driver. Stumbling back into the living room, I found June holding my phone with a wicked look on her face.

"Oh here she is now! Good pee?" she teased.

I mouthed 'give me the phone' as violently as I could and June dangled it in front of me. I snatched it off her and she pouted, but soon found solace in her concoction. I took the phone out onto the balcony. It seemed as if I should give them some alone time, and perhaps that I should have some time alone to talk to Hatton. For all he knew, we could be meeting in Copenhagen in a couple of weeks.

"Good evening. Thank you for your call. How can I help you tonight, Mr Finch?" I said, trying to sound like I hadn't been drinking prosecco and tequila for two hours. Instead, I sounded like I was manning the phones on a credit card fraud helpline.

"Sam? Is that you?"

"Yes, sorry. A flash of formality came over me, it won't happen again," I said, leaning over my balcony to watch the local drunk serenade a lamp post with 'Oops I Did it Again'. I couldn't help singing along. The man stopped suddenly and glared up at me, probably worried I was coming for his title. His look said 'if you come for the king, you best not miss', or at least he would have if he could focus his eyes properly.

"Are you singing Britney Spears?" laughed Hatton.

"So what if I am?"

"I just never imagined it. You seem the sort that would have some sarcastic feminist remark re: her singing about being smacked around while being dressed as an underage schoolgirl."

"Hm, I think that's another song. In this one, she is the biggest cock-tease on Mars, gyrating for astronauts in red PVC. You know, real world problems every woman can relate to," I said, watching the drunk shuffle onto his next lamp post victim. "Anyway, why did you call me? Sudden desire to talk about Britney?"

"No, I am at a beer tasting with Aubrey and her husband." Now that he said it, I could hear general exterior pub noise in the background, laughing, music, plus the whoosh of traffic. "They said I needed to 'get out there' again."

"Ooh! Out on the pull!" I said as if I was one of the lads, but I only really wanted to be one of the lads with Hatton if it was in one of those homoerotic Greek friezes.

"Ha! I don't think anyone will want an ageing actor who has spilt stout down his shirt."

"Oh puh-leeease," I said, turning to see June apparently slow-dancing round the room with a very eager-looking Brutus in her arms. "You are a total DILF."

Damn that tequila, it was making words leak out of me. I tensed, like a rabbit, hoping if it stays still enough it will escape evisceration by a passing kestrel. The only sound on the other end of the phone was the muted throb of a tune I couldn't name.

"Really? You think so?" he said eventually. I thought I could hear a smile, but maybe I was wrong.

"Well, obviously I didn't mean me personally," I back-pedalled furiously, so hard I was surprised I didn't fly through the window and knock over June and Brutus. "Just forget I said it."

"I probably will. I have lost count of the number of beers we have 'sampled.'"

At least he was drunk too, I reassured myself.

"You still haven't said why you called?" I said, trying to pivot away from this unfortunate topic.

"Well, because I'm drunk!" Suddenly I heard it in his voice, the words sliding out as if across ice. "And I wish you were here. And we were drunk. Can we get drunk in Copenhagen? When are you next there?"

I sighed. I did really want to go and get drunk in Copenhagen with him. Something in my stomach twisted when he said he missed me, but that very well could have been the irn bru-tequila-prosecco combo curdling.

"I quit my job!"

"YESSS! Finally! So I will see you soon then?"

"Um, I am actually going travelling this summer. You probably won't see me for a while," I said. How could I feel like I was dumping someone the closest that I had got to knowing carnally was seeing dredged out of a river in their underpants?

There was radio silence again, with occasionally blurs of sound from the bar.

"I think it's for the best," I pressed on. "Right now, I am so close to saying something I shouldn't to you, so God knows what I would do in person. The whole situation is too complicated. I have been there, written the book *and* got the promotional t-shirt to prove it." It felt awkward, but almost a relief to finally allude to what I thought was going on between us. Of course, I then immediately panicked as the only thing worse than this would be if he didn't care at all and I had imagined the whole thing.

"I get it," he said, sounding tired. "These things don't just go away though. Attraction doesn't wash out like I hope this beer stain will. I am not going to make you say or do anything you don't want to, though."

It wasn't going anywhere, but it alleviated some of my anxiety that he had acknowledged what was going on. I was almost a bit angry at him too, though. Could he not have said something a bit misogynist just to make this easier and less hot for me?

Just then, June knocked on the window, shaking the tequila at me.

"Look - I better go. See you..." I couldn't think of a good way to end the sentence.

"When you see me?" he volunteered.

"I'll see you when I see you."

CHAPTER

12

Three weeks later, June and I entered Edinburgh Airport at the incredibly unsociable hour of 6am. Checking in was relatively painless because the pets had been sent ahead on another flight. Paxton had left our travel arrangements to his new (now ex) assistant, who naively thought her job was to act in the financial interest of her employer. She had therefore booked the most inexpensive option, which was transporting our pets separately and shipping us out on a budget flight with a connection at Heathrow. Appalled at the savings made, Paxton had at least booked us into a fancy airport hotel, just three minutes' walk from the terminal.

The two of us cleared security without being searched, much to June's annoyance. In the queue, she had pointed out a hunky guard with a buzzcut and declared her intention to act as suspiciously as possible around him.

"I think they would have probably made a woman search you anyway, June," I said as she sulkily slipped her sandals back on on the other side of security.

"Don't ruin my fantasy!" she said, giving a coy wave to the officer.

"I'm glad to see your heart is mending just fine after the Professor," I said.

"After who?" asked June.

I lugged my bulging rucksack over my shoulder. The assistant had also booked the least expensive luggage options for us too and we didn't have the heart to tell Paxton.

Determined to write something new, I had packed several journals in there, alongside a wholesale-amount of mini toiletries, a motley collection of vest tops and capri leggings found at the back of my wardrobe and mismatched bikini bottoms and tops who had lost their original partners to the dangerous waters of my washing machine.

Exiting security, we walked across the Duty Free shop floor, a mandatory gauntlet you had to run to reach Departures. Bottles of whisky extended along one wooden wall, groups of American and Asian tourists browsing as if they were in the Library of Alexandria, carefully examining labels. Whisky had never really been my thing, so I managed to avoid that temptation. Plus, I knew what drink sampling could lead to, and this trip was supposed to keep me out of trouble.

A scoosh of perfume stopped us in our tracks and I realised that we had entered the Cosmetics section, a forensically well-lit shrine to impossible beauty. I coughed, the perfume catching the back of my throat. It smelt and tasted like a cross between washing up liquid and an off-banana.

"You've not got that thing that's going around, have you?" asked a perfectly preened sales assistant, perfume bottle in hand. I think she was concerned, but she maintained the standard issue rictus grin.

"No, but that perfume smells like it is on its last legs," I said, backing away before she could wield her weapon again. Now her eyes said 'go die in a hole', but she kept the smile fixed to her face with the utmost professionalism.

"Sam, stop victimising the working-class!" scolded June.

"It legitimately smelt awful, June," I said, my nose hairs quivering at the mere thought.

"Whatever, I thought it smelt ok. Let's get out of this consumerist hellhole," said June.

We sped through the rest of the lipsticks, hand creams, designer sunglasses and other things that I swear nobody actually buys in these places, only ever sneaking free tests. I was pulling June along as she offered her reflections: "Who needs 50 different shades of nail varnish? You only have 10 fingers!" and "Oh, fantastic, a poster of a white woman flogging Tahitian vanilla hand cream. She is about as Polynesian as a Lorne sausage!"

We didn't survive the temptation of the huge bags of sweets at the till though. We somehow rationalised not being able to last the one-hour flight to London without a bag of diabetes which could last a large family for a month under normal circumstances.

On the concourse, things felt a little less overwhelming; the shops all existed as independent units, so it at least meant the pockets of rampant consumerism couldn't bleed into each other.

It was still obscenely early, so there was only one thing to do: grab a pint. I made a beeline for the 'Very Scottish' bar at the far end of the terminal. Normally you couldn't pay me to frequent somewhere with tartan everything (including carpet, wallpaper and staff uniforms) that blared the Bonnie Banks of Loch Lomond on the bagpipes, but drinking at the airport is a national tradition, so needs must.

I was on a mission, trying but failing to zone out all the expensive distractions around us; what possesses people to load up on designer scarves and buy *a car* at the airport? Who honestly goes "That reminds me! I totally forgot to buy a BMW before I left the house! Thank God there's one here, that could have been embarrassing." I wished I had those problems; personally, I was always forgetting my travel adapter for my increasingly rickety laptop and having to buy one in the electronics shop before my flight.

I was muttering something about people having more money than sense when something familiar caught my eye.

'Bae for Pay' it read. My book. Here it was in the airport bookshop, sandwiched between gloomy covers of Scottish thrillers and pastel-coloured chick-lit books. Two figures clinked glasses on Bae for Pay's front cover, not that you would know that, because the company had seen fit to slap a giant yellow 'LOCAL AUTHOR!!' sticker right across the glasses.

I found myself at a halt directly in front of it. It still felt weird to actually see it in real life, like I was just having a vivid fever dream.

June had walked ahead but reversed back into view.

"What are you looking...oh. I see. Do you have to do this *every* time you see your book in a shop?" huffed June.

"We will see how you are when you publish your own Communist Manifesto," I said.

"Ha! You won't find it in chain stores. I will drop it from aeroplanes to bypass the inevitable government censorship." I laughed, but I knew June was only half-joking. "Whatever, I will leave you two alone. I am going to grab us a table," said June, heading towards the bar.

I decided to take a photo of the books for my Instagram Story. It would remind people it was available in airports and encourage them to buy it if they were going on holiday. I would post it with a GIF of a cat doing a shocked face so that I came across as whimsical rather than opportunistic.

I was flicking through the library of animated cats when I was distracted by the shriek of a baby. I cringed and turned, hoping it wouldn't be on our flight.

"Caspar Benson! Hold still!"

It was Harriet, my BFF from uni. In one arm, she held a stack of glossy magazines, in the other a baby - Caspar. He looked less than impressed and probably would have called his mother a traitor if he could say more than 'Mama' (pronounced like a character from Brideshead Revisited rather than the normal baby speak, to give him his due). I knew because this had been chronicled on Harriet's Instagram. Even though most of his face was obscured by a chemical-warfare-chic hood, there was no doubt he was Harriet's child, with the same haughty eyes and permanently pursed lips.

Part of me wanted to run out the shop to avoid any 'inopportune' interaction, but another more morbidly curious part of me wanted to know what she would say. It was probably the same part that made me write the book in the first place.

"H-Harriet, is that you?" I piped up. Harriet froze, weighing up her options. The only thing she hated more than looking bad in public was poor manners, so it wasn't a total surprise when she looked up with a pleasant smile on her face.

"Samantha! What a small world! Fancy seeing you here! Charmed, I'm sure!" It was like listening to an English as Foreign Language module on small talk. "What are the chances! Here you are, right next to a shelf of your...*unsold* books," she said.

"Truth is stranger than fiction," I replied. Harriet spluttered a bit and so did Caspar, a snot bubble dangling precariously from his nose.

"I do hope he is not coming down with that terrible virus in the news," she said nervously, producing a 'C' embroidered napkin from a huge baby bag at her feet. "You can never be too careful."

"Hence the Hazmat suit?" I asked, nodding to the big plastic hood contraption her son was wearing.

"You think I am quite ridiculous," Harriet bristled.

"No! I mean, who wouldn't want to protect such a," I trailed off, searching my mind for the most appropriate maternal response. "A...cherubic... infant?"

"You might be a writer, Sam, but you are certainly not an actress. You have never liked children. Remember when they tried to make you take care of a flour baby for an article in the student newspaper? You used it to make a cake. Which you burnt."

"Hey, that cake was perfectly edible once I cut off all the burnt bits," I shrugged and Harriet smiled a little. "He looks like the perfect mix of you and Allan, though!" That was to say that I couldn't see any of the bland Allan in Caspar. Just at that moment, he gave me a wicked grin that reminded me of someone else: Paxton, who had been involved in an ill-advised sexcapade with Harriet and her husband Allan at the reunion. Luckily, Harriet was too busy fussing over the snail trail of snot across her son's face to notice the whites of my eyes flare: could Paxton be his biological father?

Why hadn't I thought of this earlier? I should have been paying less attention to my career and more to Harriet's menstrual cycle - this was potentially very juicy gossip. I made a mental note to do some digging on social media later on to see if the dates lined up. It shouldn't be too hard, Harriet had started posting about Caspar's arrival in the world very early on, possibly during the C-section.

"Speaking of Allan, where is he?" I asked, trying to move on from any potential awkwardness.

"Oh, he is over by the magazines. He said Company Car Quarterly was out and he wanted a copy for the flight," Harriet gestured towards the magazine aisle, where identikit men in cargo shorts and striped polo shirts shuffled in waves towards the car section.

I waved in the direction of the men, but, in all honesty, I had no idea which one was actually Allan.

"Where are you flying to, anyway?" asked Harriet, semi-distracted by Caspar trying to grab an erotic thriller off the shelf. Another indication that the lascivious Paxton was the daddy, I wondered?

"Paxton," I blurted, before stopping to see if there was a flicker of recognition. There was not. "Paxton invited me to this new retreat he is involved in on the island of Belkita."

"How kind of him. He is very generous, isn't he?" Harriet smiled dreamily. I mentally underlined the moment.

"And where is the happy family off to?" I said, making to pinch Caspar's cheek, but germaphobe Harriet hugged him away from potential affection. I was pretty glad - the striplight had caught the snotty sheen across said cheek.

"We are just connecting here for a flight up to St Fillan's. Well, nearby, anyway. We have an AirBnB in the countryside - a very sophisticated cottage, not one of those shacks with a spare room - for the rest of the month. Should be heaven."

Yes, alone in the secluded wilderness with the world's most boring man and his germ-infested maybe-baby sounds absolutely heavenly, I thought.

"That it does!" I said, forcing enthusiasm.

Harriet let out a laugh. "What did I tell you about your acting?"

"OK, let's be real, then," I said, summoning my best poker face. "When are you going to forgive me for the book?"

"There's nothing to forgive!" said Harriet, the way you might address someone who put a flaming turd on your doorstep.

"You weren't happy with the book, come on!" I said, prodding the beast.

"No, I wasn't, but," she lowered her voice, "It *was* a good book, OK?" Our eyes met and for the first in a long time, we actually *shared* a smile.

"Look, our flight is boarding now, and even I am not sure which of those men is Allan, so I better get a move on," said Harriet. "But message me and let me know how it goes at Paxton's? I will send you some photos of little Caspar on his first trip to St Fillan's!"

Caspar sneezed all over her shoulder as she walked over to the magazines

I seized the snotty olive branch, smiled and waved.

CHAPTER

13

A few hours later, I was sitting with a Heathrow hotel bar, waiting for June to come back with our drinks. I was watching a muted news bulletin about cases of the Baby Botch being found at a private school near Cambridge. A horsey-looking woman was clutching fretfully at a pashmina in a talking head segment, the subtitle beneath her reading 'Tilly Smythe-Hattlebury, Concerned Mother'. I would have been concerned if she was my mother, but luckily mine was too busy plotting early retirement when I was in high school to do anything quite so embarrassing as go on the national news.

June put a glass of prosecco in front of me. I looked at it and felt a bit wistful about drinks with Hatton at the hotel bar in Copenhagen.

"Oh, you don't look pleased? I thought this was what all white women drank when they went on holiday," said June, hopping onto the towering metal stool opposite mine. "And if you think I am gonna buy you champagne, you have got another thing coming. Champagne socialism is not on brand for me."

"No, it's just what I wanted. Hatton and I always used to have it in Copenhagen," I said, taking a cheery sip.

"Ughhh," said June, raising her own glass to her lips. "I wish you had just banged him, honestly. I'm not sure if I can stand a whole summer of this lovesickness."

"I'm not lovesick!" I declared. "If anyone's lovesick, *you're* lovesick for Professor P."

"I am not! I would never speak to him again unless he left this scarf at mine," she said, producing a paint-daubed, ratty thing from her bag. "I have only messaged him to see if he wants it back. And I don't even care if he does."

"Let's just agree not to talk about either of them. We are majorly failing the Bechdel Test right now," I said, shaking my head. "Let's talk about the news. What do you think of this Baby Botch thing going around?"

"It's a narrow-minded litmus test for the complexity of the female experience.

"Eh?"

"The Bechdel Test. Sometimes in our lives we are going to talk about men more than at other points. It doesn't make you or I less of a feminist."

"Ok, whatever. Please just put that manky scarf away. Can we talk about something less controversial, like disease spreading across the globe?"

"Oh, that. I think it's one of the signs of the Fall of Capitalism."

I groaned and took a long drag of prosecco. "Why, dare I ask?"

"Think about it. GenXers, Millennials, generations abused by the capitalist machine. Now young people can't take any more of it, even physically. All we can hope for is that they are still strong enough for the revolution." June's eyes misted over.

"Is this *really* your first drink of the evening?"

"I might have had a shot at the bar," June shrugged. "You should have one too. It's the start of our holiday, after all."

I nodded begrudgingly and dismounted my stool. It was only 5pm and felt a bit early for a shot, but I was going to need it if June was already on the Communist conspiracy chat.

I walked up to the bar. It had all the personality of a Love Island contestant on mute; it was pretty in a plastic sort of way. The shiny white stools and the word 'RELAX' aggressively rendered in neon capital letters above the bar just wasn't the same as somewhere I would choose to go, like Divine Drinks or that bar in Copenhagen.

"It's just not the same, is it?" said a voice at my side. It sounded awfully like Hatton, but I was feeling cynical and doubted it could be him; maybe our experience hadn't been unique at all. Maybe it was the flat-pack furniture of relationships and happened in airport bars and boutique hotels all over the world.

I swivelled round, sceptically narrowing my eyes, only for them to spring back open when I realised it was actually him. He had grown his beard a bit since I last saw him and was in long-haul flight clothes - hoodie and joggers. I was hoping my shock would morph to horror at seeing him dressed like a member of the Beath Liberation. No such luck because the hoodie was cut to reveal a hint of muscle and healthy tanned chest. It was a refreshing change from the tattoos and track marks on my 'suitor' on Beath Walk; he routinely leaped out of doorways to claim Princess Diana had told him that we were meant to be together.

"What are you doing here?" I said, gulping hard to swallow the panic and excitement that was leaking into my voice. I regretted this grey sweatshirt with 'PET PAWRENT' embroidered on it. Why couldn't I have worn one of those stylish travel outfits trotted out in the magazines Harriet was buying at the airport?

"I'm flying out to Paris to pick up Parthenope from her French immersion course tomorrow morning. We're going to spend the summer together. Travel, do lots of educational things," he said, catching the eye of the barman, no hideous sweat patches or anything. "What brings you here?"

"Oh, I'm going on a retreat with my friend June over there." I said, pointing casually but continuing to sweat profusely. June's jaw was being propped up by her prosecco glass, at least she was as shocked as I was.

"She has a lot to answer for, doesn't she?" said Hatton, trying not to laugh.

I decided babbling would make everything better. "Ahhahahaha. Well, we have a cheap deal with the aptly named Cheep Cheep Airways. So, first we fly to Barcelona, and then we-"

"Two proseccos, please," said Hatton to the barman. "And what will June have?"

June was now waving her hands and hyperventilating. "Kittens, apparently. Or another prosecco. Whatever you have back there."

The glasses were poured in front of us robotically by a bored teenager 'Irfan: Customer Service Champion', his name badge informed us.

Hatton drummed his fingers on the counter. "Of all the gin joints in all the world, eh?"

"You want gin?" asked an irritated Irfan. His attention was largely consumed by Daddy's Girls music video on the bar's big screen. "I thought you said prosecco."

"No, it's a line from Casablanca," I said to Irfan while looking at Hatton.

"Casablanca? Is that where you two are going?" he asked, checking his phone, no doubt for very critical updates.

"No, it's a film. And we're not together!" I said, looking away from Hatton because we had just looked at each other like we were very much together. Like we were just about to go on honeymoon somewhere exotic but not actually leave our hotel room for two weeks.

Hatton suppressed a snort, just.

"Alright," said Irfan, placing the filled glasses on the bar. "What does it mean, this gin in Casablanca thing?"

I looked back at Hatton. Again, poor Irfan was ignored as Hatton passed me a glass and looked a way that combined mental undressing with a penetrating x-ray quality. "It means, God, why did you have to walk back into my life?"

"Don't try and get a free drink by pretending we're mates. I ain't walking back into your life, bruv. I have never met either of you before. I haven't even been to Casablanca!" Irfan fumed.

"No, it's a bit of an inside joke from an old film called Casablanca," tried Hatton.

"How old we talking here, like the early '90s?" Irfan asked, crossing his arms.

"More like early 1940s," I said. Early 1990s was old now? Could Disneyland qualify as a UNESCO world heritage site?!

"Oh my days! Talk about gatekeeping the conversation! Update your references. Engage in dialogue with the youth. We're changing the world!"

Hatton had been trying to flirt with me, not Irfan, but he did have a point. "Sorry," we mumbled.

"Irfan, stop harassing the customers with your bloody woke nonsense! Stick to the script!" boomed a voice from the backroom.

Irfan sighed heavily. "Thank you for choosing our bar this evening. Please leave a review on TripAdvisor and," he cleared his throat, "mention me, Irfan, your Customer Service Champion. How may I have the pleasure of taking your payment this evening?

"Oh, card please," coughed Hatton, looking for his wallet.

"Erm. I will take these over to our table," I said, grabbing the extra glass for June and scurrying off.

June let out a scream that sounded like the last hiss of a deflating dinghy. "This is too funny," she managed to rasp.

"It's not funny at all," I said, pursing my lips to the prosecco.

"Does this mean that you two are going to…"

"No!"

"Ah, another one of my schemes comes to fruition. The collapse of capitalism must be next," June said, a satisfied smile spreading across her face.

"I feel like I came in at the wrong point in the conversation," said Hatton, appearing at the edge of the table.

"Oh no, it was just getting started! Join us!" declared June with sadistic enthusiasm.

"I hope that's OK? I mean, I can take this back to my room and leave you both to it," he said to me, ignoring June's glee.

"No, it's OK," I said back, quietly, not because I was embarrassed but because it didn't feel like we were in a crowded bar for a second.

Hatton hopped onto the tall stool with a disgusting amount of ease. That put me off him. Everyone else had to climb up one butt cheek at a time, who was he to show off a secret talent? He probably practised at home to look good, I told myself, just to extinguish any amorphous feelings that might have been creeping back in.

"Er Hatton, this is June. I've told you about her, she's my best friend. She is a masseuse and so left wing she makes Jeremy Corbyn look like a Tory peer." June weighed up the description for a moment, before nodding in satisfaction. "June, this is Hatton Finch," I said, praying she would not make this any more awkward

Apparently there was no God, because June looked skywards, as if searching her brain for who he might be. "Hatton Finch...Hatton Finch... where do I know that name from?" she said, drumming her fingers on the table.

Hatton's eyes slid across to me, confused. I shrugged with a slightly manic smile.

"Hatton Finch...Hatton Finch....oh yes! I think Sam has mentioned you!" said June triumphantly.

Hatton's face crinkled in relief and I laughed with relief. And gave June a playful but sharp slap on the shoulder.

"Are you the guy who fixed her radiator? Mine is on the blink too, could you come round and have a look at it?" June said innocently.

"June!!!" I said, delivering another swift slap to the shoulder.

It just made her burst out laughing, though. "Ah, I am only busting your balls. Of course I know who you are. An ex dragged me to see that army film where your best friend was a sniffer dog or something. Plus Sam talks about you all the time." I shot her a look that was harder than any slap.

"I mean, Sam talks about you only in moderation."

I groaned.

"Well, I am appropriately pleased to hear that I am talked about in moderation. Whatever that is," said Hatton. He flicked a look in my direction, reassuring but also a bit hot. Then June crept into view between us.

"So, June, the collapse of capitalism, how's that going?" asked Hatton as if he was checking the football score.

"Very well, if this new Baby Botch thing is anything to go by," June informed him.

"Oh really? I'm just worried about my daughter, I never considered it could be ushering in a revolution," said Hatton.

"If you can't consider it, then you can't be part of it," said June, but she was the one left out. Hatton and I had drifted towards looking at each other again. Taking her cue, she said, "I think I am going to enjoy my processo alone in our room. It was nice to meet you, Hatton. See you tonight, Sam."

Then a message popped up on my phone.

June: Or not!

I swiped the message off my screen as June gave one last wicked smile from the exit. The bland pop music in the bar was replaced by throb of my blood pressure rising. My brain was spinning down a helter skelter of blind panic when Hatton finally spoke. "So, how are you?"

"I'M ABSOLUTELY FINE," I shrieked as only someone having an all-encompassing crisis can. Now my entire head was throbbing in an alarming way, but I realised that it couldn't be much more embarrassing if I indeed had a stroke in front of him, which was weirdly comforting. "HOW ARE YOU?" I shouted above the banging in my head.

"Yeah, I'm fine too," Hatton said, a distracted look of concern in his eyes. "Look, I didn't want to make you feel awkward coming over. I should just go back to my room. It has a PowerPress 3000 toaster, after all," Hatton said, sliding off the chair.

"A PowerPress 3000 you say?" I said, tumbling off my own chair like an avalanche gathering speed. "I have always wanted to see one of them in person!"

Reader: I have never wanted to see one of them in person.

"Oh really? Well, you could come up...and...er...see it now?"

"I would be totally up for that!" I said far too enthusiastically and transparently. Regaining some composure, I added, "I mean, one must keep up-to-date on the current toaster trends. Plus, we don't have one in our pleb room."

"Well, time is of the essence! I can't stand the thought of you wasting another moment of your life without experiencing what that toaster can do!" said Hatton, leading the way out of the bar.

His room was in the opposite direction from ours. Both were on the ground floor, but ours only had an unimpressive vista of the bins, while his, I discovered, had its own private door through the 'reflection garden' no one ever used because they were getting a 6am flight and really didn't want to reflect too much on that.

However, I couldn't help reflecting on the whole situation as Hatton appeared to go through every pocket possible in search of his key card. I waited by what a cheap plastic sign told me was the 'Pondering Pond', watching a crisp packet sail across its surface. Was I *really* going to do this? On a scale of 1 to Brexit, how bad an idea was having a one night stand with Hatton? Would it get whatever this was out of my system, or would I spend the rest of the summer obsessing even more? What if I had got the wrong end of the stick and he really just liked toasters?

"Here it is!" he said, triumphantly pulling the card out from a zip pocket on his joggers.

"Oh, yay," I said, still distracted by the intrepid crisp packet.

Hatton pushed open the door and I followed, although my mind was now definitely somewhere else; it had taken a sharp left turn on Anxiety Avenue, straight onto Spiral Street and was now on the Highway to Hyperventilation. However, the swankiness of the room managed to penetrate even that; a four poster bed, a lounge area bigger than my living room at home with Chesterfield furniture, a widescreen TV and there was nothing mini about the bar, which was a well-stocked free-standing drinks cabinet. Then there was the breakfast bar, filled with gadgets, including the fabled PowerPress 3000 toaster. It looked more like a small armoured vehicle than a toaster, to be honest. I could more easily imagine Lily and Brutus riding it through a warzone than it producing a breakfast snack.

"Ah, I see you're admiring the fine piece of machinery," said Hatton, walking up beside me as I realised I had gravitated towards the toaster.

"It looks like it is about to do a tour of Iraq. Do I need to thank it for its service?" I said, bending down to look at its reinforced steel veneer, which threw my warped reflection back at myself.

"It's quite something, isn't it?" he said, bending down so the toaster threw both our reflections back like fun-house mirrors; my eyes were two different sizes and my nose was sliding to the left, whereas his nose took up most of his face, his eyes exploding outwards like a hammerhead shark. Well, that was enough to shrivel the libido of the most ardent lover, so I shot back up away from the horror show, but Hatton seemed undeterred, twiddling a couple of the knobs on the machine.

"You can pop some bread in and put it on a timer so it has the toast ready for you in the morning. And you can manage it from an app on your phone!"

Had I stumbled into a QVC ad for this bloody toaster? Maybe he was just obsessed with it and he had forgotten all about our conversation. I leaned against the 'mini' bar as he continued his sales pitch, my eyes frosting over.

"It has eight different settings and you can even make grilled cheese in it! With every purchase, they apparently donate a toastie to a needy child in Malawi. How philanthropic!" he said, my nether regions more closely resembling the Kalahari desert with every word.

"Yeah. That's really something," I said, trying to muster enthusiasm.

"I'm all out," he said, turning away from the toaster with a tired look on his face.

"Eh?"

"That's all I know about the toaster. I googled it on the way up here. I got worried that you were actually interested in the toaster after all and I didn't want to come off as a total pervert, so I looked up its Wikipedia page."

I started to laugh. I tried to stop, but that just made it worse, like when a teacher would tell you to stop laughing at whatever banal teenage thing you were peeing your pants over and it would only spur you on.

"I'm sorry," I spluttered, hysterical tears beginning to prick my eyes.

"It's not *that* funny," he said, grabbing me round the middle as if we were playing cops and robbers.

"It's just," I wheezed, grabbing onto his shoulders to steady myself. "I was worried *you* were a secret toaster obsessive and I was just a filthy-minded pervert."

I looked down at the accidental hug we had found ourselves in. Thoughts that would get me jailed in Saudi Arabia streaked through my head. Maybe I *was* a filthy-minded pervert, even if he wasn't a toaster obsessive.

"If I hear another word about that toaster again, it will be too soon," he said, pulling me closer.

"I'm ok with that. In fact, I don't think we should say another word to each other the entire evening," I said, closing the last shred of daylight between us.

"I will just pretend you're not here then," said Hatton, looking past me as if he had just been struck by blindness. "Looks like it's just me and the toaster tonight!"

I steadied his chin and kissed him hard, a sort of Glasgow Kiss without the blood and broken bones. It was a result of wanting to shut him up but also not being able to hold it back any longer.

"Could the toaster do that?" I asked as he looked at me, as dazed as if I had, as they say in the Dear Green Place, nutted him in the heid.

"Well, I wouldn't put it past it..." he said with a smile I was determined to wipe off his face with another 'Glasgow Kiss'.

CHAPTER

14

A few hours later, I awoke with a start to the smell of burning and the sound of George Michael's Careless Whisper.

Perhaps this was the welcome you got at the Gates of Hell, I thought, groping around in the dark. Sign me up, sounds like great fun, I thought, until I caught the PowerPress 3000 in the middle of some sort of elaborate light display.

I had been existing in those few fleeting moments when you first wake up after something big happens before your memory boots up. The toaster, which had produced two slices of toast while blasting George Michael music, brought me back to reality, even though it was a work of perverse science fiction. I mean, who thinks, I know what the world needs, a toaster that is also an alarm which also plays banging '80s tunes?

Yes, I had slept with Hatton, but I couldn't deal with that right now. The clock on the PowerPress3000 told me that the time was 5.45AM. My flight was at 6.30. June would never let me hear the end of it if I missed the plane. Then she would tell Paxton, and he would probably do something like tell everyone else on the retreat my name was Sam Finch and I was just married and to please ask me about it because it was my favourite topic of conversation.

In a panic, I leapt off the sofa and felt around on the ground for my underwear. I suppose I should have at least been grateful that I was wearing one of the super fluffy bathrobes we had found in the wardrobe the night before, because now my arse was in the air as I tried to fish my bra out from underneath the coffee table.

Hatton was propping himself up on an armrest and jabbing violently at a remote control. "That's enough of that, George," he said, just as the saxophone began to swell in the song before promptly being cut off by a click of a button. His eyes were still superglued shut like one of those baby animals that doesn't open them for like a week after being born.

"Just come back to bed, or the sofa, or whatever I am lying on," he murmured, rolling over.

"I can't!" I hissed, pulling up my yoga pants. I could not verify their appropriateness for yoga, but I could tell you they accommodated aeroplane bloat and the subsequent farting episodes most tolerably.

"Yes, you can. You can do whatever you want to do. You're a strong, independent woman," he mumbled into a cushion, pulling his dressing gown tight around him.

"I'm a strong independent woman with a fucking flight to catch in 25 minutes!" I cursed, struggling to jab my arm through a hoodie sleeve. It was only as I caught a whiff of Hatton-smell (a combination of some sort of fancy herb that they put in gin and the sea, in case you were wondering) that I realised it was his and not mine, but I was too far gone for that, there was no time to change.

"Oh God," said Hatton, scrambling to his feet. "You can still make it, you are a strong, independent woman, after all," he said, feebly picking through the remnants of last night; room service plates and two bottles of wine on the coffee table, the duvet pulled over to the sofa, and, oh yes, the towels, because we had decided showering together was something business associates did all the time after said bottles of wine.

I was already heading for the door now that I was vaguely appropriately dressed for society, but also partly because I didn't want a more intimate goodbye. I knew it wouldn't really be a goodbye, I would probably miss the flight if I was any closer to him than halfway out the door, which is where I was when I turned and said:

"See you in Copenhagen in September, champ!"

I slammed the door just as he was standing in the hallway in his robe holding my bra, which I had completely forgotten about up until this point. Out of view, I managed to simultaneously run and cringe my way down the hallway, unable to overcome that I had actually used the word 'champ', as if I was his baseball coach in a '90s family film. What had happened the night before was *definitely* not for family viewing.

Luckily we had checked in our bags the night before, so all I had to do was grab my bag from our room, throw my card key at the checkout desk and sprint as fast as I could towards the security area without arousing suspicion and being shot by an overzealous border guard. I did all this, catching times on clocks that seemed to slip out of my grasp like those drooping ones in Dali paintings.

It was 6.26AM when I reached the CheepCheep gate, which was, of course, located so far from the main terminal area that you could probably charter a flight to get there. 'FINAL BOARDING' flashed above me as I jibbered incoherently about not wanting to be called Mrs Finch and thrust my passport and e-ticket at a very perturbed looking check-out assistant.

I boarded the plane, greeted with a sly smile from a CheepCheep Airways air hostess, who was clearly trying not to laugh at me. I must have looked a right state, just out of bed in a hoodie that clearly wasn't mine, plus sweating as if someone had just asked me how well I knew Hatton Finch.

It does really make you reconsider a lot of your life choices when you are doing the walk of shame down a budget airline flight aisle and gradually realising how rough you look from the scandalised glances of the cabin crew and passengers.

I saw June out of the corner of my eye as I stuffed my bag in the overhead compartment, looking refreshed after a good night's sleep, but also struggling to contain her obvious glee at my hot mess. I slumped in the seat next to her and pulled the hoodie over my head, getting another whiff of Hatton and cringing even more.

Soon the safety presentation that no one listens to began.

"Nice sex hair," whispered June surreptitiously, like she was whispering at the back of the class.

"How do you know? I have the hood up!" I replied.

She whipped back my hood. "I saw that absolute bird's nest on your way down the aisle. Damn, Sam, your hair makes you look like an Amy Winehouse voodoo doll made out of pubes."

I pulled the hood back up sharply. "My hairbrush is in the hold luggage. I did not expect last night...to happen," I told her, while the elderly woman in our row looked at my hair with great alarm whilst crossing herself.

"Well, what happened then?" asked June, much more tenderly and quietly than I expected.

I decided to answer, just to distract from the lingering thought of imminent death in this tin can of an aeroplane. "Well, we went back to his and there was this toaster, and it was kind of funny, we both thought the other one was super-interested in the toaster-"

"Ugh, can we skip to the sex bit, please? This is like when they have an unnecessarily elaborate set-up on PornHub. Boring!" said June, ignoring the increasing horror radiating from an elderly woman behind us, whose judgemental little eyes poked between our seats.

"Sorry," I said meekly to the woman, who looked at me like I was the whore of Babylon in return.

"Gory details, please," said June

"Fine."

"No, it was kind of sweet. He," I said, trying not to smile so much, "he said the last time he had sex with someone new was 25 years ago, so he wanted to apologise in advance."

"Lol, at least you have something in common, I suppose," June giggled.

"Hey, you know I almost-sort-of did it with that journalist in Berlin last year," I said, crossing my arms.

"Sam," June said, giving me a pitying yet reassuring stroke of the arm. "That's the novelist version of 'I shagged a girl on holiday but you don't know her because she goes to school in Canada."

"That's neither here nor there," I said, growing red because I had been so sure I had gotten away with that one.

In front of us, an air hostess was beginning the pre-flight safety demonstration that no one ever listens to. She held up a seatbelt above the uninflated life vest around her shoulders, a name badge reading 'Pauline' poking out of it. She sniffed and began to mime along with the pre-recorded spiel.

"Tell me more, tell me more!" sang June like a proper Pink Lady, clearly willing to take her chances in the event of an aviation emergency.

Pauline glared at her and pulled the belt extra tight, as if in warning.

"Well..." I said, lowering my voice, but clearly not low enough for the stewardess, who indicated the nearest exits with a force that suggested she wanted to push me out one of them. June was still egging me on, poking my side. Our strict schoolmarm Pauline did not look too enthralled by this either but tolerated it. I realised I was just going to have to mime the evening with Hatton for June, but the props were limited. I looked around me, all there was was an in-flight magazine, June's water bottle and a sick bag. Not the most suggestive selection of items, but it would have to do. I would just have to trust that June and I had been friends long enough that she could extrapolate my meaning from some crude miming. There was a good chance she would too - we always killed it at charades because of all our in-jokes.

As Pauline blew into the little pipe attached to the vest, I held my finger up to signal 'wait' and flicked through the magazine in hope of finding another prop. I was lucky - a sachet of cocoa butter hand cream that I would never be able to afford fell out of page 56. Ok, maybe I can do something with these, I thought. June, still paying absolutely no attention to the safety demonstration, elbowed me to get on with it. I rolled up the magazine and gave June a wink. She gave me a thumb's up. I nodded and grabbed the sick bag, with the sad realisation that this was going to have be my vagina in the mime. Hatton seemed to be getting all the glory with a thick magazine willy and here I was with a flappy bag for vomiting acting as my vagina. June raised an eyebrow, but I realised I had missed out a vital detail, so put down the sick bag and slathered the magazine in the hand cream. June, a strong advocate for female pleasure, gave me a silent round of applause and I returned the thumb's up. I turned to see the old lady still peeking through from the row behind us, but this time she gave me an approving wink.

The only downside to the glossy-magazine-as-substitute-penis prop was that it was now too slippy to handle properly and had taken on a life of its own. I managed to wrangle it into the grip of one hand, which June took to be a depiction of events the night before, and she wasn't entirely wrong. I squeezed it tighter in preparation for shoving it into the sick bag, but this just made it pop out of my grasp completely. June and I followed it as it made its ascent above our seats, arcing into a firework-like spatter as it caught the harsh cabin lighting. I made a grab for it but it was too far away now; I could only watch as it began its descent towards Pauline.

Then everything slowed down as the full horror revealed itself. The magazine unfurled in the air, droplets of hand cream rolling towards the flight attendant. Unaware, she pulled on the air mask like it was a weapon in a slow-mo fight scene. Now the pages of the soggy magazine were close enough to fan her face, if they had not been gummed up with hand cream. Her nose twitched, perhaps at the scent of cocoa butter. It was still quivering when the magazine made impact and everything speeded up again. It smacked her face with a noise a cross between a spank and a squelch, leaving globs of cream from her formally neat bun to her starched collar. Pauline froze, airbag in hand, as the magazine skimmed the top of three rows of seats, sending the occupants ducking for cover, surrounding passengers emitting 'ews', 'yucks' and sniggers.

Pauline stood dripping hand cream for a few moments, while the crowd began to murmur and turn towards June and I. We shrunk back into our seats and Pauline's eyes flicked over to us.

"Sorry," I squeaked. June appeared to be choking to death on a laugh.

"I am this close to having you removed from this flight," she informed us, illustrating her point with a tiny gap between two (now well-moisturised) fingers.

"I really am sorry! I promise nothing like that will happen again!" I said, patting myself down in search of a tissue to offer her. I could swear the woman behind us was now tittering.

"Now sit back, relax and enjoy the flight," chirped the voiceover, just as Pauline's eyes filled with vengeful rage.

Just then, an air steward appeared at Pauline's side, gripping her arms to her sides. "Don't do it, Pauline, they're not worth it. Remember what the boss said - we can't have another social media scandal with people being thrown off the plane!"

Pauline nodded reluctantly, no doubt remembering the story in the press last week. The cabin crew ended up in a (livestreamed) running battle with a stag do on a flight to Malaga, the entire flight being arrested by Spanish police on arrival. She was led back down the aisle like a broken trolley by her colleague, but at least she had dewy skin thanks to the hand cream.

"ANYWAY," said June. "You sure it was a one-time thing with Hatton?"

"Wha?" I was still distracted by Pauline's venomous stare. I shook my head. "Yes!" I said as forcefully as I could while every fibre of my physical being tried to stop me. Meanwhile, my mind grasped for #reasons. "He is far too old for me for starters, he's 39!"

"Sam, I'm 39. I'm not exactly ancient and I am your best friend. Plus, you're almost 30," said June.

"Why is everyone so obsessed with me turning 30?" I huffed. "What happens? Do I turn into a pumpkin at the stroke of midnight?"

"I'm sorry, you're right," said June as the plane rumbled along the runway. "I mean, I hate to quote from noted child predator R. Kelly, but age ain't nothing but a number. Just, y'know, as long as everyone is of legal age and able to consent, contrary to what that human cesspit would have you believe."

I leaned my head against the window as the plane tiptoed off the ground. I had wanted to nap on the flight, but how was I meant to do that with nightmarish visions of R. Kelly?

CHAPTER

15

We arrived at Belkita Airport that afternoon. It was probably the biggest structure in the country; from the sky, its landing strip cut through the centre of the island like a geoglyph with a Brazilian. Well, it was a holiday island, after all.

Getting off the plane, we were greeted by a series of loud bangs and smoke coming from the terminal.

"What was that? Are we under attack?!" I said, gripping June's arm on the hot tarmac.

"Ha! I don't think so," June said, tapping her beach read, A Durkheimian Ethnography of Belkita. "It says here that fireworks are a key part of Belkitan culture, as well as a disregard for health and safety. Each flight gets an...er...explosive welcome."

"But it's the middle of the day, you can't even see the fireworks in the sky!"

"Ugh, white people," muttered June. "Who are you to judge their use of fireworks? We have been through this before, you people use them to celebrate murdering the last person to enter Parliament with honest intentions."

I laughed nervously, not because June had called out my whiteness, but because I was reminded of Dean. His biggest role before being my 'date' to the reunion in Bae for Pay was starring as a boy whose face had melted in a firework accident for a government information film. I wished I had the sort of brain that took snaps of memorable moments on holiday instead of deciding to fire up a slideshow of your most embarrassing moments.

I was distracted though by a sudden fanfare of drums and singing coming from the main building, cutting through even the airplane engine noise. Seconds later, a welcome committee of scantily clad dancers burst through the last rags of smoke from the fireworks, their instruments and well-placed local foliage the only things containing their modesty. There was a lot of them to contain, too. None of them looked like the lithe Belkita boy on the speedboat in the brochure. Instead, thighs jiggled in time to the music and stomachs rested over the top of drums.

We walked down a red carpet, the drummers and singers on either side, and a sun-bleached 'Welcome to Belkita' banner lazily flapping in the wind above us.

Inside, it was just like any Passport Control area across the world. As an EU country, and in the last few months before Brexit, we were unsurprised when all the UK passports were mysteriously rejected by the automatic machines and we all had to file into a lengthy queue overseen by a much less welcoming committee of Border Patrol guards. As we lined up, I saw them handle passports with plastic gloves and spray them with disinfectant.

We were now international pariahs, between Brexit and the Baby Botch outbreak in the UK all over the news. In the queue, my mind drifted off; would I even be allowed back into Copenhagen in a few months? Where was Hatton? Would he get back in?

I scolded myself as I handed over my passport for examination by an officer who picked it up as if I had given her a used hankie, doused it in disinfectant, then slid it back with equal disgust.

The lack of luggage meant we got to skip baggage collection and head straight to the arrivals area. A full-faced lad was holding a sign saying 'SAM CHAMBERS + JUNE' and I was reminded that I myself still didn't know what her surname was. Sure, I had seen flashes of letters on her passport or driving licence when she got ID'd in bars, but she would quickly tuck the document away, declaring she only really had the one name, "like Cher, Madonna or Stalin." I could imagine her in an outrageous outfit with a toyboy on her arm while she ran Russia, so it was hard to argue with that logic.

Our driver was JoJo, according to his nametag drooping sadly from his polo shirt, which clung to his soft chest as if it might just melt off his body in the heat at any second. He eagerly took our bags from us and wrapped us in a hug that felt like being locked in a steam room.

"Benciula e Belkita! Welcome to Belkita, my friends! Follow me to the minivan," he said, striding off as we dabbed his perspiration off ourselves.

The carpark looked like something that would be attached to a small dusty diner on Route 66 compared to the sprawling car cities attached to airports back home.

JoJo was unlocking his minivan, which looked as if it had seen some armed conflict, shrapnel-sized holes covering the exterior, as well as burn marks.

"What happened to your van?!" I asked.

"Oh, firework accident at my 18th last year," he laughed nostalgically, throwing our bags in the back. He then bundled us in the back too, which would have set off serial killer alarm bells if he hadn't been so jovial.

We landed on a couple of seats with stuffing protruding out the sides. Ripped fabric from the ceiling dangled overhead. Maybe this *was* his murder van and he was going to kill us, just very cheerfully.

"What about this?" I said, swatting the material out the way.

"You ladies are responsible for that!"

"I beg to differ," I said. If I must be butchered in the back of a van, I would not be victim-shamed too.

"Your pets! I took them to the fort yesterday. The little one, what's he called, something Roman..."

"Brutus?"

"Yes! That's the name!" said JoJo, starting the sputtering engine. "He got loose and went a little crazy."

I sighed. "I'm sorry about your van, JoJo."

"Oh, it's OK. It is the lady that I felt sorry for."

"The lady?"

"Yes, I was taking other teachers up to the fort yesterday. Young Brutus was very taken with the lady and began chasing her around the van. Unfortunately we were driving through a village party, many fireworks were going off. I couldn't stop the van until about 10 minutes later. Then

I looked round and *that* had happened. The poor lady was fending him off with a headrest!"

I probably should have been more mortified, but one time Brutus had got loose at the Beath Community Nativity and humped the plastic Baby Jesus, so this was small fry.

"What do you mean 'other teachers'?" asked June, looking up from her phone.

"Oh! Er, did I say 'teachers'. Ah, in Belkitan, our word for 'teacher' is very close to our word for 'tourist'. Excuse my mistake," said JoJo, glancing back and forth in the rearview mirror.

"These words don't look very similar," said June, who had clearly been googling.

"Look! Another firework display!" shouted JoJo, pointing at the clear sky. Maybe it was evasion. Maybe it was someone's 18th birthday party.

June was now scrolling through the Belkita Tourism Authority website. She stopped at a picture of the ripped speedboat driver. "Any idea where we can meet this fine specimen?" she asked, thrusting the phone towards the driver's seat.

"Oh, that's Tony. He lives in England now."

We both muttered our disappointment.

"Yes, that is how all the women and many men react. Tony is not typical of the Belkitan man, I am afraid," JoJo chuckled over some '80s tunes now blaring out of the radio.

"How so?"

"Belkita has an obesity rate of 30%," revealed June, showing me a listicle on her phone. Wow, that woman could Google.

"Wow, that's...almost as bad as Scotland, am I right?" I said. June googled for confirmation.

"Yes," confirmed JoJo. "We are chunky fellows. As we say in Belkita though, 'We cushion your landing when you fall in love with us." He gave a Beyonce-style jiggle which was quite seductive in its way and I didn't think it was such a bad thing Tony lived in England now.

The Beyonce moves gave us much to consider for the rest of the drive, as did the spiralling dusty road JoJo was driving up. With each corner we rounded, we got a better view of the jigsaw of pastoral green and desert sand that made up the island, as well as views of the brilliant blue nothingness of the sea swallowing up the horizon. The converted fort, where we would be staying, steadily grew from a dot to a full-fledged sandstone complex, too.

"Wow, this looks like somewhere from one of the video games that glorifies the Crusades," I said, peering out at its turrets, which in turn peered imperiously out to sea, presumably so they could smite anyone who didn't believe in Jesus at several nautical miles.

"It is!" confirmed JoJo.

"Really?"

"Yes, the citadel in Christ's Secret Service was based on this very complex! What a game! The way their heads explode!" marvelled JoJo. "Now, if you look over here, you will see the town square where St Paul harpoons a Barbary pirate in Level 3..."

And so passed the rest of the journey, an anachronistic tour of what didn't happen in world history.

CHAPTER

16

"My gorgeous guests of honour!" called Paxton from a turret like a randy Rapunzel.

We waved up at him as JoJo took our bags through the fort's gate.

Paxton disappeared from his fairytale tower and materialised at the top of a set of stairs on the other side of the gate. He bounded down towards us and something about the way he scrabbled downstairs reminded me of Brutus.

"Where are the pets? Did they make it OK?" I asked as he ran towards us with open arms.

"Sam Chambers, I have missed you too, you magnificent creature," said Paxton, herding us into a three-way bear hug. "And they are fine."

He released us from his grip and bellowed "RELEASE THE HOUNDS!" before chuckling to himself. "Ah, I have always wanted to say that."

Paxton turned with a flourish, like a circus ringmaster welcoming his lion to the stage. Leni and Brutus appeared at the top of the stairs and howled at the sight of their mothers. It was a strange chorus, Leni's howl a sonorous Barry White to Brutus' Prince on helium. June and I shrieked in unison, barging passed Paxton, only to be knocked over by our furry sons. Brutus covered me in slightly oedipal kisses and took great interest in attempting to hump my arm, while Leni pinned June to the floor, lying across her like a 60kg weighted blanket that meant she could never leave again.

"Where's Lily?" I asked, shaking Brutus off my arm.

"Well, Sam, I am very well, thank you for asking, your concern for an old friend who flew you out here on his own dime is touching," Paxton said, clutching his hands to his heart.

"Yes, Paxton, thank you very much for the trip. And I am so glad to see the syphilis isn't tertiary yet. Or is it? It's always hard to tell with you," I said, pinching his cheek affectionately.

"Hey! They have never been able to conclusively prove that that is the cause of the family madness!" laughed Paxton. We laughed too, but you were never 100% whether that sort of thing was a joke or reality for him. "And Lily is upstairs. She likes to sun herself in the bar and judge people in the people in the swimming pool."

"Aw, just like her mother," June said, wiping away a fake tear.

"Sounds great, shall we join her?" I said, already imagining an ice cold glass of white wine.

"Oh! Er, JoJo will show you to your rooms first," said Paxton. "Drinks are at 7pm. We have a lot to catch up about, so make sure you are there on time."

"OK…" I said, feeling uneasy. Paxton had never been bothered about time; his three year 'Gap Year' after university was proof of that.

I looked him up and down for a sign of what he was planning, like a tell in a game of poker, but he remained unflappable. Then I remembered that he was almost professionally gambling away the family fortune at this point and had probably learnt a thing or two in the casinos.

"Paxton, sir, my uncle made that sign for the entrance. It's in the back of the van, where should I leave it?" said JoJo.

"Oh, just leave it in the van. I will get someone to put it up later" Paxton said, ushering JoJo away. "Why don't you go and help yourself to a refreshing lemonade?"

"What sign?" I asked, trailing behind.

"Come on! I want to see these rooms!" said June, dragging me off. I kept looking at Paxton though, who continued to smile sweetly. I didn't know what he was planning, but I didn't like it.

"Look at this!" said June, as if she had just been presented with Young Stalin covered in whipped cream.

I mouthed 'I'm watching you' at Paxton and turned to see what she was salivating over. In front of us was a courtyard with a giant water feature in the centre; a mermaid and a merman atop a tower of shells, pouring bottles of 'wine' into the water below.

I squinted at it. "The merman looks awfully like..."

"Tony, yes. He posed for it last summer," confirmed JoJo.

"Tony's a busy boy. Who's the girl?"

"His sister."

June and I both made icky faces at each other, the same ones we made when we tried to binge watch Game of Thrones that time.

"It's not their fault that they have good genes!" said JoJo, walking down the hall. "They cannot help being the two top models in the country."

"In the country? Tony doesn't even live here now," I said, scurrying after him.

"No, neither does his sister. She moved to Eindhoven about six months ago."

JoJo threw our bags in an antique elevator. "It's 90 years old!" he told us, and it looked every year. It was a nonogenarian with brittle bone disease; the metal lattice door opening with brutal cracks, our bags eliciting groans from the floor. "In you go!" he said, pushing us, despite more objections from the lift. "Nobody has died in there! It's all terrible rumour," he said, waving us as the doors juddered. Then it became awkward and he had to pull the doors shut whilst I wondered if I should have written a will.

What would I leave and to whom? I wondered as the lift creaked upwards unevenly. June? But she would likely die with me. Oh God, who would take care of the pets? Paxton couldn't take care of a broken nail, let alone a pet. I spoke from experience, a ragged cuticle had somehow escalated to him having to get the tip of his ring finger removed in Fourth Year. My parents? I wasn't sure if Brutus the snow dog would adapt to warmer climes long term. I grabbed a wobbly railing and felt my heart sink.

Then the doors opened on our floor and my entire death fantasy was moot. Oh well. I made a mental note to compose a will when I wasn't so tired from travelling.

"So, this email here says it's all contactless because of this Baby Botch stuff. You're in Room 12, I am in Room 11. Just download this app," June said, flipping her phone so I could see. "And touch your phone to the keypad on the door."

I began to download the app. "Why are they so bothered about the Baby Botch? It's a retreat. The average age is probably 55, and that's with us bringing it down by a few years."

"Well, we're all young at heart, aren't we? No one wants to be reminded of how old they are. You of all people should know that! Have you forgotten that you are lurching towards 30? Or has the dementia set in?" June said, tapping her phone to her door.

"Remind me, how old are *you*, again?" I said, pressing my own phone to my pad.

"I am timeless," winked June, gliding into her room.

I shook my head and pushed open my door too.

There is nothing quite like when you first arrive in a hotel room. The excitement as your new home from home is revealed, the seal to your cosy bubble as the door clicks behind you. This was no exception, the tiled floor cooling me as I kicked off my sandals, as well as the breeze fluttering through the gauze curtains from the balcony.

A four-poster bed with more billowy curtains danced in front of my eyes. I wondered how long it had been since I slept as its gravitational pull sucked me into its crisp cotton sheets. I knew I should probably shower - I wasn't sure how long it had been since I had one of them. I glanced at my phone as my head hit the pillow - two hours until I had to meet Paxton at the bar. Plenty of time to sleep *and* shower, I decided as my phone screen smudged into a blur between my heavy eyelids.

CHAPTER

17

Two hours later, there was a knock on my door and drool on my pillow.

Sleep-deprived Sam was such an optimist. I could barely get out of bed and to the office on time(ish) without snoozing six or seven alarms. Why did she think I would be able to self-regulate a nap and perform basic hygiene?

Another knock came, followed by barking. I wondered if I had somehow managed to offend the Belkitan government during my short stay and was about to be 'disappeared'. At least I would be tortured and disposed of in a picturesque spot, I thought as I staggered to the door.

I pulled it open a little, a sunbeam spearing my face.

"Come on!" said June as Brutus and Lily scampered into my room. "Urgh, you look like a mole person and smell like a pair of pants after a spin class."

I nodded in agreement. What else could I do? I caught sight of my look in the hallway mirror and a whiff as I turned. She was completely right.

"I need to shower," I mumbled, picking my way through the pets at my feet back towards the bathroom.

"There's no time!" said June, grabbing my arm. Finally, I registered that she was freshly showered, spritzed and in a floaty tie-dye dress she had picked up in a kibbutz a couple of summers' ago. "It's already 7.10. Plus, it's only Paxton, he won't care what you look like. What's his motto, 'any hole's a goal'?"

I groaned and gripped my head. "I need to wash my hair!" I pleaded, one hand stuck in a massive tug. June ignored my protestations and pulled me out into the corridor, leaving the pets to their business, which was Brutus reclining on the bed, languidly trying to seduce Lily, who was much more into climbing the four-poster and shredding the curtains.

"You *do* need to wash your hair," confirmed June, holding a clump out for inspection. "This is the worst case of untreated sex hair that I have ever seen. You might need a medical shampoo. But not now. Let's go to the bar."

I shuffled behind June, an overdressed sex yeti to June's wispy summer angel. In the decrepit elevator, I rolled up my sweatshirt sleeves in a desperate attempt to escape the heat. "The bar better have air conditioning," I muttered.

On the ground floor, we followed gold signs for the bar like they were the road to El Dorado. A cool glass of wine for my parched lips and a bucket of water for my sweaty, dishevelled head was what I needed. A drift of mariachi music and cool air guided us around the last corner, where we were met with a huge sign: Tito's Tavern.

Just in case we were in any doubt about the Mexican theme, the 'T's were shaped like cacti and topped with sombreros. A couple of waiters shuffled about, presumably because their own sombreros came down so far over their faces. One passed us with a tray of limp, microwaved nachos, passing a 'Specials' board that simply read 'TEQUILA'.

One of the waiters spotted us and shambled over. "Welcome to Tito's Tavern, ladies. A slice of Mexico in the Mediterranean. I am Lorando," he said, tipping his sombrero to us, revealing slicked back black hair and an imperious look that was a cross between English butler and Mafia enforcer.

We both kind-of curtseyed, unsure how to respond to his formality amongst the knock-off Mexicana surrounding us.

"We are meeting Paxton, the owner?" I said, tugging awkwardly at my sweatshirt, which I was suddenly aware smelt of a flight's worth of airplane farts.

"Ah yes," said Lorando, checking the reservations book. He leafed carefully through the book, as if about to begin a sermon, but the reverence was ruined by the 'I LOVE CANCUN' sticker on the front cover. "Mr Paxton is on the verandah, please follow me."

Lorando replaced his sombrero and strode through the restaurant, mustering as much dignity as he could. We followed behind, trying to absorb the assault on the senses that was Tito's Tavern. A donkey piñata snagged on my hair and I had to fight it off, which only led to my hair looking more of a disaster, the colourful tissue paper a garnish on the hot mess. Meanwhile, June was regarding a large mural of Salma Hayek frolicking in a cocktail glass with a healthy dose of skepticism.

"Interesting decor," she told Lorando, jerking her thumb at it.

"Yes," Lorando said, his jaw muscles clenching. "Our previous owner was quite the fan of Mexico."

I spied novelty fluorescent yellow tshirts displayed above the bar. Normally I wouldn't have been caught dead in one, but I was worried that I was starting to smell like death. "Can I take one of these?" I asked a sombrero-ed youth behind the bar. He nodded with a defeated air, as if mourning the death of fashion. Using a stick, he fished one from above and handed it to me.

"How much is it?"

"It's all on Mr. Paxton," he said, studiously polishing a glass, as if he couldn't quite bring himself to look me in the eye. Did I really look *that* bad?!

June and Lorando were now almost out on the balcony. I could make out the back of Paxton's head at a table.

"Turn around," I instructed the bored barman. He sighed heavily and turned towards a wall of tequila bottles. I decided to quickly change my top as I walked out; Lorando was now out of sight, and June and Paxton had seen me in worse states of undress over the years.

"Sam! Get out here! NOW!" shouted June.

"I'm coming!" I called back, freeing myself from my fleecy prison. A welcome waft of air con hugged my stomach, but my head was caught on the 45% OFF!! Tag on the neck of the top.

"Sam! You NEED to see this!!!" June shouted again.

"I can't see anything!" I said, feeling my way through the door to the balcony.

"Uhoh! Let me help you!" said June as the warm evening sun hit my bare skin.

"What is it?" I huffed as June tugged the top down.

There was a yellow flash as the material and I was finally free. I blinked as the sun hit my eyes, trying to make out a familiar shape seated at the table.

It wasn't Paxton, too tall for that.

I blinked again.

It was Hatton.

CHAPTER

18

"The look on your face, Sam!" said Paxton, throwing an arm around my shoulders, which were just about in the armholes now. "I can tell you are surprised. You also look a little like you are about to pass out, but that must be the jet lag." He hugged me closer. "Or maybe it's the smell. What is that? The bottom of a laundry basket?"

Throughout his little monologue, Hatton and I looked at like two actors beamed into the wrong play and expected to carry the scene. Hatton pushed his seat out and stood up, his mouth moving but nothing coming out.

June, sensing the situation, improvised. "So, Paxton, what is Hatton Finch doing here?"

"These two are so funny together that I had to bring them both out for the summer. It will be like having my own personal streaming service, all the time," said Paxton, ignorant of, or perhaps choosing to ignore, the palpable awkwardness. "It will be hilarious."

"You don't know the half of it," June said to herself, helping me into a chair.

"Wh...why....didn't you tell me?" I managed.

"Or me?" said Hatton, sitting back down too.

"I thought it would be a fun surprise when you found out. Actually, I am kind of surprised it didn't come up in conversation before now," said Paxton, lying out on a nearby sun lounger.

"I don't think they have been doing much talking of late," sniggered June, helping herself to a carafe of wine on the table.

"What was that?" said Paxton, who was distracted by Lorando delivering a rubbery plate of nachos to the party.

"She said we haven't done much talking, we have been so busy of late," I ad-libbed, a look of relief coming over Hatton's face. "I thought you said you were doing something educational with your daughter in Paris this summer?" I said to Hatton, but making eye contact with a floor tile off to his left.

"Er, well, no, I just said I was meeting her in Paris. I suppose we...didn't get into the specifics when we last saw each other," Hatton said with a gulp. "But we are doing something educational this summer, that's right."

"What is it?" I said as June poured me a glass of wine. I took a cooling sip.

"Well, this is it," Hatton said, gesturing to the building.

I almost spat my wine out. "Er, I don't think going on a jolly in the Mediterreanean can really be classed as educational, but ok. Whatever you need to say to pay less taxes. Rich people, amirite?" I laughed nervously, nudging June for back-up. However, she had decided to take a holiday from her own socialist ideals and laugh *at* me.

Paxton leapt up from his chair. "Sam! We need to have a chat..."

"What about? What's going on?" I said, beginning to wonder if I had really woken up or if I was just dreaming all this in the hotel bed upstairs.

"Hatton's right. He will be teaching here this summer," Paxton said enthusiastically, as if his exuberance could polyfilla over confusion and emotional betrayal.

"Yeah, my daughter is going to be attending the summer school too," explained Hatton.

"So what are we doing here? I thought this was a retreat?" I turned to Paxton.

"Yeah!" demanded June.

"Well, I may have been a little economical with the truth," said Paxton as he smoothed back his hair. "It would be a great honour if you two ladies would stay here for the summer and teach too." He tried to smile pleadingly, but it didn't work because people like Paxton always get what they want and they know it. "OK, I get it, I can't use my seductive charms on ya, but you gotta help me out of this bind, my parents made another massive donation to St Fillan's…"

"That is the most First World Problem I have ever heard. Actually, why is that even a problem?"

"Well, St Fillan's were pleased, overjoyed in fact. The money meant they could finally start a university campus somewhere sunny that the senior management could go on pointless corporate jaunts to. And, well, there was this cheap old hotel in Belkita with enough rooms to be turned into student halls *and* conference rooms that could easily be classrooms " Paxton said, gesturing around us with a salesman's charm. "And my father said to the VP of Donations, in between taking shots at some incredibly endangered species in Kenya, "Can you not give my boy a job out there?" So, here I am."

"Doing what?" I asked.

"Pfft. I don't know. Strategic logistics scholastic...plastic fantastic. Something like that. I wasn't really listening. But I did agree to get staff out here so they could run a summer school for teenagers heading to college in the Fall - no matter what it took."

"Subterfuge and false pretenses?"

"Bingo!" smiled Paxton. It was an infectious smile, but not in a good way - the chicken pox of smiles. It latched onto me and I felt the corners of my mouth itch and begin to lift. I shook it off and said "I'm not staying." I still found myself curious though, against my better judgement. "Why a summer school?"

"The Principal wants to build a villa out back and they are all rich brats - sorry Hatton," said Paxton.

"Oh, don't worry, it's perfectly true," he admitted.

"So, I knew that poses a problem for June. And you have always hated kids, even when you were a kid. I have seen that photo of you in kindergarten looking disdainfully at the children in the sandpit."

All true, June and I nodded. Then the anger at the betrayal bubbled back up.

"Come on, June. Let's get the next flight back to the UK." Hatton looked a bit sad, but I committed to storming past Paxton. The little weasel clung onto my arm though, like an incredibly rich but pathetic sloth.

"Don't go! Please!" he wailed. "I have to make a success of this!"

"No you don't," I said, trying to shake myself free. "You literally live a life free of financial consequence to any of your actions."

Paxton was now stuck to me, like the Great Gatsby of limpets, one arm winding tighter around my forearm, the other balancing a martini.

"Everyone thinks I am a failure!" he cried.

"No, we just think you're irresponsible, there's a difference. Now let me go," I said through gritted teeth, like a mother whose child was embarrassing them in public. "June, help me out here!"

June was tracing the rim of her wine glass. "Well, maybe it wouldn't be the worst summer in the world, would it?" she said, flinching at the end of the sentence, as if waiting for a crash - perhaps me throwing Paxton at her. "I mean, sun, sea, other...things," she said, jerking her eyebrows in Hatton's direction. "Don't worry about me, I am certain that I can find some way to undermine capitalism."

"Don't go on my account," piped up Hatton. "I am sure we could have a very good relationship. Working. Working relationship. Professionalism." He cleared his throat and tugged his shirt collar.

"God Dad, you're so awkward, it's embarrassing," said a lanky girl appearing from the bar. Her spine was shrugged into a question mark, almost physically asking if her father could be any more mortifying. It was hard to tell exactly who was the father she was declaring embarrassing though as her black hair (with standard-issue Gen-Z middle parting) gave a shiver of indignation. I looked around to see who the embarrassing dad was, her disdain seemed to ooze over us all collectively, plus it was hard not to notice that she didn't really share an obvious physical resemblance with anyone in the room.

I tried to glance nonchalantly at Lorando, who was clearing some plates away from the next table. Was he the embarrassing father in question? Could you even clear plates away in an embarrassing manner?

"Yes, yes. Don't worry my darling daughter, you won't die from embarrassment. I will just kill myself after dinner and spare you any more horror. Does that work for you, or would you prefer I just hurled myself off the balcony now?" said Hatton. So *this* was Parthenope. She shot a look at her Dad that stopped just short of putting him out of his misery right then and there. While the dysfunction unfolded, I subtly brought out my phone and brought up Hatton's Wikipedia page, scrolling down to 'Personal Life':

'Hatton Finch married actress, model and wellness coach Electra Lawson-Finch on 14 February 2003 after four years of dating. In 2006, they adopted a child from Guatemala, a girl named Parthenope Aglaia Aubrey Maple Lawson-Finch.'

That explained it, I thought - Hatton had also mentioned being cagey about his daughter's privacy, so she was never papped with her parents. I coolly placed my mobile back on the table. Parthenope had her phone out now though and was filming the balcony. She turned around and zoomed in on the mural of Salma Hayek. "Ew," was her pronouncement.

She flipped the camera screen and began to speak into it. "So I'd like to report some child abuse. My Dad is making me have dinner in this hot mess."

"If a tree falls in the forest but no one was there to put it on TikTok, did it really happen, eh Parthenope?" said Hatton, craning into shot.

"Go away, Dad!" she said, quickly turning the camera off. "The DILF comments I get from sad middle-aged women when you appear are so cringe," she shuddered as she slumped into the chair next to mine.

"Who are you?" she asked, about as interested in the reply as she was in family bonding. I was tempted to reply 'one of those sad middle-aged women who has, rather embarrassingly, called your Dad a DILF to his face', but thought there was enough tension going on anyway.

"Oh, me? I am Sam Chambers," I said with a big smile, a strange need to impress her coming over me.

"Sam is an amazing writer," said Hatton. I smiled more, then caught June looking at me and put on my best poker face. "We work together and get on really well."

My phone buzzed.

June: Wow! He managed to say that last bit without using air quotes! He must be a good actor.

I turned my phone face down on the table whilst trying to telepathically tell June I would kill her if this continued.

"I will be teaching here this summer too," I said, regretting it almost as soon as I said it. What else did I have to go back to, though? As June had said, it could all be good material for my next book.

"You will?" asked Paxton. I nodded in resignation. Hatton's eyes brightened but he also seemed frozen, like an animal discovering that the brightly coloured snake it ate was really delicious but also poisonous. June did a little dance in her seat.

Parthenope had still passed no comment on the revelation of my identity, but my British desire for politeness made me push the conversation. "And you must be Parthenope?"

"Ugh, I hate that name," she grumbled, wriggling uncomfortably in her stripy crop top.

I was about to ask why, even if it did seem a bit suicidal, when I saw Hatton get up from the table and throw open his arms. "Aubrey!" he called as I turned to see another woman join the scene.

I recognised her immediately as Aubrey Markowitz, Hatton's friend and the indie director/star of their first film. She was older than how I was used to seeing her, which was in '90s throwback shots when scrolling through Instagram. There were plenty of accounts dedicated to her younger self, long wavy blonde hair virgins would have combed vigorously while dreaming of their future husband 200 years ago, her Princess Diana figure slipped into high-waisted jeans that would have meant severe thrush for a mere mortal. Not for Aubrey though, who danced through fields in them or posed legs akimbo on a backwards-turned director's chair.

She was easy enough to find in the past, but it was more difficult to find her now. Aubrey herself was known to shun the limelight of social media. Turning to news articles, there were fresh tracks; a small indie film here, an appearance at a festival there. Oh, and the protests. She was always at a protest, whether it was stopping pipelines across Native American land, against the deportation of refugees and even in outrage about that Pepsi ad with Kendall Jenner. In interviews, she refused to be pinned down on which country she lived in, often giving some whimsical answer about 'a fairy kingdom'. I wondered how people engaged her for these events in the absence of solid contact information - was it a very chic carrier pigeon?

Some people could get hold of her, Hatton for one. Now she was here in the flesh, There were streaks of grey going through her curls like reeds through a river, but the high-waisted jeans still fitted, now accessorised with a blazer that said 'I occasionally do lectures and have to look semi-professional but wish I was smoking cannabis right now'.

She hugged Hatton warmly and pulled off her blazer as if it itched her skin. "What a beautiful hotel!" she fizzed. Parthenope snorted. Aubrey gave her a look of reproach, but they both ended up smiling at each other; Aubrey obviously occupied the 'favourite aunt' position in Parthenope's painfully cool soul.

"How's Dave?" asked Hatton, pulling out a chair for Aubrey.

Another quick Wikipedia established that 'Aubrey Markowitz wed her husband, David Cohen, the Democratic Senator for Vermont, Cynthia Beck, on 31st August 2015.'

"Oh, he is ok. Big election campaign coming up but he is golfing upstate, of course. Meanwhile, I am absolutely exhausted after the flight. The beds in First Class are just so uncomfortable!"

Hatton nodded gravely. June muttered 'rich people' under her breath. Aubrey regarded my own dishevelled state with a look of alarm.

"I am a victim of CheepCheep Airways," I shrugged. June muttered 'And Hatton Finch' just low enough for only me to hear.

"You poor thing! They are a terrible airline. Or so I have heard," said Aubrey, as horrified as if I had told her I had been dragged here tied to a team of wild horses.

"Aubrey, this is Sam Chambers," said Hatton with a start, sensing simmering class resentment from our end of the table.

"Oh my goodness! You should have opened with that, Hatton!" she said, shoving him out the way. She took my hand and looked me in the eyes very earnestly, even if her nostrils twitched a little from my questionable odour. "Hatton gave me a copy of your book. I adored it!"

I felt myself blush and looked away from her wide puppy eyes. Hatton was looking at us with a satisfied smile that said 'I knew they would hit it off'. I snapped my eyes back to Aubrey, who had let go of my hand and was rifling through her bag. "It's here somewhere. I thought it would be fun to reread it on the plane," she mumbled to herself. "Ah! Here it is!" she said, producing a copy of Bae for Pay before hugging it bashfully to her chest. "Would you...would you sign it for me, please?"

"Of course!" I spluttered. "I can't believe you liked it. You're, like, a proper professional artist who has won awards and everything."

Aubrey's eyes, which had previously sparkled like fairy pools, froze over. "You are an artist too. Don't let anyone else ever tell you otherwise."

"OK, I won't," I said as I signed the book. It felt like I was agreeing to a contract with her.

"Please tell me that you are teaching here too this summer?" she said as I handed the book back.

"Yes, I am," I said, turning to Paxton. "For my sins."

"What will you be teaching?"

"I don't know, Paxton, what will I be teaching?"

"Creative writing! What else?" he announced.

"The written word is dead," said Parthenope to no one in particular, filming her manicure glinting in the sun.

"Parthenope! Don't be a Philistine," scolded Aubrey. She turned back to me excitedly, like a kid making a new friend on their first day of school. "I'm going to be teaching filmmaking."

"Hatton will be teaching stage combat and June will be teaching Politics and History," said Paxton.

"Aw, really?!" said June, clapping her hands together.

"It's hard to argue with 33,000 YouTube subscribers," replied Paxton. "As MetalFan36 said, "You're a legend who saved my A Level."

"Damn right I did! I'm sorrynotsorry about the episode on why your family is what's wrong with Late Capitalism," shrugged June.

"It's ok! I loved the bit where Barbie got run over by the Russian doll driving the tank," said Paxton. "Who wants a drink?"

The answer was everyone, so Paxton eagerly obliged as the setting sun caught glinting metal off to the left. I turned around, squinting to see a sign now above the entrance:

ST FILLAN'S UNIVERSITY
THE PAXTON PREPARATORY ACADEMY
BELKITA CAMPUS

CHAPTER

19

Paxton was ordering another pitcher of Tequila Sunrise at the bar when a man in one of those sweat-wicking gym tops and a pair of cut-off terry cloth shorts appeared beside him. At any given time, there are at least three of him in any gym across the country, observing their personal training clients with a glazed look. Paxton turned to him and his eyes lit up though as they took each other in a bro-hug.

"Who's that?" asked June.

"He looks a little familiar," I admitted. "But I can't place him."

"James!" cried Aubrey, jumping from her chair when she saw the new man. Hatton waved at him. As Aubrey made her way over to 'James', I asked Hatton, "Who is he?" I was partly curious, partly just glad we had a neutral and distracting topic of conversation.

"He's Aubrey's PT," said Hatton, also looking relieved. "I think he is going to be doing some wellness thing with the kids."

"James is ok, even if he keeps trying to make me drink those mackerel smoothies," volunteered Parthenope.

"They are great for the skin *and* building muscle!" said James, who had walked ahead of Hatton with a tray of drinks. Another pitcher and glasses for us, a lonely glass of water that I presumed was for him. He saw me looking and said, "The barman refused to make the smoothie on 'humanitarian grounds'. Some people just have no taste." He pulled down his sunglasses from his forehead, but hesitated for a second. Did I look familiar to him too?

Maybe Paxton could shed some light on the situation. He spent far too much time with his alcohol-sodden socialite aunts growing up and as such had become a walking version of Who's Who, remembering every significant (and insignificant) social connection in his milieu.

"Oh, it looks like Paxton needs a hand with that tray. I will go and help!" I improvised, backing away from the table as everyone began to share out the drinks.

I caught Paxton at the bar, who was piling bar snacks onto his tray. "Who's this James?" I asked. "I know him from somewhere." Paxton, who had a crisp packet in his teeth like a naughty puppy, spat his pack onto the tray. I grabbed a handful of snack to lighten the load.

"You must remember James Crane!" Paxton scoffed. "Is this what happens when you approach 30? Your mind starts to go? Jeez, what are you, three months older than me? If this is my future, someone make me an appointment with Dignitas!"

"James Crane? Your roommate from First Year? But he looked like a malnourished noodle that shopped in Gap Kids!"

"Yeah, he looks a little different these days," said Paxton, with a nod towards James' biceps, which writhed like sleek pole-dancing otters with his every movement. They were distracting and verging on grotesque, but I had something else on my mind.

"Wait, didn't he drop out or something after First Year? What happened there?"

"Oh, he fled prosecution and went back to Aruba," chuckled Paxton, as if James being on Interpol's most wanted list was not a big deal.

"I'm sorry, he what?" I said, stopping just out of earshot of the table.

"Don't you remember? Wow, the dementia is more advanced than I feared, Sam."

"Any more of that and I might become so senile that I forget all social niceties and flip your drinks tray, Paxton."

"Wow! Touchy! Well, I suppose you and I only started hanging out properly in Second Year after I joined the newspaper," he said. "James was long gone by that point, but you must have heard the story. The police chase was on the news, for Christ's sake!"

"Police chase? In St Fillan's?" I asked dubiously. I would surely have remembered that happening. Then again, a police chase in St Fillan's would be a blink-and-you-miss-it affair; it only took three minutes to drive from one end of town to the other.

"No, it wasn't in the actual town," said Paxton. "It was on the way to that private airfield that is on the drive up from Edinburgh. What's it called..." Paxton clicked his fingers to summon the answer.

"Invertay," I filled in the gap. Why I remembered that and Paxton didn't was a mystery - he was the one who flew home from it for Christmas every year.

"That's the one!" Paxton confirmed. "Maybe the dementia is catching. Anyway, a few of us thought it would be fun to steal the Principal's vintage sports car in First Year."

"I remember something about that!" I said, relieved that I had recovered some memory, not shocked, because this was typical Paxton. "Was that the car he tried to write off as a business expense; an 'emotional support car' so he felt confident on official engagements?"

"The very one," said Paxton, smiling nostalgically before snapping back into storytelling mode. "Well, we decided to break into his garage and take it for a spin one night after a few bottles of absinthe."

"Drink driving, Paxton? Come on, that's not cool," I said, hushing my voice as James looked over in our direction.

"I may be a louche dilettante but I have never had a DUI in my life!" Paxton preened. "James had just started his health kick, so he was our designated driver for the evening. He was also the only one skinny enough to get through the loose tile on the garage roof."

"I think I see where this is going," I groaned.

"It was all going so well until the Principal sat up in the backseat with one of his lady friends," sighed Paxton.

"Not his wife?"

"Of course not!" snorted Paxton. "Poor James got the fright of his life, shrieked, put the car in reverse and drove it through the back wall." Paxton laughed heartily, like a god watching mortal chaos of his own doing.

"What happened next?" I asked, ripping open a mini bag of popcorn from the snack pile.

"Well, then he really started to panic," said Paxton, the whites of his eyes flaring at the memory.

"Started to panic? So putting it through the back wall was part of his five year plan?"

"Sam, oh my God. Wait until you hear what happened. You will think rats fleeing a sinking ship is a military manoeuvre," he laughed like a muted hyena, in case we attracted more attention from the table. "So James, the Principal and his lady are all screaming at each other. James' fight or flight response kicks in. Spoiler alert - it's flight. He drives off, but neglects to remove his passengers first."

"Oh dear," I said, squirming, but Paxton was telling the story so vividly that it *was* just like watching a car crash - I couldn't look away.

"He drove about 15 miles before the Principal and his floozy managed to bail out at a zebra crossing."

"How come this wasn't in the news?"

"The Principal didn't want the drama. But James' story isn't over."

"How much more of a hash of things could he make?!" I asked, bewildered. I flicked my eyes away from James so he wouldn't catch on what we were talking about.

"Once James commits to something, there is no stopping him. Even with panicking," Paxton said, almost with admiration. "I, meanwhile, struggle to commit to one brand of bourbon. It's something I am working on, actually, my commitment issues-"

I burst out in a guffaw. I loved how Paxton was so self-deprecating yet sarcastic sometimes, it really sounded like he was going to a therapist or something. "Come on, Paxton. The others will be wondering why we are still hanging out at the bar. We haven't got time for your jokes. Even if it was a good one, you almost had me going for a sec."

"What do you...I mean...it's not...Ha! As if I would ever try and improve myself, right? My defects are my USP. I am like a really sexy version of an old cabinet that fetches more money at auction because John Wilkes Booth drew a bullseye on it and used it for target practice."

"Back to the story, Paxton," I prompted, but I made a mental note to return to this later. Was Paxton actually trying to unravel his Citizen Kane-Great Gatsby complex?

"Right, so James was convinced he would be thrown in jail. Can you believe it, he didn't even think about blackmailing the Principal, like any normal person would," Paxton snorted in disbelief. "Talk about a schoolboy error!"

I shovelled another mouthful of popcorn into my gob.

"He went to ground for a few days. His parents had sent him to some military academy where he was systematically bullied for having a BMI below 20, but boy did that guy know how to make a tent out of a deer carcass. Eventually, he got to a payphone and his father arranged a private flight out of the country. Their family motto is, 'Consequences are for the weak.'"

I felt a rash coming on, an allergic reaction to this much privilege in one conversation.

"Funny thing was, his family had to face the consequences of his dad's insider trading when they lost all their money and he was put under house arrest for five years. So now James is making his own way in the world, working as a personal trainer."

"How enterprising," I muttered. "It's positively Dickensian."

"You guys! What's the hold up? Get back out here!" called June. I jumped and looked up. Hatton was looking straight at me. Then he wasn't. Parthenope was regarding everything with disdain. James was showing a disinterested Aubrey how to use a chair for tricep presses.

CHAPTER

20

"You have to stay up til dawn! I command it. I'm the boss, after all!" boomed Paxton as I yawned. Us 'teachers' had travelled hours to get here and were tired. An occasional evening breeze, which had swept rather grandly and romantically from the depths of the Sahara all the way to the island, also reminded me that I still smelled awful. My eyes were drooping shut as Aubrey regaled us with a ribald tale of selecting the freshest onions at her local farmer's market when Hatton shook my shoulder, lightly but just enough to bring me back.

Half asleep, I blinked at him, trying to work out where I was. My brain grabbed on to the last time I had seen him - in bed 18 hours beforehand. I laid my head on his shoulder and murmured "Set the toaster for tomorrow morning."

"What did she say?" said Paxton, his voice rising at the whiff of gossip. The volume jolted me well and truly back from the Land of Nod. I sat bolt upright to find Parthenope looking at me like I was diseased and Paxton's sharp little whitened teeth glowing across the table. I looked up at Hatton and we exploded apart.

"Oh, Sam. Her herbal remedy must have interacted with the alcohol," said June, always quick off the mark. She grabbed my hand and began to lead me away from the table.

"I hope she is alright!" said Aubrey fretfully.

"Oh, she will be fine. Just afraid of flying. I gave her a traditional Thai tea before take-off. Silly me, forgot it doesn't sit well with alcohol," prattled June.

"Huh, weird. She wasn't too scared to fly to Denmark on a bi-monthly basis," said Paxton, throwing his voice so we would hear as we left the balcony, but keeping his eyes fixed on an uncomfortable Hatton.

"The poor dear! An early night will help," Aubrey nodded sympathetically.

James appeared immune to the gluttonous temptations of the lives of others, and was telling a dead-eyed Parthenope about an article he had read claiming the marathon actually originated in Belkita, not Greece. I wanted to interject with a high bullshit rating since the entire island was less than 26 miles in circumference, but I had to keep up my act, so I meekly stumbled away with a sleepy wave.

"Nice save," I said to June when we were back in the hotel lobby.

"I think I fumbled it a bit, but it was a distraction."

The sandstone walls of the corridors were glowing in the soft lighting and the air felt thick and strange, but not necessarily unpleasant; filled with the hum of cicadas or some other sort of insect that would never survive the cold in Britain and a heat that hadn't got the message about the sun going down.

"What a day," I groaned, dragging my feet up the stairs.

"What a *summer* it is going to be! Who needs Netflix when I have your personal life to keep me entertained?" said June, dancing up the staircase.

"Your support is touching," I said as we walked the extravagantly thick carpet (why?? The coldest recorded temperature in Belkita was 10C) towards our rooms.

"I'm only joking. Mostly. It won't seem as bad after a shower and a good night's sleep, Sam. I mean, it will still seem pretty horrific, but you might want to kill yourself from the shame a bit less when you don't smell so bad," June informed me as she opened her bedroom door.

I rested my head on my door, exhausted and partly hoping all those YouTube conspiracy videos were right and we all had microchips in our forehead and mine would open the door. I thought about trying to construct a witty reply, but it was taking all my energy to fish my phone out of my pocket. "Good night, June."

"Night!" she called as her door closed. I opened mine to find Brutus skittering along the smooth floor. I presumed a snoring cat-shaped bump under the covers was Lily, who seemed to be making herself at home. I decided to have a quick shower, the smell really was quite offensive now, before taking Brutus out for his evening pee.

I peeled off my biohazard clothes and considered burning them, wishing I had been cool enough in high school to take up smoking just so I would have a lighter to hand at this moment. Brutus, ever the pint-sized pervert, loved the aromas emanating from the offending items and began rolling in the clothes pile with great fervour, paying particular attention to the underwear. This just made me feel even dirtier, so I jumped in the shower and began to lather myself with the complimentary shower gel and shampoo provided. I felt the past 24 hours slip off me and down the drain. I gave a satisfied sigh and stood under the water for a few minutes, cleansing myself of any trace of the eventful day.

Then Brutus barked at me, his paws pressed against the shower door. He was never one to pass up seeing a woman in a state of undress; June told me he had somehow made his way into her massage room many times when she dog sat once. However, I could tell by the way he was cocking his head towards the door that he needed to visit his own bathroom, the great outdoors.

"Ok, ok, one minute," I said, sadly turning off the shower and drying myself off. I smiled when I smelled my skin though, the rank smell of the day replaced by a sweet floral scent that the shower gel bottle informed me was 'Belkitan Camomile and Honey'.

Brutus hopped from one tiny paw to the other, claws clipping on the floor as I grabbed a summer dress out my suitcase and pulled it on. I had already covered the floor in soggy foot prints and didn't want to make it any wetter, so quickly clipped his collar to his lead and took him downstairs.

I noticed the bar was now dark and deserted, a lone fan wafting long curtains by the balcony.

Meanwhile, a far less glamorous engagement lay ahead of me; searching for Brutus' freshly plopped poo under a blanket of twinkling stars, which were pretty but just not bright enough to illuminate his faeces. I was combing a patch of scrub like I was on a crime procedural when my poo-bag-clad hand seized upon something firm but a bit squishy. As I grabbed on, I realised it was also approximately the same size as Brutus, and able to move. I screamed. For a second I actually thought that a mutant poo had come to life. Then I realised it felt more like a sturdy shoe than a big poo monster, which was reassuring but also oddly disappointing.

Whatever it was wriggled away, flashing out the other side of the bush. Brutus barked as if to say, "Catch that zombie poo!" and I clutched the flimsy plastic bag to my chest, as if it would offer me some protection from the beast of the bush.

The leaves rustled and branches cracked. Brutus barked and I closed my eyes as one final but useless shield and braced myself for a (scatological?) assault. Then I literally had a knee jerk reaction and thrust my leg out, connecting sharply with something unfortunate, which let out a yowl not unlike Brutus.

A dark figure limped out of the bush, hunched over and whining. I readied myself for another kick when it said, "Jesus, where did you learn to kick like that? I've been kicked in the nuts by Jean Claude Van Damme in hobnailed boots and it didn't hurt as much!"

This was a favourite anecdote of...

"Hatton?"

"Yes," he wheezed, staggering under the warm glow on a streetlight, which only highlighted how pale he had gone.

"I'm so sorry!" I said. I stepped forward to check he was ok, but the movement of my leg made him flinch away.

"You aren't coming anywhere near me! It was like being smacked by a Centaur!"

"Fine! But can you blame me? Someone jumped out of a bush at me! What were you even doing in there?"

"I was hiding," Hatton told me, regaining some of his composure and the colour in his cheeks.

"From what?" I asked.

"Paxton."

"Why? Was he trying to have another one of his threesomes?" I said, not sure if I was joking or not.

"Don't think so, but he was trying to drag us all down to the beach for a rave. He had glow sticks and everything. Having a seizure on the beach thanks to bad ecstasy hasn't really been my thing for about 15 years so I politely declined."

"Ha! You call it 'ecstasy'. What an old timer."

"Can you hear that? I think it's the sound of you hurtling towards 30. Next stop middle age," Hatton hit back. He was obviously recovering just fine, even if his ego was bruised. "Anyway, Paxton wouldn't hear of it though and insisted it was a traditional Belkitan custom to take Class A drugs under the stars. I managed to give him the slip in the car park though while he was trying to persuade a taxi driver to join us."

"So you hid in the bush?"

"Yep! All that time crawling around in the dirt for Afghan Hounds finally paid off," he said wryly, bending down to pet Brutus. He was referring to a military comedy-drama he had been in a few years ago, in which he played a maverick dog trainer in the American Army stationed in Helmand Province. It was marketed as M*A*S*H for the new millennium but was more a mish-mash of tropes and stereotypes; someone just one week away from retirement was always being blown up by a dastardly terrorist who was dressed like the sheikh in The Clash's Rock the Casbah video.

I realised that I had been playing the intro to Rock the Casbah in my head for a while and that I really should say something that addressed the wider situation. Hatton was still petting Brutus, maybe he was thinking of something to say too? Or maybe he just thought Brutus was cute? Everyone else did.

"So...what a day!" I eventually arrived on.

"God, yeah!" said Hatton, standing up. He hedged his bets with a smile and a tired shrug of his eyebrows.

"I mean, this time 24 hours ago, we were..." I pressed. I wasn't sure why, it was probably easier if we just lived under a thick, scummy layer of denial for the next three months/the rest of our lives, but I already felt like I was suffocating under it. We needed to work out how we would handle this.

"Admiring the finest toaster this side of Japan," he said, but there was subtext dripping from his words.

"Yeah, I mean, we really admired the hell out of it, didn't we?" I laughed. "But, it's just, I don't know, the toaster was great and all, but I'm not sure if we should use it here?"

"Given the choice, I would have my toast every morning from that thing. I would probably start eating breakfast in the evening just so I could use it then too. But, it is more...complicated to use it abroad."

"Yes. First of all, we would need a travel adapter," I said, offering a practical note on an entirely metaphorical conversation.

"Plus Parthenope is here. I don't want to confuse her. Or embarrass her, but I think the ship has already sailed on that one," he said, looking very serious, but also as if he wanted to be convinced otherwise, like someone hoping a salesperson will help them justify an impulse buy.

I nodded vigorously and picked up Brutus, just to give myself something to do. My first instincts had been right all along, I didn't need another bizarre 'almost relationship' that would blow up in my face, especially with all these added complications. "You are completely right," I agreed, mentally abandoning my cart with Hatton still in it.

CHAPTER

21

The next morning, I headed down for breakfast alone at about 9am. June had texted me to say she had already been eaten. June is a morning person, she is also an afternoon and evening person, always up to something. She once told me her deepest, darkest secret was that she really admired the fact that Margaret Thatcher only slept four hours a night and aspired to emulate it.

I, however, was not an early bird. I never caught the worm, instead grabbing whatever was vaguely breakfast-related out of my fridge on my way to work.

Despite the beautiful morning, the island paradise had not reformed me. However, keeping things professional with Hatton had gone well so far; mostly because I had been asleep for eight hours, but I hadn't even had an incredibly graphic dream about him, which was pretty good going, I told myself.

As I walked down the stairs to Tito's, where a note in my bedroom told me breakfast would be served 6.30am-9.30am, I thought about how adult I was being; choosing to neatly fold my feelings away back into my emotional baggage, unlike the actual clothing which had already exploded out of my rucksack and all over the hotel room floor.

Everything would be fine, I assured myself, descending the stairs with steely resolve. I would be just like one of those elegant but emotionally repressed women from a 1940s film, like in Brief Encounter but without the almost throwing myself in front of a train.

Then I saw Hatton and Parthenope going into Tito's. I realised I was very much not fine with the whole thing. My emotional baggage was threatening to pop open, the zip straining to contain it all. I was not a cool 1940s lady and I could not do breakfast with them. My eyes flicked around the lobby and latched onto James, who was intently examining one of the paintings on the wall, much more classical and tasteful than the Hayek mural only one room away.

I quietly slinked down the last few stairs and scurried over to James. Reaching his side, I looked at the painting in front of us; I guessed it depicted a Greek God smiting another in a state of undress, the men sparring in what appeared to be strategically draped bedsheets. I didn't see the appeal, but it had obviously caught James' attention. Asking him about it seemed like the perfect opportunity to stall going into the restaurant and an awkward encounter with Hatton and Parthenope.

"Painting catch your eye?" I asked as casually as I could, pretending it was normal to start conversations with almost complete strangers about legitimised 18th Century pornography.

James turned to me, looking me up and down. It wasn't the same gaze he used on the picture, but it was just as critical. I call it 'PT eyes', scanning me for micros, macros, BMIs and body fat percentages, working out where I was on the scale from orthorexic ornament to being winched out of your own house by the fire brigade.

In the end, he settled on regarding me with a smidgen of disdain and an arched eyebrow. "Yes," he said. "Aubrey has another D'Agosti at home, but I think this is one of his later paintings. Anyway, I am going for breakfast."

He made to move off, but I grabbed his bicep, which was shaped and felt like a boiled ostrich egg. I glanced around to see Hatton and Parthenope waiting to be seated. James looked at me reproachfully, but I didn't care, I needed to stall him.

"Er...how do you know that it's a late D'Agosti?" I asked feebly.

"Well," said James, removing my hand from his arm like it was a bird poo, "I am pretty sure that he used the guy on the left in a few of his earlier paintings." James gestured to the younger of the two slightly swaddled gentlemen. He was being wrestled by the older model, who was strangling his swan-like neck with an end of their bedsheet-togas. A look of terror shone in the whites of his eyes, but his puny sapling arms were doing little to claw away the murder weapon.

"He is much more developed in his later work. Great quads and traps. Wish I knew what his workout regime was," James said, leaning in closer to inspect a thundering thigh muscle.

"I imagine going through that every day is a great workout. Survival of the fittest?" I said. James continued to study the painting, as much to tell me to go away as he appreciated it. I couldn't face a Full English or a Full Belkitan (whatever that was) with Hatton and Parthenope though, so I pressed on. "Why did D'Agosti paint men homoerotically throttling each other?" I asked.

"Typical," muttered James, his well-developed forearm twitching as if he was barely restraining himself from strangling me.

"Excuse me?" I said, a little outraged. I had been described as 'weird', 'not her again' and 'it', but never 'typical'.

"Just because I'm gay, I'm meant to know why he liked painting naked wrestling scenes?" James retorted, sporting a murderous scowl like the killer's in the picture.

"No!" I spluttered. The thought of James' orientation hadn't even crossed my mind, so preoccupied was I with avoiding my own sexuality. If I had thought about it, it was only to observe that he looked like one of those muscle-bound guys who peacock around the gym telling women how to lift weights. "I had no idea you were gay...I'm just..." I trailed off to catch Lorando leading Hatton and Parthenope to a table. "I'm just really interested in Art History." I said. I wasn't - I just wanted to buy enough time to see if Lorando sat them at a two-seater. If he did, I could go in and safely navigate my way to a lonely little table somewhere. If it sat three or more, social niceties might compel us all to share. With James, who was convinced I was a raging homophobe, just to make matters worse.

"Well, if you didn't know I was gay, you are just as clueless as Aubrey. Were you not listening last night when I was telling everyone about my partner Keith?"

"Er, I was a bit distracted last night. And sleepy. Hang on, Aubrey doesn't know? Haven't you worked for her for years?" I breathed a sigh of relief when I saw Hatton and Parthenope led to a two-seater table, but now I was interested in James' story. Breakfast could wait.

"Don't get me wrong, she's a lovely woman with the core strength of a 16-year-old gymnast, but she is a bit oblivious. Keith and I have been together for years and she still goes on about how wonderful it is that we are such good friends and flatmates."

"Have you ever told her directly?"

"No. At first, I felt a bit awkward correcting her. I thought, she will get it eventually. But no. And now it's definitely too awkward. She would be so embarrassed if I told her that Keith and I are not just best friends sharing a one-bedroom apartment. I have never met someone with such woeful gaydar."

I nodded and turned back to the painting, the two men frozen in battle forever. This was going to be a long summer.

"Anyway, I need my protein pancakes," said James, walking off towards Tito's. I watched him go, presuming he wouldn't want to eat with someone who put sugar on their cereal and drank juice from concentrate.

"Come on!" he barked at me; the same tone he no doubt used when instructing clients to throw a tyre.

CHAPTER

22

It was a surprisingly pleasant breakfast; I avoided eye contact with Hatton *and* James only glared at me once for going back for extra hash browns. After that, we had a few hours to kill before our first 'assembly' with our new students.

As I left breakfast, my phone vibrated.

June: Meet me at the pool!

Well, that was my free time taken care of, then.

Back in my room, I rifled through my bag contents. Being in a country where no one knew me had emboldened my swimwear selection; I had gone to Primark and bought what could be loosely defined as a bikini. However, in true fast fashion tradition, it looked like the leftovers of a much larger garment. It seemed to be the thing all the wannabe celebs were wearing when I hate-read the Daily Mail on my lunch breaks, and, dare I say it, I actually thought I quite suited it. June had even complimented me on it, but I had to tell her it was a recycled creation from Etsy to avoid her (very correct) judgement about my social responsibility.

It was one thing being body confident in a hotel full of people you would never see again, but it was something else entirely in a resort filled with judgemental teenagers, a hawk-eyed personal trainer and a very recent ex-lover. I cursed Past Sam for not buying one of those Nigella Lawson all-in-one black water moo-moos. I had no other choice than to truss myself up in the bikini, even though I looked like a pale and pimply supermarket chicken. The addition of sun cream just made me look like I was basted and oven-ready. I pulled the same summer dress I had thrown on the night before over it, hoping to make it to the pool edge, quickly whipping it off and submerging.

June lolled against the neck of an inflatable flamingo, drifting across the pool. She lowered her sunglasses, which were a pair she had proudly had since the '90s; huge, blue and bedazzled with rhinestones. Their origin story was very on-brand for June - she won them off a FARC female soldier in a drinking competition.

"Your steed," she said, gesturing to an inflatable unicorn perched on the pool edge. June took a long sip of her mojito and flipped her sunglasses back into place with a well-practiced snap of the neck.

Hatton sent a ripple of water across the pool as he surfaced like a stylish otter by the ladder. How did he do that without looking like a llama caught in a flash flood, I wondered, when I looked like I had been in a rodeo in a rainstorm trying to get on my unicorn. He had the air of a merman in a perfume advert, his hair wet, but looking like a celebrity hairstylist had slicked it back with expensive product.

"I'm going to the bar, do you two want something?" he asked.

"Bring us a couple more mojitos," replied June.

Hatton nodded and walked off towards Tito's, a trail of wet footprints evaporating as quickly as he left them.

"Do you two want something?" mimicked June when he was out of earshot. "Two mojitos and you scrubbed, shaved and sent to my room, Mr Finch!" she said before taking a long, satisfied drag of her mojito, until all that was left was melting ice.

"Ok, no more mojitos for you," I laughed nervously. My unicorn had drifted close to June's flamingo, so I pushed off her pink inflatable with my feet and sailed across the pool. June's flamingo meandered off, as if it was trying to remember where it had put something.

"Oh come on, I don't really fancy him. Not in the way you do," scoffed June, wiping a bead of water off her prized sunglasses.

"Idon'tfancyhimI'mtotallyoverit," I hissed unconvincingly, banging my hand off the pool edge for added emphasis. I felt like a judge losing control of a disorderly courtroom.

"Yeah, you do," June replied, casually but with conviction, like an unshakeable witness in the dock. Reclining on her flamingo, she continued, "You look at him like he is a half-price bottle of Zinfandel."

"Oh, Jesus," I groaned.

"No, not Jesus! That piece of fine Judean man meat died when he was only 33. You're into older men, Sam Chambers." June had now turned into the prosecution, her eyes boreing through her FARC-approved sunglasses, hotter than the sun that was burning my skin, that must be why my cheeks were boiling.

"I am not!" I retorted.

"You can't fool me," June said, regarding me with a scientific intensity, her huge glasses like those safety ones researchers wear doing experiments. "You're zany for zimmer frames! Hot for Horlicks! Vibing for Viagra!"

Hatton chose this opportune moment to come back into earshot.

"Who is...vibing...for Viagra?" he asked with some trepidation, crouching down at the poolside with the already dripping mojitos.

"Sam," informed June, spinning over in her flamingo and plucking a mojito from his hand.

"Yes, I'm actually a 92-year-old impotent geriatric. I've just had really good plastic surgery," I said, not missing a beat. However, I still avoided eye contact with Hatton and served June a death glare as I retrieved my cocktail.

"Yes, it's a wonder what they can do with surgery these days. I'm actually the reanimated corpse of Vasco de Gama," Hatton said, standing up with a flourish.

I laughed at the turn into the absurd, perhaps too loudly, because I could feel June looking at me again. I stopped abruptly. Hatton looked at June a little strangely, like she was the class troublemaker who kept moving her desk back whenever he wasn't looking. The sound of lapping water, normally so fluid and easy, felt jagged and awkward in the silence.

"Are you two not going to address the elephant in the swimming pool here?" huffed June. "Enough jokes about plastic surgery and Vasco de Gama. My teasing is for your emotional health. Are you not going to talk about what's going on with you two?"

Hatton and I shared a stilted glance and his mouth moved, but no noise came out.

"Ugh, June, look, to cut a long story short, I kicked Hatton in the balls last night in the carpark but we sorted it all out and we aren't going to see each other any more! Now go back to getting pissed on your flamingo."

Hatton nodded vigorously. "What she said."

"Ugh, you two. I can't even," June muttered, mostly to herself, as she dismounted her flamingo and made her way out of the water.

"Ok..." said Hatton. "Well, I better get going. I like to get in an Olympic Weights session and a meditation podcast before lunch." He gave a boyish shrug that made his wet hair fall forward, like it was alive and well-rehearsed in appearing pant-droppingly roguish at a moment's notice. I fixed my eyes on my cocktail and waved as casually as I could, hearing him pad off to the gym.

"Well, that's one for the spank bank," declared June.

"What?" My next tactic to throw June off the scent was just to be as obstructively confused as possible.

"Oh, I'm off to get all sweaty and bulgy with big boy weights then be super sensitive with a podcast!" she said, hulking her sinewy shoulders forward and flopping her fringe over her glasses. "That's going straight in the spank bank, right between young Stalin and Jeremy Paxman berating Tories on Newsnight."

"Was that meant to be an impression of Hatton?" I said dumbly.

"Wasn't it a good one? You know him so much better than me...biblically and all!"

I sighed. I could see why she had waited until she was out the water to make a comment like that, I would have toppled her flamingo if she was in the pool.

"June!" I hissed, then lowered my voice because I could hear what sounded like kids' voices drifting up from the carpark. "I'm not going down the weird pseudo-relationship road again, OK? Hatton and I have agreed."

"Oh come on, *please!* I'm bored," pleaded June.

Just then, Paxton bounded into the pool area. "Ladies! The students are arriving! Put some clothes on, you saucy wenches, and prepare for your first classes!"

CHAPTER

23

Parthenope sat in the front row, but you knew she wasn't a swat, just above everything else going on behind her. You could tell she had a princess complex because she was literally wearing a tiara straight out of an early Disney film, or at least a good imitation. She wore it in frosted blonde hair, which I had overheard her tell one of the other kids she had dyed 'ironically', but I was pretty certain that her love of it was genuine by the way she carefully brushed it in the corridor. And at the table the night before, come to think of it. And at that very moment in class, too. She must have seen me looking because she gave me a classic cool girl dirty look, the one that says, "Yeah, I'm brushing my hair *during class.* I cannot be tamed."

I smiled at her in defense, at which she raised a pencil thin dark eyebrow. Did every girl have to go through a phase where they compulsively removed the best part of their brows? And did she just hate me because she was 18 and I was human in her vicinity, or did she know what was going on with her Dad?

Parthenope plonked a bag on the table with a bang and I was momentarily wrenched from my anxiety back into the room. Then I had flashbacks to the Koolux bags of my own youth. Some things never change; the bag, although this time a dinky little metallic rucksack, was unfit for containing anything more than a hairbrush.

I pulled my eyes off Parthenope, making my way to the flip pad at the front of the room. Surely she had no idea about any of my anxieties, she was so tightly wrapped in her cosy duvet of teenage angst.

A couple of other kids had filtered in and sat behind her. Paxton had told me it would be a small class. 'Bespoke' was what he called it, as if I was going to measure them all up for suits as part of the package. A quick glance at the register told me there would only be three students in the class, which felt claustrophobic, almost worse than if I had been thrown to the wolves of a class of 30. I started to feel hot and itchy, like I was under a microscope that was pressing into me, but I swallowed hard and tried to press on.

What would I say, though? "Good morning, class," would be too close to admitting that I was really old enough to be teaching a class instead of taking it. I looked around the room - was I so much older than these kids? Annie, in her crop top and '90s 'oriental' silk skirt, certainly dressed more maturely than I did; the last time she would have been willingly seen in the embroidered Moomin top I had selected for the day was probably before she could vocalise her displeasure. And just because I was wearing Mom jeans, it didn't mean I was old enough to be an actual mum.

While this train of thought trundled on relentlessly, on another track, my brain was flicking through different ways to greet the class at high speed, as if they were all station names blurring behind a locomotive. Eventually, I settled on the casual "Hi, everyone!" Then I gave a wave that was meant to be breezy and fun but was more spasmodic than anything else. The kids would have a field day with that, I was sure. I doubted things had changed much since I was in high school; every idiosyncrasy of a teacher was there to be mercilessly mocked. This would surely snowball into a reputation as the teacher with the nervous tics, which would no doubt cause me to actually develop nervous tics, and then there would probably be an informal school competition to do the best impression of me by Week 4.

Trying to move swiftly on, though it seemed the negative thoughts had been swirling for an eternity, I said, "Let's do the register." I brought up the list of the names on the tablet Paxton had thrust into my hands before class.

What a novelty, I thought. Back in my day, these were all done on paper. Maybe I was getting old after all.

I scrolled through the register, which was meant to be done alphabetically by first name, another change since my school days. Oddly, there was no 'Parthenope', though.

"Parthenope, I can't find you on the register..." I said, already feeling her disdain seep into me.

"Ugh, I told that short guy who runs the place I wanted to be called Annie," she huffed, sinking into her seat, scandalised and uncomfortable.

"Bzzzmgrntamlq, *Parthenope!*" said a boy behind her, his face sliding into an easy smile which immediately marked him out as the class heartbreaker.

"Yeah, I know, right?" she laughed indulgently.

"I'm sorry, what did you say?" I asked.

"B-zzz-mgrnt-amlq," the boy repeated.

"I...I don't know what that means?" I replied.

Now all the class were laughing at me and the room suddenly felt very hot.

"It's his way of saying lol, like what old people say," explained Annie with great relish. I would have lolled if not being confronted with my own mortality.

"Yeah, now we use random letters to show we are making laughing sounds. My signature sound is Bzzzmgrntamlq." I nodded dumbly as the boy's eyes narrowed on me. "Hey, I saw you with Hatton Finch earlier? I loved him in Afghan Hounds! It was one of my Dad's favourite films, we watched it all the time," the boy continued, insinuating himself into Annie/Parthenope's personal space with a lingering hand on the shoulder, which she did not bat away.

"Yeah," she replied, smiling thinly, excited by his touch but trying to appear bored by his question.

"Really, it's just you, y'know, don't..."

"Look alike? Yeah, I've heard that before. I'm adopted," replied Parthenope/Annie, like a bored air stewardess reading the flight safety speech for the thousandth time. "They say they love me just as much as a biological kid. Then again, they did call me Parthenope, so..."

Approving laughter flitted around the room, impressed by Parthenope/Annie's virtuoso defense move of metaphorically punching herself before anyone else could.

I nodded as I checked her into the class. "Annie it is," I mumbled, remembering that Parthenope was one of the sirens in Greek mythology; one of those random bits of information a degree from St Fillan's gives you. She might have wanted to be known by it, but she was already living up to her birth name; flashing Bambi-eyes at the suspected heartbreaker, who smiled at her like she was a fan in a crowd.

"Jesús Ruiz," I said, moving on swiftly to the next name on the register. It was the guy Annie was making eyes at. The name was quite apt, because he clearly thought he was Jesus, turning away from her and beamed a boyband smile in my direction.

"That's me. My mom named me after this pretty cool guy. You might have heard of him. Fed the 5000, pissed off this guy called Herod, came back from the dead?" He mugged for laughs and Annie was only too happy to oblige with her own version of Bzzzmgrntamlq.

"Thank you for that potted history, Hey-sus" I sighed, making sure to pronounce his name correctly.

"Call me *Jeez*-us." he said good-naturedly, as if he was telling me a nickname.

"Oh! It's ok! I did a couple of semesters of Spanish at university, I don't have a problem saying your name properly...I think?" I said, beginning to wonder if my Spanish was rustier than I thought.

"Oh no, it's not that. I just prefer Jesus," he replied. "I'm rebranding. It's for my follow-up to my debut album. It's called the Second Coming."

"Oh, are you a singer?" I asked, imagining Christ coming back for a third time just to put an end to this blasphemy.

"Don't you know who I am?" scoffed Jesus.

"Our Lord and Saviour?" I replied. "I always thought when I saw you that there would be more hellfire, what with the rapture going on. Also that you'd have a beard. But life never turns out how you would expect."

Jesus' chuckle was as slick as his hair. "I love a woman who can make me laugh!" he declared. Annie looked at me as if I was both Jimmy Savile and a romantic threat.

"You sound like an ageing divorcee at a singles bar," said a bespectacled boy to his side.

"How did you know? I got that line from my Dad," replied Jesus, with genuine shock.

I decided it was best to move on quickly to the next name, but regretted it almost immediately. "Koala Freebird Merryweather Gould," I read out, imagining poor little koalas dying in forest fires in an attempt not to laugh.

"Present," came a clipped voice on my left. It was the kid with the glasses, if you could call him a kid; he was one of those people who was probably born in tweed and glasses, their body clock already set at 40. Koala looked not like his cuddly namesake, but a sick baby bird in a suit, his translucent skin covering a network of blue veins and an incredible science nerd vibe that was about to burst out at any moment.

"I too will change my name officially, in due course," he informed the group. "I have been incredibly busy the last year attempting to get emancipated from my layabout parents."

That's where I had heard his name before, I realised. The Merryweather Gould's ran hugely successful Freebird CBD, it had been in the news recently that they had sold it and were using the proceeds to build a commune in County Clare somewhere.

"Do you want to change it now?" I asked. "Everyone else has."

"No, I'm taking time to fully consider my options," said Koala.

"Any ideas?"

"Something dignified and traditional, like Nigel."

Jesus sniggered. "And you said *I* sounded like an ageing divorcee."

"Ok!" I said, attempting to avert possibly the weirdest school fight in history. "And last, but I am sure not least, we have Melody Johnson!" The only student left wordlessly raised her hand with a sweet smile, before tucking some bronde hair behind an alice band. Now here was a middle of the road name for a middle of the road person. I was relieved she seemed so delightfully beige. The many murder podcasts I listened to told me that it was always the unassuming ones like Melody who went mad and killed everyone. If she did, I was sure I would have my hands full with the other three up until that point, though, so death might actually be a sweet release.

However, we had survived the registration process, so maybe there was hope yet. Perhaps we would get to the end of the class without Annie actually shagging Jesus in the middle of the room while Koala vomited in disgust and Melody was just...there.

In bed the night before, I had been thinking about the best way to begin the class - after I was done over-analysing every interaction I had had with Hatton in the last 48 hours. As I drifted off to sleep, I had thought how nice it would be to ask them all what had inspired them to take a course in creative writing. I was wrong.

"My parents are making me," said Koala, shuddering. "They think it is important to 'embrace creativity." He then gagged. Maybe he would be sick after all.

"I saw your photo on the Vintage Vixens Instagram account and thought you had a bangin' bod," said Jesus, leaning back in his chair, observing me as if I was a freshly prepared steak dinner.

"Jesus, this is probably the least problematic bit of what you just said, but 'Vintage Vixens'?" I asked, pulling out my phone and typing the term into Instagram's search bar.

"Yeah, it's this account dedicated to hot older women. There's you, Meryl Streep, Susan Sarandon, young Germaine Greer..." explained Jesus.

He was right. There I was, drinking wine in my bra and pants (June had sneaked a stealth photo and put it on her Insta - thanks). On the grid, I was sandwiched between Meryl Streep getting her hair washed by Robert Redford in Out of Africa and Susan Sarandon prancing around in a corset in Pretty Baby.

"I mean, I am flattered, in a way, to be objectified alongside these very talented and beautiful women, but they are all about 50 years older than me," I said, scrolling through for confirmation; Meryl at the Oscars when I was one year old, Germaine leading a protest for women's rights about the same time my parents were but a glint in the milkman's eye.

"Yeah, but they are all about your age in the pictures," said Jesus, now disturbingly engrossed in the feed himself. "I'm not a pervert, 30 is my absolute upper age limit!"

In that case, I couldn't wait for the stroke of midnight on my 30th birthday, when I would turn into a pre-menopausal, invisible Cinderella in the eyes of Jesus. Pity it was still six weeks away.

"What about you, Parth...Annie? Why did you want to take this course?" I said, turning to her with overcompensating brightness.

"My parents are having issues. I'm about 80% sure they have broken up. My Mum is trying to 'find herself' on a reality TV show and my Dad feels guilty about, well, everything. So, here I am," she said, without looking up from her phone - apart from to see if Jesus was looking at her.

"Melody!" I said, swivelling away from the Finch family car crash. "Let's try and keep it vaguely related to literature," I said wearily. "Like wanting to be an author, or even learning the alphabet, for example."

"I want to study English at university and this course will look good on my CV," she said in the pleasant tone of a personified bland, milky tea.

"Thank you," I said, smiling with relief.

"Wait, Annie, is your mom like 80% single then? I could be persuaded to flex my rules in her case," said Jesus.

Annie sort of smiled, but her face twitched too, unsure whether it was good or bad that Jesus fancied her mum. On the one hand, it was still another (older) woman. On the other hand, in the hormone-addled mind of a teenage girl, it was her mum, which at least inferred in some sort of Ancient Greek incest way that he found someone close to her attractive. Could it be just a hop, skip and a jump to fall in love with her daughter? I prayed I wasn't around to find out.

"Come on, guys, not now. If you're good, we can spend the last lesson deciding whose mum is hottest. I'll even bring in some pics of my Mum on holiday in Ibiza in 1993 if you behave yourself, Jesus."

"Deal," said Jesus, producing a notebook from his jean pocket (I had been beginning to wonder if he was both pleased to see and had a horrible medical condition). "I'm ready to learn! Let your genius seep into me," he said.

"There will be no seeping of any variety in my classroom, Jesus," I said, putting down the tablet and walking over to the whiteboard. Finally, we were moving on to the actual lesson. Finally being the operative word, this whole performance having taken up a good 25 minutes of a 45 minute class. I wondered if they were doing it on purpose, I certainly had back in the day. In high school, we used to ask our very recently and proudly divorced single mother Politics teacher if it was true all men were scum, knowing her reply would take up a good chunk of the class. Many mock exams were missed that way. Was this the rich kid version of that?

I was determined not to let the class get any more off-track, but there wasn't much time to turn the focus fully to writing. Paxton's lawyers were insisting that we all go over health and safety with our class because there had been a few cases of the Baby Botch at a local school. Some of the parents were getting antsy about their little darlings getting diseased. There was no need for these regulations, I thought, as I told them all not to share food to avoid possible cross-contamination, they all had so many unique dietary requirements. Plus there was very little chance of them associating with any of the local plebs when they could continue their digital codependency with friends back home thanks to their phone.

A disinterested fog fell over the class as I spoke, their eyes glazing, which was a symptom of the Botch but also boredom. I could have said 'your trust funds have been liquidated' by the end and they wouldn't have noticed.

I glanced at the clock at the end of my safety briefing. 40 minutes gone already. Everyone else's eyes had gravitated towards the clock too.

"Ok everyone, it's been...interesting meeting you all. Our next lesson will be on Thursday at 10am. I want you to meet me all on the beach."

Melody nodded absentmindedly, Annie was clearly dreaming of a shirtless Jesus, who was still salivating over Vintage Vixens and Koala wrote the note in a filofax as if under duress.

CHAPTER

24

"How did it go?" asked Paxton, shifting from foot to foot outside the Goat Conference Room.

"It was ok," I sighed, suddenly noticing the sweat marks on my top, which suggested otherwise. "It took most of the class just to get through the register though. Remind me, Paxton, why are you doing this, again?"

"I'm going straight, Sam. I want to be a proper business man," he replied, adjusting a bow tie that looked like it had been put on by a three-year-old influenced by Dadaism.

I laughed, but he looked at me seriously, like a real, stern headmaster. He lowered his voice, and leaned in. "I'm not kidding!"

"But why?" I blurted, unable to reconcile my enduring image of Paxton, literally swinging from a chandelier, with this stuffed suit. Paxton sank his fingers into my arm and dragged me back into the classroom, like a tiny pigeon turned bird of prey.

"Hey, come on, what was all that about?" I asked, snatching my arm back in the now empty room.

Paxton paced dramatically back and forth across the worn, slightly stained carpet. "This may come as a shock to you, Sam, but do you remember that night at the reunion?"

"Yes..." I said. Was this going where I thought it was going?

"Well, you know, I had a little rendezvous with Harriet and Allan. Mostly Harriet, Allan was kind of in the background, like a desktop wallpaper framing a porn video."

"Unfortunately, yes..." Was he? Could he be?

"Well, Caspar, the son of Harriet and...well, the child, was conceived that night."

It was true! My suspicions at the airport were right. "What about him?" I asked, innocently flattening a crease in a table cloth.

Paxton took a deep breath. "He's my son."

"NO!!!" I burst out, adding a gasp that came out a little too hammy, but Paxton didn't notice.

"Yes, it's true. Harriet had her suspicions, we had a DNA test done," Paxton said, tugging at his bow tie.

"Does Allan know?"

"Harriet told him, but he changed the topic to the latest Peugeot model being recalled," Paxton said, flopping into Jesus' seat.

"Wow, sounds like he is deep in denial," I said, assuming my place at the front of the class once more. "What are you going to do?"

Paxton shrugged helplessly. "I don't know. They are going away for a few days, Harriet is hoping that she can get through to him."

"But, what are you going to do about Caspar?" I pressed.

"Well, he's why I am doing all this. I want to be able to provide for him. Properly, not just with my family's millions."

"They're always handy to have for a rainy day though, aren't they?"

Paxton conceded with a tired nod.

"I wonder why Harriet told you," I said, flicking through a prospectus, as if it would tell me. "Sure, you're loaded, but she seemed to have her suburban dream with Allan. You know, semi-detached, and not just from reality...company car, stable husband and finally the baby...Why not keep quiet and keep it all?"

"Harriet's more complicated than that," Paxton told me, now the one teaching me a lesson. "You always pigeon hole people. To you, she was a party girl at uni to you, now she is a Stepford wife. People can't be categorised that easily."

"Wow," I said, genuinely taken aback. "Thanks Paxton. I'll be sure not to write you off as a rich kid playboy, you're clearly also a budding psychologist! Where will you be setting up practice? Your armchair, I presume?"

Paxton pushed his desk away with big delinquent energy. "Whatever. You wouldn't understand. Your most complicated relationship is with white wine!"

"It is not! My relationship with red wine is much more complex! Why does some of it stain my teeth? Why are other ones totally fine?"

"I'm sorry, that was a little unfair of me," said Paxton, putting his hands up in surrender.

"It's ok, you're under a lot of stress," I said, putting a sympathetic hand on the rumpled material covering his shoulder.

"No, I mean, it was unfair of me to say that when you are clearly having some complicated relationship with Hatton Finch," Paxton leapt up, a sly smile streaking across his face.

I pulled my hand away and crossed my arms in defence. "That's not true at all, Paxton!" I said as convincingly as I could, which wasn't very.

"Oh come on, you've clearly boned. Or want to. You could have cut the sexual tension with a combine harvester it was so thick last night," Paxton said, finally just undoing his tie and leaving it draped around his neck.

A creeping quiet fell over us. He was smoking me out.

"It only happened once and it's not going to happen again," I said in a small voice.

"I KNEW IT!" Paxton shouted over me. "You guys were dynamite on TV! That's why I wanted you out here. It's like having my own version of Love Island but without the plastic surgery and suicides. Hopefully."

A smile flickered across my face. I shook my head and looked around as if someone could overhear, "It's not like that, Paxton."

"Yeah right. And I'm a self-made man!"

The door swung open and I flinched. Annie appeared, looking sullen, but no more so than usual.

"Forgot my bag," she explained, slipping across to the shiny monstrosity like an unwilling extra onstage.

"No worries, see you later!" I said, smiling and trying not to perspire too nervously/guiltily.

Annie looked me up and down with about two parts pity to one part allergic reaction. "Uhuh," she replied.

With a skulk, she was gone, the door closing behind her.

"Aw, you're gonna make such a great step-mom!" Paxton gushed with sarcasm.

"Oh, shut up, baby daddy."

CHAPTER

25

A couple of days later, I was walking down to the beach for the next lesson with the class. June was missing wild swimming and had decided to tag along.

"So Paxton is the father? The dirty dog!" she said, her flip-flops shuffling down the dusty road to the beach.

Well, I couldn't *not* tell her. The gossip was just too juicy.

"Yeah. And you thought my love life was going to be entertaining this summer," I said, rubbing SP30 into my shoulders, which just seemed to baste them, making them shiny targets for the mid-morning sun.

"What's going on there then?" asked June matter-of-factly, the way she might ask a client what aches and pains they wanted her to concentrate on.

"Nothing, I hate to disappoint you. I have mostly been in my room planning classes the last couple of days," I said, my skin an alabaster testament to this. "How are yours going?"

"Fantastic, thank you for asking. I'm really enjoying it, so much so that I don't mind you asking solely to deflect from my question!" said June, rubbing a stray bit of sun lotion into my arm.

"Ha! Really? What's been going on?"

"Well, we have only had two lessons, but I already have the son of a Tory peer singing the Internationale and putting it on TikTok," she said with a salute. "Wow, look at that view!" June's arm shot away from her forehead and towards the sea now spreading out in front of us, calm and deep blue, the colour seeping into the cloudless sky. "See you later, I'm going for a swim! Put on another layer of SPF 30 in an hour, ok? We can't have you looking like a leather bag by the end of the summer!" June called, skipping off towards the water, shedding her Daisy Dukes and crop top as she went, revealing a red bikini with Hammers and Sickles printed on each breast. You had to give it to her, she was always on brand.

As I followed her down the dune she had just nimbly skied through, I saw Jesus reclining at the bottom of it, his eyes almost jumping out his head cartoon-style at the sight of her.

"Eyes back in your head, Jesus," I said as I passed him.

"Come on, Sam, you know I only have eyes for you!" he said, clambering to his feet.

"Well, I would like to donate them to a more worthy cause. Can you put them in the post to a blind charity?"

"That biting wit is hard to resist. Are you trying to seduce me, Ms Chambers?"

"I must, for both legal and moral reasons, emphatically state that I am not trying to seduce you and whoever let you watch The Graduate has a lot to answer for."

Jesus' eyes were already trailing off behind a woman in a thong bikini. He shook himself back to reality and sauntered off towards Koala and Melody, who were standing underneath a 'BEWARE OF THE DOLPHINS IN MATING SEASON' sign, which had a graphic aroused-dolphin-chasing-human pictogram attached. But who would warn the dolphins about Jesus? I wondered.

Koala and Melody stood in a silence. It was hard to imagine two people who had less in common, apart from maybe Koala and Jesus, who was now trying to give Koala a bro hug. Koala stiffened like an unwilling cow being herded through the abattoir as Jesus took him in his arms. Then Jesus offered him a fit bump, but Koala just looked on, affronted and confused. Jesus just carried on smiling as if he had been asked for a selfie by a fan.

Melody smiled politely at them both - that was it. I was starting to want her to do something, anything a little out there. It was all just so *bland*. Maybe she was a dolphin using a deepfake to catch victims.

"Hi everyone," I said, joining the group. "That's almost all of us....where's Annie?"

Jesus shrugged, "Beats me."

"Over there," Koala said reluctantly, pointing his finger like he was gesturing to an unsightly growth. I followed his hand to find Annie lying on a beach towel in a dental floss bikini, surrounded by professional paraphernalia that reflected and deflected light off her in the most flattering fashion possible. A male photographer, at least 15 years older than her, was snapping away.

Fearful that he was even more predatory than the dolphins and Jesus combined, I rushed over to break up the photoshoot. "What's going on here?" I said, putting myself between the man and Annie.

"God, leave him alone. I hired Ernido to take some pics for the 'Gram. He's a nightclub photographer normally."

"Yes, but there's not so much business in the clubs right now with that Baby Botch thing," explained Ernido, flicking through photos on his screen.

"So you're a nightclub photographer turned child pornographer? She's only 18!" I told him.

"So? She's not a child, she's 18!"

"Well, she will always be a baby to her dad. He is Hatton Finch, the actor, and he kept all his guns from Vietnam Vets 2: High Noon in Ho Chi Minh. He likes to use older men sniffing around his daughter as target practice. Now show me that you're deleting all those photos and get out of here."

Enido deleted the photos with trembling hands in front of me. Annie fixed her eyes on me and redressed, violently knotting her sarong like a garrote.

"I'm so not happy right now," Annie said, clearing up any confusion.

"Wow, that's a turn up for the books. You're usually so full of rainbows and sunshine. Right, let's get on with class for today," I said.

"What will we be doing?" Koala asked earnestly, pulling out a tablet to make notes on.

"Well, you won't be needing that for starters," I told him.

Koala looked down at his device in confusion, like I had just told him we wouldn't be needing our heads anymore, so we were just going to chop them off now. "Wh...wh...what do you mean?" he asked, a clammy film on his forehead sizzling in the sun.

"I just want you guys to spend the next half an hour observing the beach, what's going on, that sort of thing. I don't even want you to take notes. We will meet back here in 30 minutes, ok?"

Jesus was already heading toward a group of bikini-clad girls frolicking in the surf. Maybe he would walk on the water to reach them. Now that *would* make a good story. Annie was following him like a disciple. Koala appeared to be short-circuiting, sort of mechanically rotating left and right in desolate horror. Melody just smiled and did as she was told. I somehow found that the most disappointing.

I looked around the beach, the sand was a burnt orange, sun loungers and towels creating a mosaic effect. I knew I had forgotten something important; with no towel, my ass would just fry on the hot sand, and I was too cheap and Scottish to pay 15 Belkitan Nokos for a sun lounger. Oh well, it seemed like there was no choice but to sit under a parasol at the beach bar, because I was not too cheap to pay 15 Belkitan Nokos for a club sandwich and a beer.

I picked my way through the plastic furniture, none of which quite matched, and found a table out of the sun but with a clear view of the kids. It was right next to where all the fishing boats were unloading their catches and smelt like anchovies, but it would have to do.

I could see that Jesus had coaxed the girls out of the water and was now introducing them to the group, who at best looked indifferent (Melody, of course) and at worst silently seething (Annie). Koala just looked on with pity, a pious priest above the pleasures of the flesh.

Maybe I should write some of this down, I thought, but I had left that lovely collection of notebooks in my room. What a pity, I had had such high hopes that the fact they were furry *and* glittery would somehow give me the motivation to write another book. I really should have beaten myself up about it a bit more, but a waiter was passing, so I waved him down to order my lunch. He took my order with a bright smile and a disposition as sunny as the sky.

"Can I have a tuna melt and-"

I heard a large splash behind me followed by what was presumably much cursing in Belkita. A crowd gathering round the small marina. Old fishermen with skin like battered briefcases were laughing and pointing. I considered going over, but if I left, they might forget about me and then I would never get my sandwich. I settled for dragging my plastic chair round, scraping it across the cement floor.

Eventually, whatever had caused so much hilarity lost its charm for the fishermen, some of them heading towards the beach bar for a pint, others drifting off towards their own crafts. The crowd now dispersed, I could see a very wet Hatton, and a very red-faced Lorando, had been at the centre of the comedy. Hatton looked like he had been through a cycle in the washing machine. He was offering sodden apologies to Lorando, who was patting him on his shoulder as if to say 'it could happen to anyone', but his eyes were still roving around the bay, catching the last mocking glances of the local fishermen. Finally, his eyes crossed with mine and Lorando smiled and waved, smothering his embarrassment in a tight layer of customer service. He looked back awkwardly at Hatton and decided to drag him over to me.

Hatton was mouthing "I'm sorry" to me and also Lorando whenever he turned around to keep tabs on his wet prisoner. "Sam! How are you enjoying your stay in Belkita?" asked Lorando, letting go of Hatton and wiping his wet hand on his 'Captain Lorando' t-shirt.

"Oh, it's been very nice so far, thank you, Lorando," I said, casting a concerned eye over the dripping Hatton. "What happened to you?"

"I fell in trying to tie the boat up," Hatton said, almost as embarrassed as his daughter was by everything. "I think I really showed up Lorando. Again, I'm so sorry."

"There is no need to apologise! I should not have been so presumptuous. You played a champion fisherman and wrestled that tuna in It Takes Tuna to Tango, I just presumed you had sea legs."

"I do, it was just-"

"There is no need to explain," Lorando said, touching a finger to Hatton's lips. "You sit down here with Sam and dry out. Order yourself a rum to warm up too. This is my uncle's bar, tell him Lorando sent you, it will be on the house."

"Oh, that's a nice idea Lorando, but I was just about to leave!" I said, getting up with a start.

"Your sandwich," said the smiling waiter, sliding my meal onto the table. I grimaced, partly because my lie had been exposed, but also because I had been called ma'm.

"Thank you," I said quietly. "I forgot I ordered this." That was probably the worst excuse since Paxton 'tripped and fell' into his girlfriend's best friend in Third Year, but it was all I had.

"Ah, Darin!" exclaimed Lorando.

"Uncle!"

"Go and get this man a rum, eh?"

"Of course! I will get you one right away, sir," said Darin, scurrying off, still smiling.

"Excellent, I better be getting back to the hotel, lunch will be served soon. You two enjoy yourselves here! See you at dinner," Lorando said, heading towards his car.

We both watched Lorando go until his car had completely left the beach, which is more significant than it seems because an entire primary school class went across a zebra crossing before he reached the main road. It was awkward, but we both clearly felt it would be less awkward than actually interacting with each other.

"Well, I'm a bit dryer now, I think I will head off!" Hatton said, standing up.

"Your rum, sir. Enjoy!" said Darin, placing the drink on the table.

"Oh, thank you, but I better be going."

"But, Sir, to refuse a drink is the ultimate snub in Belkitan culture! We used to put people who did it on prison ships!"

Hatton looked at Darin then back out to sea again, then sat down. "I think I have spent enough time on the water today, thank you for the rum."

"No problem!" said Darin brightly, heading over to a burnt British lady who was waving a menu at him.

"Oh well, cheers," said Hatton, who looked like a deflated balloon in his wet t-shirt.

"There's no need to look quite as depressed about the concept of having lunch with me," I said, picking up my sandwich. A greasy bit of tuna spurted out, slithered down my top and onto the floor. A passing street cat hoovered it up.

Hatton watched the cat chew with a sort of reserved horror. "Do you need me to put it in your mouth and say 'here comes the choo choo train?"

"No, surely that's what got us into trouble in the first place?"

Hatton snorted, rum wetting his shirt, which had only just started to dry again.

"I know we said we wouldn't...play here comes the choo choo train abroad-"

"Belkita doesn't even have a railway, for a start," Hatton offered.

"But we can't avoid each other completely. In fact, it will look more suspicious if we never talk to each other. So, the least we can do is have a civilised lunch."

Hatton nodded. "That sandwich does look good. When it's not being eaten by a cat on the floor."

"Do you want some?" I said, taking half and pushing it over to him on a napkin.

"Ok..." he said, picking it up. "So what brings you to the beach?"

"We're doing a class here," I said, taking a sip of beer.

"Well, I hate to be the bearer of bad news, but you seem to have forgotten the children."

"Oh no, they are over there," I said, relieved to see them in exactly the same location I had spotted them at just before I got distracted. "It's independent learning. I'm going to set them some homework at the end of the class."

"I'm sure Melody Johnson's barrister father is thrilled he is paying thousands of pounds for this."

"Well, he can sue Paxton if he isn't happy," I shrugged. "How do you know her dad is a barrister?"

"He's a celebrity divorce lawyer. Aubrey said I might want to..." he trailed off.

A Belkitan beach bar didn't seem the place to unpack all that he inferred. For starters, we only had cracked plastic furniture and this really required a psychiatrist's couch. "What about your classes? How are they going?"

"Urgh, could be better. We are doing stage combat but they are all absolutely terrified of touching each other. It's like a school dance but worse, somehow." Hatton took a dejected bite of his sandwich. "Anyway, how are things with you? Are you writing something of your own too?"

"Who, me?" I said, mid-mouthful.

"Yes, you. It's literally in your job title - Sam Chambers, author."

"Oh, I have been too busy writing lesson plans," I said, the same way people in the office used to say they had been so busy when I had personally witnessed them playing Solitaire for six hours.

"Yes, letting the children loose on the beach is indeed a complicated piece of pedagogy," Hatton said with more than a trace of skepticism as he brushed some crumbs off the table.

"I don't have anything to write with," I sighed, irritated as if I was covered in the crumbs he had just swept away. "I left my notebooks at the hotel. By accident."

"Yeah, yeah," said Hatton, "Your subconscious isn't getting away with one. Garçon," said Hatton, waving at Darin, who bounded over like he was presenting a kids' TV show.

"What are you doing?" I whispered, with only a hint of panicked menace. I even managed to smile at Darin.

"Have you got a spare notepad?" asked Hatton.

"Errr...Sure!" said Darin, reluctantly yet cheerfully producing one from his pocket.

"Sam would like it."

"No I wouldn't!" I shot back, smiling apologetically at Darin. I waved away the suggestion like it was a mosquito. Hatton grabbed my hand and steadied it on the table.

"A notebook would be nice, if you wouldn't mind, Darin," I mumbled. Darin's smile twitched at the corners, but he still acquiesced with dimpled cheeks, taking a notebook out his back pocket and placing it in front of me.

I looked up at Hatton, who also looked pleased with himself. "She probably needs a pen, too, right?"

"Ok," said Darin, sliding a spare from behind his ear and onto the table. "Just don't tell anyone, ok? This Baby Botch thing means we are not meant to share pens anymore."

I pressed the pen to my lips and said "Shh!" only thinking afterwards that I might have smeared Baby Botch all over myself.

"You sure you want to do that, you might catch something," said Hatton. He looked concerned, or maybe it was just that the rum he was sipping was strong.

"Why? It's the *Baby* Botch. I'm almost 30! That's positively ancient by social standards. Darin even called me ma'm," I shuddered.

"He called me sir, too," Hatton lamented.

"Sir is distinguished though. It's powerful, it has gravitas. Thanks patriarchy," I said, taking a gulp of beer for fuel. "Ma'm is a retired schoolmistress with acute spinal arthritis!"

Hatton laughed, perhaps a little too hard. My eyes beamed a sarcastic 'thanks' at him. "That's funny, you should write it down."

It was funny. Maybe I should. I grabbed the no-doubt diseased pen and reluctantly scribbled 'schoolmistress with acute spinal arthritis' across it. "Happy now?" I asked Hatton.

"Yes, I think I am," he said. It was all very earnest and I didn't think he was talking about the notepad, but then I thought, wow, Sam, what an episode of undeserved confidence to think you are such hot shit that it's all about you.

"The lesson is over," said someone behind me. Now *that* was a retired schoolmarm voice. It was Koala, of course. Hatton looked up at him, curious yet skeptical, like he was being shown a mermaid skeleton at a roadside attraction.

I looked around. "Am I hearing voices again?"

"Oh God you're not a pothead like my parents, are you?" moaned Koala.

"No, I'm just a lush. I could have sworn I heard someone say class is over, but, since I'm the teacher, it must have been me, right?"

"I tire of your middle-brow millennial humour, Ms Chambers. I have rounded up the rest of the class and left them in the carpark. Now, I wish to go back to the hotel and work on my emancipation case."

"Fine. You do realise everyone is going to hate you for this, right? Jesus will have your head down the toilet by sundown," I said, getting to my feet and leaving some money on the table.

Koala gave a remarkably casual shrug. "I didn't come here to be liked, I came here because my parents are misguided druggies with more money than sense. Besides, studies show that hate is just a visceral manifestation of respect for those with IQs under 150."

"What studies?" I asked, waving goodbye to Hatton, who was now concentrating very hard on his phone and biting his lip, shaking with what must have been laughter or a sudden fit.

"My own. It's been this way my whole life" said Koala proudly. I nodded as if I understood. We approached the rest of the group, who were all on their phones. Jesus had one vengeful eye trained on Koala, though.

"Ok, everyone, party's over, time to go back to the hotel," I said. Jesus and Annie began to shuffle with dramatic apathy, Melody floating behind. Koala was already halfway up the road out of the beach.

"What even was the point of that 'lesson'?" Annie asked Jesus, laughing at the end just to show that she wasn't actually a nerd that cared about her education.

"Thanks for asking, Annie!" I said with a cheerfulness I used to reserve for passive aggressive emails. "I want you all to write your own account of what happened at the beach today and send it to me by Friday. We will all meet individually during our next class to discuss."

"*Homework?*" Jesus asked.

"Yes. Don't complain, I have just let you dick about on the beach for an hour."

A martyred expression crossed Jesus' face. "Fine," he said, "You're just lucky you're a hot teacher, I would never do it if you were a total dog."

CHAPTER

26

One time I saw someone reading Bae for Pay on the train to Copenhagen Airport and I wanted to die. It was like watching someone dissect your own brain. The girl reading it seemed interested enough, she didn't set it on fire or throw it out a window, but I couldn't help feeling incredibly uncomfortable.

So I could only imagine how it would feel as an angst-ridden teenager to watch your teacher read your work for the first time, or, God forbid, make you read it out in front of a class of your peers; adolescents have an unfortunate habit of turning into Scar's hyenas in such situations. I emailed the class, outlining their task as follows:

From: Sam.Chambers@paxtonacademy.org

To: Annie@paxtonacademy.org; Jesus@paxtonacademy.org; Koala@paxtonacademy.org; Melody@paxtonacademy.org

Subject: Homework

Message:

Hi Class,

I hope you all enjoyed our lesson today. As mentioned, your homework is to send a piece of writing about the visit to the beach and send it to me by Friday. I will then review it and circulate it around your classmates. Please read each other's work and come to class prepared to discuss it.

Send me a message if you have any queries.

Thanks,

Sam

Within minutes, an email popped up in my inbox.

From: Annie@paxtonacademy.org

To: Sam.Chambers@paxtonacademy.org

Subject: No way

Message:

I will write you something but there's no way I am showing it to other people!!!!!!!

I sighed almost as heavily as Annie probably did writing the email. I decided to wait a while before I replied. As long as the rest of the class didn't balk at the idea, then, sure, Annie could play the coveted part of the difficult bad girl. I inched closer to the bedside table to put my phone down, pinned as I was to the mattress by Lily and Brutus, who had decided I was the perfect spot for an afternoon siesta. I managed to manouevre close enough without disturbing them, laying my phone down next to the notepad and pen Hatton had insisted I have at the beach bar. It was too hot to go outside, and the streets of Belkita were always dead from 12pm to 2pm anyway. If I was going to make the kids write, I probably should work on something too. Not that I would show them. Was I just as bad as Annie?!

It seemed such a shame to disturb the pets. As I shifted, they both looked at me like I had just eaten a dog sandwich with a side of cat in front of their very eyes, or, just as bad, given them their flea treatments.

"I'm sorry, but Mummy has to have creative expression," I explained. "Also Mummy has to earn enough money to buy you those expensive treats you both like so much." I took the notebook in hand and blinked her begrudging acceptance. Brutus barked at a lamp.

Picking up the pen felt strange and heavy. It was as if I was a weightlifter trying to hoist a PB after injury. What would I even write about? A mix of dread and anxiety began to fill my stomach. I hadn't written anything more than one officious email to my students in months. Plus, they say those who can't do, teach, and look where I had ended up.

Hatton had believed in me though, at least enough to commandeer a notebook. I was still getting comments on my Instagram asking when I would be writing another book too.

I tested the pen with a scribble, still unsure of what I would actually write. It didn't work, a little ink puttering out to an imprint of the ballpoint almost immediately. That was that, then. I flung the notebook down. This was clearly cursed from the outset. Then a thought began to buzz at the back of my head - I was pretty sure I had a pen in my rucksack. I picked it up off the chair at the hotel desk no one ever uses and rooted around the bottom, feeling an assortment of tampons, hair ties and coins until I found a pen. I pulled it out triumphantly and walked back over to the bed to begin writing, still unsure about what, though. I looked at the pen as if it might tell me. Then the writing on the pen itself caught my eye - 'Copenhagen Coastguard'. Now I remembered getting it after we jumped in the water a few months ago! I had been asked to sign a form promising never to enter the Danish waterways again. Suddenly it was clear where my story would start:

"When you are approaching 30, there's nothing quite like watching teenagers prancing around in thongs to make you want to throw yourself into the sea..."

Soon I had scribbled my way through the tiny notebook and went in search of the nice journals I had brought along with me. My phone buzzed and I flicked through the notifications - the rest of the students confirming they would do the assignment. I momentarily paused my search to reply to Annie:

To: Annie@paxtonacademy.org

From: Sam.Chambers@paxtonacademy.org

Subject: Re: No Way

Message:

Hi Annie,

That's ok, you don't have to share your work if you don't want to. I will keep it confidential.

See you in class,

Sam

There was no reply but I could almost hear her disappointed muttering. The only thing worse than authority imposing itself on you is when it turns out to be quite reasonable, especially when you are a teenager.

CHAPTER

27

The stories rolled in. I sat down on my bed, copies laid out in front of me. My hair was still wet from a swim and dripped drops across them as I got myself comfortable. It was yet another hot day on Belkita though, so the paper and my hair dried quickly as I made my way through my class' submissions.

Annie:

It was so awkward!! Sam just left us on the beach and I had no idea what to do! My Dad says to give her a chance - he brought up something called the Dead Poets' Society and told me to look it up on the internet. Like I am going to do that!! The Wifi here is crap anyway! It's so annoying, I have to stand at the end of the carpark to get enough signal to upload an Instagram Story!!! What is all that about?!?! I don't know why I even bother, all the comments are just about how tanned I am now. It's like, thanks, like I didn't notice!!!

So many exclamation marks!!!!!!

Anyway, Jesus, he's so cool, right, he was talking to some absolute local skanks in the water.

Tell us how you really feel, Annie...

The others were being boring so I decided to follow Jesus. They were all so tanned! I actually thought about pretending to be nice just long enough to take a photo with them! Then I could upload it to Instagram and prove to everyone that I am not *that* tan!! It's not my fault Hannah Linder from my music class needs to wear Factor 50 when it's cloudy in London! And why does she need to bring it up at least once in every TikTok video? Oh, what's that?!?! It's the sound of no one asking, Hannah!

Identity crisis!! Exclamation marks!!!!

That's enough about her. I'm not going to give her Victorian lady skin any more airtime, she will already be buzzing that I have spent so much time writing about it!!!

So Jesus made a joke, it was really funny and we all laughed at it. I definitely laughed harder than all the local girls! I can't remember what he said but it was really funny!! Jesus is the best.

Wtf Annie, Jesus is as about as funny as being assaulted with a tyre iron!!! God, the exclamation points are catching.

The local girls said they didn't want to join Jesus in the hot tub back at the hotel (why?!?!?) so we walked along the beach. I told Jesus they were so weird for not wanting to come back to the hot tub with him and he said "Lol I know right?" It's so nice to find someone who just gets me and thinks exactly the same way as I do!! He is just so gorgeous as well, like a baby lamb with big eyelashes and sex appeal. Is it weird to say that? I better never say that to Jesus.

Why are teenage girls like this?! You are far too good for Jesus. You deserve the actual Jesus, not this cheap imitation who is perving on other girls right in front of you and has the personality of an unneutered goat. You don't know it yet because you have only been exposed to a small selection of douchey teenage boys, but there is so much better out there.

I was gonna say that I would totally go in the hot tub with him but then he might think that was weird too so I just laughed instead. Melody laughed too so I looked at her like 'I will be the only one in that hot tub kthxbyeeee'.

MELODY IS NOT THE ENEMY!! WOMEN SUPPORT WOMEN, ETC.

I walked ahead with Jesus after that. On purpose!! Hahaha. We didn't really talk, it was like we were so in tune with each other that we didn't need to!!

It was not

Then it was time to head back. Koala dragged us all over to the bar to find Sam, which was super annoying because Jesus and I were definitely having a moment.

No, you weren't

I saw she was with my Dad, and I was like, no, it would be too embarrassing to go and speak to them, you have to go alone, Koala. Plus Dad is always a bit weird around her.

Ok, Annie, back in your lane! Let's return to how hot Jesus is!

Also it gave me some more time with Jesus.

Thx bbz

He was looking at the menu and I asked if he preferred Coca Cola or Pepsi. He said he only drank Fanta and I just thought God he is so unique I am in love.

Give me strength and/or vodka

Jesus: There were four absolute hotties in the water, so I went over to introduce myself as soon as Sam was out the way...don't want her getting jealous! There is plenty of Jesus to go around, after all. I could come in wafer form, chicas!

I think I was just a bit sick in my mouth

I was laying it on thick with this one girl who had an ass like Jennifer Lopez if she was a centaur.

This is actually a sort of good metaphor, if very objectifying

It was truly magical. Then Annie popped up and burst my bubble-butt fantasy. I would tell you what her ass is like but I have honestly never noticed. AND the beach girls didn't even want to go back to the hot tub with me. Maybe I am getting older and losing my virility? One of the execs on my last film told me not to waste my time because a male reaches his sexual peak at 16. I think he was full of BS though because he had a 21-year-old model sitting on his lap when he told me that and he looked about 85. AND I just had an absolutely filthy thought about the maid cleaning my room right now. I think I'm ok.

It's like reading a definition of 'problematic'

Also poor Annie, he doesn't even notice her...

I walked along the beach in search of more babes after that. I think Annie was there, I can't be 100% certain, jiggling boobs and butts kept swimming into view, like sexy jellyfish. Let me tell you, I was stung by all of them.

Again he's actually not bad at imagery, it's a pity it's all so questionable

Then that killjoy Wallabee or whatever his name is told us it was home-time.

Lol Wallabee! Howling

Remind me to pants him next time I see him around the pool. He is such a massive cock-block too, he marched right up to Sam in the middle of the restaurant even though it looked like she and Annie's Dad were going to have a little afternoon delight. I learnt that phrase from that movie exec, I didn't get it at first but now I know *exactly* what he was talking about...

I can't believe he went there. Well, I can. When I say Jesus has sex on the brain, I mean it like when someone has water on the brain, an alarming and fatal condition.

Koala:

10.23am, Thursday 23 March, a godforsaken beach, Belkita

Sunny, approx. 23C, clear skies, SE wind

Ms Chambers pulling some sort of Rudolf Steiner on us. Lamentably, my parents would love it. Stranded on beach with classmates. Despise them on principle. All they care about is sex. Melody OK though - she has never actually spoken to me.

Jesus and Annie went into water. Sadly, they survived.

Ok, I did snort at that bit.

Don't know what Melody did. Saw interesting assortment of crustaceans in rockpool. One had blue spots on its back. Took photos to identify later. Quite enjoyable.

Realised the 'lesson' was almost over. Gathered the degenerates. Found Ms Chambers at bar with Mr Finch. They look at each other in weird way. Took photo to identify later.

All this seems like, I can't believe I am writing this, Classic Koala. Emotional detachment, judgement, written like Captain Scott's high school diary. Must remember to destroy any photography.

Melody:

The sea sparkled like a diamond as the sun burned in the sky. Holidaymakers sat on the beach, soaking up the rays of the sun. A seagull swooped down, gliding across the calm sea. The sand was soft and warm between my toes and the air smelt like sun lotion and beer.

So far, so boring

Over by the marina, there was a crash and a splash. Local men gathered around, gossiping like fishwives. A man pulled himself out of the water and sprawled on the deck, as limp as a dishrag. When he stood up, I realised it was Annie's father, Harlon(?) (note: confirm name with Annie).

Yawn

The spectacle over, the fishermen scurried back to their boats. Annie's father looked embarrassed, or maybe he was red from the sun. A man beside him, I think he is a manager at the hotel, looked embarrassed for him.

He saw Sam, Ms Chambers, our teacher (note: check what we should call her) sitting at the bar and walked over to her. He took a seat at her table and they shared some food. They looked happy, like a couple on their honeymoon.

OH FFS

HOW CAN MELODY SPOT THIS WHEN SHE WOULDN'T KNOW AN ORIGINAL METAPHOR IF IT...URGH...HIT HER IN THE FACE?!

I tossed the essays aside and flopped back on my bed. I was frustrated with myself for a few reasons: Why wasn't I better at hiding these things? Why was I getting myself into another situation that could only end badly? And, why was I so mean? Here I was, deriding my charges, calling them boring and sniggering at their names. I never used to be like this. Sure, I was a classic Chandler who used humour as a defense mechanism, but not outright mean.

Maybe I *was* becoming a Karen. I groaned, grabbing handfuls of hair in my hands. I wasn't ready for that, but, though I could not admit it, I was starting to like the idea of a fringe.

A cold horror swept across me.

CHAPTER

28

A few days later I was running through the hotel lobby, on the verge of being late for class. June had lent me her Trotsky biography and I was just getting to the juicy bit where he starts an affair with Frida Kahlo and lost track of time reading it by the pool.

I crossed paths with Hatton in the reception area. I thought I would get away with a mildly harassed wave as I scuttled past, but he wasn't having it.

"Where are you going in such a hurry?" he asked, standing stock still.

I pumped the brakes and halted beside him. "Class! It starts in...well, about 90 seconds ago," I said, glancing at my phone for confirmation. My body swayed, hoping that would be enough to encourage him on his way too.

"Oh yes, Annie said she had one this morning. I should get a move on too," he said, distinctly not getting a move on. "I'm meeting my class down at the beach to practice some Krav Maga in the water. It's good resistance training."

I nodded politely, my mind drifting to Hatton emerging from the water in a clinging wet t-shirt. My hands played nervously with the edge of the tote bag I had over my shoulder. In it was the Trotsky biography, my laptop, the journal I was quickly filling up and...the notebook he had made me take at the beach the week before. I had been carrying it around with me all week as a sort of lucky talisman for creativity.

"Oh! Look what I did!" I said, rummaging in my bag.

"What?"

"This!" I said, producing the full notebook and handing it to him. Hatton took it and flicked through the first few pages, a big proud smile growing across his face.

"Thats, that's amazing, Sam. Well done!" he said, handing it back.

That was weird, I didn't feel any of the usual self-conscious horror of showing my work to someone else. I fanned myself with the notebook. "Thanks!" I said, distracted. "I should really get to class now though."

"No, yeah, me too," said Hatton. We didn't move.

"Come on! You're late!" said a harassed Paxton storming between us.

"Are you feeling ok, Paxton? Is work ethic a symptom of the Baby Botch?" I joked, looking for Hatton's reaction. He was still looking at me. He laughed. I smiled. He smiled. I smiled again, then-

"I have no time for your tomfoolery, Samantha Chambers!" sniffed Paxton. "Now get to class!"

Hatton and I shared one last delicious glance of conspiracy and broke off to go and teach our classes.

Paxton moved off with me, marshalling me to my classroom. "Easy!" I said, shrugging him off. "You need to chill out Paxton. Go and have a martini or something."

He mumbled something dismissive in reply, typing away on his phone. I used the opportunity to slink away, creeping towards my classroom as quickly as I could.

"Oh! Before you go! There's going to be a staff social tomorrow night at Tito's. Starts at 7.30. *Try* to be on time!"

I gave him a thumbs up as I entered the class. At least Paxton always threw a good party, even if he was an anxious mess.

The students had already arranged themselves into a small semi-circle at the front of the class, pulling chairs out from the desks. Annie was talking at Jesus, who was playing on his phone. Koala was regarding them with contempt and Melody was shuffling print-outs of the assignments.

"Sorry I'm late!" I said, plonking my bag on the table. There was no real reaction from the class, who continued flirting, scrolling, disdaining and shuffling. "Right, well, today we will be reviewing a few of your assignments."

"Not mine!" said Annie. Jesus' eyes drifted from his phone to her. Annie looked pleased.

"No Annie, we won't. But I would like you to stay after class so I can give you some individual feedback."

Annie made a noise that reminded me of a popular but disappointed alpaca, a sort of high-pitched braying grunt of complete derision and inconvenience. Jesus was still looking at her and Annie knew it; her too cool for school act obviously got his attention. I felt a bit of sick at the back of my throat.

"Let's crack on with the lesson. I'm going to presume that you all at least have the wherewithal to at least pretend you have read everyone else's work, yes?"

The class looked at each other and laughed nervously.

"I'll take that as a yes, then," I said, opening my laptop. I opened the folder and saw Melody's submission at the top of the list. "Melody, let's start with your piece. Can you tell us a bit about what was going through your head when you wrote it?" I said with an encouraging smile.

Melody chewed her bottom lip - she even drew a little blood, but smiled. "Um, I was thinking about my A level revision notes."

"Really? What was it about the sunny beach in Belkita that made you think of them?" I tried to keep the sarcasm out of my voice, but it was hard.

"There was just a lot of stuff about nature and using similes and metaphors?"

"My tutor gave me those same recommendations," confirmed Koala.

Annie mugged at Jesus as if to say 'Isn't studying for your future the most tragic thing you have ever heard of?' I gave her a glare and she turned sweetly to Melody and said, "I liked the bit about the sea sparkling."

"Yes, you do describe the setting very thoroughly, Melody," I said. Melody daintily dabbed her lip and smiled. "But I would love to see you give the same sort of descriptions about the people in the scene too." Melody's smile fractured a little. "Let's take a look at Jesus' piece, he has a few good examples of that." Melody normally looked at Jesus like he was a cute but naughty puppy, now she looked at him as if he had just ripped her A level notes to shreds right in front of her.

"Jesus' writing, despite being incredibly lewd and worrying, really captures the physical appearance of those around him - see the Jennifer Lopez centaur comparison, as well as revealing his own personality through his descriptions."

"I meant to do that," Jesus said proudly, if a little confused.

"Does anyone want to share their thoughts on Jesus' or Melody's work?"

"I thought Jesus' piece was, like, really insightful," said Annie, catching his eyes. "And, so funny too! The way you pretended that you didn't really notice me!" Annie's laugh was high-pitched and shaky, like it was about to fall off a cliff if Jesus didn't catch it.

Now Jesus looked even more confused. "That bit wasn't a-"

"Koala, did you enjoy Jesus' work?" I interjected. It seemed unfair to let him outright and absentmindedly break Annie's heart in front of the entire class.

"I'm not going to dignify that with a response," tutted Koala. Jesus' eyes lit up as he planned the ways he would torture the poor boy.

"It doesn't really seem like your cup of tea, actually, does it? Your style is much more sparse and Hemingway-esque."

"I used my words economically," Koala said, lining his pens up on his desk.

"Would you like to expand on that?"

"No."

A long, uneconomical silence filled the room.

"Well, I think that you are a really interesting selection of writers," I said. "Melody captures setting very well, Jesus' style is full of personality and Koala boils his text down to the most important information. You all interpreted the same scene very differently; I want you to work on developing your own unique style but learn from your classmates too."

They all looked at each other as if to say 'you must be joking', but, determined as ever, I made them spend the rest of the class editing each other's work. Towards the end, some of them were even smiling and scribbling thoughtfully.

The end of the lesson came and I signalled for Annie to join me at my desk. She slumped into the chair in front of me. It was all classic bad girl - if she hadn't been exactly on time and submitted her work well in advance of the deadline. She shot a glare at me that was both daring and defensive.

"So?" she said.

"Well, Annie, your-"

"It's rubbish, isn't it?" she said, hopefully.

"No!" I replied. She looked downcast. There was nothing less cool than being good at something. "You're a little too fond of exclamation marks, but your writing is very honest, which is a great quality." Annie looked pained, like I told her that her childhood home had burnt to the ground. She might not have wanted to hear it but it was true. I didn't really want to read any more rhapsodies about Jesus but she did have a refreshingly honest approach to sharing her feelings, which should be encouraged. "You make your feelings about other girls incredibly clear, even if you call them 'absolute local skanks' and get hung up on how tanned strangers on the internet think you are. Maybe you could think about the role of other women in your narrative. I'd like to hear your thoughts."

Annie fixed her eyes on a crack in the wall the way you might do if trying to stand on one leg, but also hated absolutely everyone and everything.

"I can't say I see the attraction to Jesus," I continued, "but you really capture the way you feel about him very well."

"Ok, yeah. Great. You said you wouldn't show it to anyone, right?" Annie said with a squirm.

"Of course not. Sharing the manuscript is entirely optional. The important part is self-reflection. What did you learn from the writing exercise?"

"How am I supposed to know?" Annie said as if I had asked her what Napoleon Bonaparte had for breakfast on 3rd October 1774. "Anyway, why do I keep overhearing stuff about you and my Dad?"

"How would I know?" I blurted. Annie stared, as tense as a cat about to pounce on a mouse.

"Sounds like we both have homework to do," she said, with absolutely no intention of doing hers.

CHAPTER

29

A few hours later, June was sitting on my bed stroking Lily while I brushed my hair.

"Paxton really needs to take a chill pill, doesn't he?" she said, rubbing Lily's tummy. "This morning, I made a joke about a class field trip to Cuba and he actually used the phrase "I am not amused, missy."

"Yeah, I think all this having a proper job nonsense is starting to get to him," I said, putting some aftersun on my face in the vain hope it would fade it from porky pink to bronzed goddess. I had spent the afternoon writing at the beach and had lost track of time, again.

"I will make him my signature Hammer and Sickle cocktail tonight, that ought to loosen him up a bit," said June, a wicked smile bursting onto her face.

Then my phone buzzed.

Hatton: Come to my room now! It's an emergency!!

Apparently there was a familial fondness for exclamation marks.

"Shall we head down, then?" said June, taking her hand away from a disappointed Lily.

"Erm, you head down. I will see you there."

"Sam, no amount of aftersun is going to overcome your Celtic colouring," June said, pinching my cheek just to make it a little redder.

"No, it's not that. I have just got a text from Hatton and he says he has an emergency in his room."

"He...has...a bedroom emergency?" giggled June.

"No! June! I'm sure it's not like that," I said, feeling my cheeks go even redder.

"Ok, and I am Priti Patel!" scoffed June. "Just don't be too long, you promised we would take a shot every time Paxton had an anxiety attack, remember?" She wrapped a silk scarf she had found in a Clerk Street charity shop round her shoulders and smoothed out its tassels.

"See you soon," I muttered as she left. Why was I going to his room? I asked myself as I slipped on a pair of sandals. I didn't have an answer; it was up there with the worst of ideas, like invading Afghanistan. Why *did* Annie keep overhearing stuff about me and her Dad? Probably because I pulled shit like this.

A few minutes later, I was knocking on Hatton's door and trying to act normally, whatever that is when you have been summoned to a 'bedroom emergency' of the Third Sexiest Man of 2007. There was some shuffling and light swearing, then the door opened to reveal Hatton in a pair of tight black underpants.

"Help me," he said, standing in the doorway like an appeal for celebrities who have lost all their clothes in a very discriminating natural disaster. He was more tanned than the last time I had seen him in his underpants, that was for sure.

Hatton also swam in the pool for an hour each morning and it showed in the tan lines hovering an inch or two above the elastic waistband of his underpants, which carried a name I was too poor to recognise. Hang on, was he flexing on purpose? Was June right? I wasn't sure how I felt. On the one hand, this 'keeping it professional' malarkey was getting old fast, on other hand, where had he got this move from? 1970s pornography? I expected a pizza delivery boy to turn up at any second.

"What do you need help with?" I asked, snapping into a tired eye-roll.

"I'm fat and nothing fits," he moped, folding his arms across his nipples. He was staring at a pile of clothes on the bed, a mishmash of materials far too good for a mere mortal like me. What use would I have for seven silk shirts if I was a man, or jeans in six different cuts?

"You're joking, right?" I sniggered.

"This is no time for your so-called sense of humour!" he sniffed, rifling through the pile of carefully curated luxury.

"You're being serious? You're having a fat day?"

"Yes, whatever you want to call it," he said, pulling out a pair of white chinos and holding them over his legs. He looked in the mirror pitifully, like his reflection was a former acquaintance he has spotted homeless in the street...who had also got fat.

"Well, you're not allowed," I said, giving him a stern look in the mirror.

"As Parth...Annie, God, I keep getting it wrong, but she's at the age where you have got to respect these things, plus, looking back, I do think 'Parthenope' maybe was a bit unintentionally cruel. Anyway, *Annie* keeps telling me, I am allowed to experience my truth in all its inconvenient complexity."

"No you're not, not when you have the body fat percentage of an orphan in a charity advert," I said, pushing him out of the eyeline of the judgemental mirror.

Then I saw myself. Were my hips *really* that big? Was that my arse drooping out the back of this skirt? Jesus, I thought. First, taking the Lord's name in vain, then, thinking that Jesus was going to have a field day when he saw me in this. I pulled my skirt down a bit in search of a more flattering angle, but I just seemed to smoosh my butt and leg into a mutant bleg.

"Your arse looks fine," Hatton said, looking at a Paisley-patterned shirt with an unsettled expression.

I hurried away from the mirror and busied myself with the pile of clothes. Hatton Finch said my arse was 'fine', I thought, smiling to myself. I mean, it was kind of already implied, we *had* slept together. But how many women could say that their ass had received that specific designation, and could I get that as a badge on my LinkedIn?

"You look fine too," I said, trying to hit 'fine' in the way you might describe the weather, rather than a foxy lady in a blaxploitation film, but I could hear my voice faltering. The result was that I sounded like a tuba with laryngitis. Hatton looked at me sideways so I set off pacing around the room in search of a good idea, or at least an alternative topic of conversation.

Hatton's bed caught my eye, and not in the way June would insist it did. It was the same joyless standard-issue khaki bedspread Paxton had kitted out each room with, but it had given me an idea that just might work.

"Where do you keep your pyjamas?" I asked.

"I'm not Judy Garland. I can't just take a vat of valium and go back to bed for three weeks because I am feeling bloated!" he said, a vein throbbing down his neck and into his shoulder. This was the point in books where we would give into our passions and make out on the bed, but he was actually pissed off and I really wanted to prove I was right, so there you go.

"Pah! You're just bitter Renee Zellweger got an Oscar when you do just as good an impression of old Judy," I said. "Now where do you keep your pyjamas? Behind your pillow?" I walked over to the top of the bed. Hatton's eyes followed me and I wondered if he was wondering if my intentions were pure. I swiped a pillow to the floor with my best remorseless cat stare, revealing that he did indeed keep his pyjamas there, which consisted of a semi-folded lump of black fabric.

"Put these on," I said.

"Seriously?" he said incredulously, like I had just told him that I was going to solve world peace with a dildo and homemade marmalade.

"We're only going downstairs for a drink with friends. Plus, you feel comfortable in them, don't you?"

"Yes, but by that logic, I should just go in my duvet," he said, turning his attention back to the tangled Rubix cube of clothes.

"Your pyjamas are about 10 times nicer than most people's best clothes," I said. It was true; Hatton was one those people that slept in clothes most mere mortals only dreamt of while wandering around Primark. I knew because everyone's standards had been slowly slipping over the last week or two and now most of us rocked up at breakfast in our pyjamas; a plush Noel Coward smoking jacket and pin-striped line trousers for Paxton, oversized punk t-shirts and fluffy sandals for June, my trusty Bananas in Pyjamas ensemble for me and tailored cotton drawstring pants and a marl V-neck for Hatton.

"I can't go down in my pyjamas, everyone will judge me!"

"Pfft. They don't judge you at breakfast! Throw that linen jacket over it," I said, picking it out from the clothes pile, "And that desert scarf thing that you think makes you look like an honorary Palestinian."

"I told you in Copenhagen, I *am* an honorary Palestinian. Yasser Arafat gave me a medal and everything," he said, cautiously taking the jacket off me.

"Put your pyjamas on. Go on, do it for Palestine!"

Hatton smiled and began to get changed. I turned away out of automatic politeness, even though I had seen it all (and more) before. What if he wasn't getting changed? What if I was going to turn round and find him naked on the bed in a gimp mask brandishing a vat of Vaseline? Then my eyes settled on a photo of him with Electra and Annie/Parthenope on his bedside table. Oh, yes, that.

I turned round brusquely and kept my eyes on the floor. "You done?"

"Yes," he said, distractedly.

I looked up to see the cause of his consternation - himself. He was approaching his pyjamaed reflection in the mirror like he was checking out a secondhand car. If he had wheels, he would have kicked them and asked how many miles they had done.

"Not bad, considering," he pronounced.

"That's what that fashion magazine said about my style too," I said, walking into the mirror's gaze. "Actually, it was 'Why does she always wear compression leggings when she very clearly has never had liposuction?'"

"No, but you have dressed up today," he said, turning away from his reflection and gesturing to my outfit, linen capri pants I only ever wore on holiday and a vest top I wore all year round, layering it up and down as needed.

"That's because I get really bad heat rash wearing leggings in this weather," I said, patting down my inner thighs for emphasis. "I learnt the hard way."

"Right," said Hatton, watching me as if the rash might be catching. "Shall we go to this thing, then?"

CHAPTER

30

A few minutes later we entered Tito's as Paxton hurried out on his phone.

"What's up?" I asked.

He stabbed his free hand towards his phone while glaring at us.

"Ok..." said Hatton. "Can I get you a drink?"

"Yeah, sure. A pros..." I said, getting caught up in romantic memories of Copenhagen. Then I remembered the family photo in his room. "A beer, thanks."

Hatton looked a little confused, but nodded and headed towards the bar. I looked away from him to see June sitting in a booth with James. He was grabbing his chest in his hands and hulking forwards while June nodded eagerly, chewing on the straw of her cocktail. She got distracted as we approached and wiggled her eyebrows at us.

"Don't start," I mouthed at her as we approached the table.

We got there just in time to hear the end of James' monologue. "....And that's the exercises Vladimir Putin does to get those pecs."

June wasn't listening though. "Oh hi Sam, did you manage to help Hatton with his bedroom emergency?"

"A bedroom emergency? What's that?" sniggered James.

"Nothing. June's just trying to be funny. And failing. What were you guys talking about, anyway?"

"About the workouts of political leaders. Angela Merkel is lethal with a kettlebell," he said, grabbing an imaginary one. His biceps undulated like walruses about to fight each other.

"No!! Don't be silly, tell me more," I said, banking on the fact people love to talk about themselves.

James murmured some protestations but June piped up with, "Go on, it *is* a funny story."

"Alright," he said, knocking back his orange juice. "Aubrey is great, don't get me wrong. She never complains, even when I make her do 100 burpees in a row. And she has the quads of Lance Armstrong when he was on the drugs but she got them with squats and strategically eating spinach."

"But?" I asked, leaning in so I could hear the juicy gossip over the plasma screen TV. Normally it just showed silent football matches, but it was blasting a Belkita Broadcasting Corporation news bulletin from a distinctly cardboard-looking studio 20 minutes down the road.

"She is just a little...unobservant. For example, Keith and I have lived together for four years. We call our pug dog our son. He, Keith, not the dog, kisses me on the lips in front of her. And yet for some reason she thinks we are just bros who share a one bedroom apartment. At first I thought she was a homophobe, but no, she just lives on Planet Aubrey."

June nodded in confirmation. "James introduced us. I mentioned growing up in Thailand a few minutes in and she looked at me in complete surprise. She said she never would have guessed. I mean, you think quite visibly being Asian might have been a bit of a giveaway."

"Really? You guys must be having me on. I thought she was really woke and aware of the world around her-"

"Sh! Here she comes!" said James, heaving with laughter.

Aubrey approached the table with Hatton. Apparently true to character, she seemed totally unaware of James' quite obvious laughter, even Hatton was looking at him funny, and he hadn't been party to the conversation up to this point.

Hatton slid the beer over to me and made as if to let Aubrey in to sit next to me. To the untrained eye, it was chivalry, but I knew he was having the same pang of awkwardness as me. Aubrey didn't register his offer, instead scooching in close to James. Hatton smiled apologetically and shuffled in next to me.

"Oh James, how is Kevin? I meant to ask during our session today, but I was struggling to breathe from all the prisoner lunges," said Aubrey, sipping on a gin and tonic.

"Kevin is well, thanks. He sent me this cute picture today," James said, showing us a photo of his partner with his dog. They were in a park and there were heart emojis over their eyes and 'We miss you!' flashing above their heads.

"Oh, isn't that nice!" said Aubrey. "You know, you're lucky to have a friend like Kevin."

The rest of the group, including James, stifled sniggers. Even Hatton had worked it out from the picture alone.

"Yes, yes I am, Aubrey," James sighed.

At that moment the television grew even louder and our group turned with irritation to see why. Lorando came over to our table, dripping with shame like a dog that has been caught ripping up the sofa. "Excuse me, my humblest apologies, but you must listen to this announcement, our President is addressing the nation."

Now we all bristled with interest, turning our heads towards the screen.

We saw a short man in a pinstriped suit approach a podium. I was wondering what on Earth it was when Paxton burst in and scooched Hatton up even closer to me so that he could get a butt cheek on the seat too.

Then the President began to speak gravely. The room fell silent.

The only problem was that he was speaking in Belkitan so most of us had no idea what he was talking about. Some statistics appeared on screen and he started to speak more rapidly as lines reached dizzying heights on a graph projected behind him. Lorando would occasionally mutter what were presumably Belkitan swear words under his breath each time the President paused. After a few minutes of this, the President bowed his head to the audience at home and disappeared stage left, only to appear as the credits were running, guided by a researcher, to the actual exit, stage right.

"What do you think that was all about?" Hatton asked the group.

"Oh, I'm sure it's nothing," Aubrey said cheerfully. We all looked at each other like 'WTF' and I am pretty sure June actually said 'yeah, right' under her breath.

"Lorando!" said June, waving him down as he hurried past.

"Yes, June. How may I help you? Another cocktail perhaps?" he said, distracted and breathless.

"No! Don't be silly. What did they say on the news programme?"

"Is it as bad as we thought?" asked Paxton, tugging at his collar.

"Yes, Mr Paxton, the President has introduced new measures."

Paxton ran his hands through his hair, which was looking a lot thinner since we came to Belkita.

"What do you mean by 'new measures'?" asked June.

"This bastard Baby Botch!" cursed Paxton.

"Yes, there are now cases at four high schools in Belkita. We only have six in total, so the situation is quite serious," informed Lorando. "They are closing the schools to stop the spread."

We all looked at each other round the table, hoping someone had more answers. "Does that mean that this school will close too?" I asked, seeing everyone else was as confused as I was. I looked down and realised Hatton and I were tightly holding hands underneath the table. How had that happened? We snatched them away just as June caught sight. Great.

Lorando shook his head. "It doesn't look like it. Private schools will be allowed to stay open, but…"

"But what?!" demanded Paxton, his hair now frazzled and standing on end.

"But we must remain on campus at all times. Staff and students."

Paxton sighed with relief, shrinking like a popped balloon. "Oh well, that's fine, then. Who wants another drink?"

"What do you mean 'that's fine'?!" demanded June. "You haven't even consulted your workers! Lorando probably has a wife and children he would like to see."

"It's no trouble at all!" said Lorando. "I don't mind, it's my duty here at the hotel."

"No, it's Paxton's duty as your employer to treat you well. He got a few of us here under false pretenses too, and now he wants to lock us up with a bunch of hormone-crazed adolescents and throw away the key. I am so not leaving a good review on Glassdoor once this is over." I looked on at June in amazement, I hadn't seen her this animated in months. In fact, the last time I had seen her this fired up was when the right-wing candidate for the Mayor of Beath made the unfortunate decision to do a TV interview outside her shop and she held up a giant sign saying 'CAPITALIST SCUM' in the background.

Paxton smirked like an unimpressed political opponent. "I'm not out-of-touch with the working man," Paxton claimed unconvincingly. "Actually, that's a lie. But I'm not a bad person. Ok, that's a lie too, but I'm like 'Bad' in the Michael Jackson sense. No! Not *that* way!" he clarified as we all looked a bit horrified. "I mean like the song he sang about being a bad-ass motherfucker."

"Qualities every parent looks for in a Principal," said Hatton, rubbing his head in his hands.

"What I mean to say is that you're all free to leave, if that's what you want. I will even keep paying your wages until the school folds, I run out of money and have to flee the country in a speedboat. But aren't there worse places to be locked up for a few weeks?" Paxton said, pulling a netted curtain aside to reveal a glorious orange sunset streaming in from across the bay.

"And I really don't mind spending a few weeks away from my wife and children. The triplets are three and they only communicate in farts and biting. And they're so bad that my wife says if I come near her again, she will castrate me with a scythe. It will be a working holiday for me," said Lorando. We all looked away from this vivid portrait of his family life.

"The hotel gym is pretty good too," relented James.

"It will give us the opportunity to get closer to each other too," said June, glancing down at my side. I looked down too and saw that my hand had crept closer to Hatton's again. They were actually touching. He saw too and we both pulled them away quickly while everyone else was still digesting the news.

"What's this Baby Botch thing anyway?" asked Aubrey. James placed a comforting hand on her shoulder and said, "I will explain later."

CHAPTER

31

It turns out that everyone enjoys drinking during a pandemic. If you're over, like, 20, that is.

"My Dad says you are all drinking in Paxton's room tonight. Do I need to stage an intervention?" asked Annie. Our class was finishing at 4.30pm on a Friday and she must have noticed my rapid-fire delivery of the homework. We had taken to pre-gaming in Paxton's pad because he had awarded himself the hotel's Executive Suite, complete with its own walk-in wine fridge. Tito's Tavern, like all bars in Belkita, was under strict rules to only sell two drinks per customer as the Baby Botch spread. No one was entirely sure what the government thought would happen if you had three glasses of wine instead of two, plus the average age of a Botch patient was 15.5 and you had to be 18 to drink anyway. Lorando told us one evening, "The government is taking no chances. There is still the slim possibility an adult could catch the Baby Botch." Then he apologetically poured our last glasses and collected our government-issued drinks tokens.

"Come on, Annie. What else are we meant to do? We've also been locked up here for two weeks," I said over the clattering of chairs being put away. "Don't tell me that you guys aren't all going to be drinking in the car park tonight."

"No," she said with a hair swish, at once dismissively directed at me and seductively aimed at a still disinterested Jesus. "We don't use alcohol to chase away our demons."

"What do you use? Pitchforks? Fire?" I asked.

"We're not all emotionally repressed like millennials and..." the words stuck in her throat, "boomers. We have therapy? And medication."

"Yeah, I have been on ADHD meds since I was, like, eight," said Jesus, who had grown listless in the lockdown; this statement wasn't even followed up with a declaration of his still hyperactive sex drive.

"Me too! And stuff for my depression," Annie said brightly.

"I still use my SAD lamp, even though we have 12 hours of sunshine a day here," said Koala, the most rebellious thing I had heard him say.

"Junkie," I said, with a wink that made him purse his lips before they collapsed into a laugh. He was coming along nicely. He still wrote as if leaving a terse record of a disaster, but there were glints of humour pushing through too.

"I once snorted cocaine off a Member of Parliament!" piped up Melody. We all turned to look at her in shock - not that we believed the claim for a second, but we were stunned at this use of dry humour. It certainly wasn't taught alongside simile and metaphor on the A-Level syllabus.

Our shock cracked as quickly as it formed and we all laughed. Even Annie said, "Good one, Melody!"

I said. "If you're all not too drug-addled, can you all remember to bring your revised chapters to the class on Thursday?"

There were mutters of 'yeah, yeah' over the scrape of chairs as they left the room. I went over to the window to watch the wonderful Belkitan sunset that had persuaded me to stay. It was beautiful but also made me feel itchy; it was a major First World Problem but we were all starting to feel trapped in the four-star hotel. It was a bit like being a strange assortment of animals left behind at a deposed dictator's abandoned personal zoo, pacing pointlessly around our cage, only with slightly less chance of cannibalism. Plus, as the boundaries grew tighter around us, the more they blurred in here. Not only was I casually discussing drink and drugs with my students, I was beginning to wonder if it really would be so bad if something started up with Hatton again. The answer was quite clearly yes but it didn't stop me dreaming about it when Koala went on another rant about the youth of today.

Paxton had also been in a better mood since the country had shut down. The courses were being delivered as normal, and all the parents had agreed their darling babies should stay here instead of attempting to get home and possibly being infected on the way. So far, no one had displayed any of the classic Botch symptoms. This, plus a steady stream of martinis, calmed Paxton's nerves. I knew I would find him with one already in hand, probably looking at his phone. There always seemed to be a new message from Harriet, which he quickly flicked away whenever he spied you approaching the bar. I wondered what he and Harriet were working on. Was she leaving Allan? It seemed unlikely. As terminally dull as he was, I always thought they would be together until the end. Harriet wasn't exactly the biggest fan of change; one time a bar ran out of her favourite sweet potato fries in St Fillan's and she went hungry because she didn't want to risk 'not liking' the cassava alternative. Even though she was trying to fit into her graduation dress and saved up her days' calories specifically for that purpose. Paxton was the human equivalent of a cassava chip (perhaps dunked in gold, but a cassava chip nonetheless). My curiosity was piqued though, and I resolved to try and wheedle some information out of Paxton before the night was over.

That's why I headed over to his room a little early. Some one-on-one time was needed to draw it out of him. His door was unlocked; it was easier than having to constantly open it for new guests, also it allowed the pets to wander in and out. An evening wasn't complete until June and Leni were harmonising to Joan Baez, Brutus was snapping at Paxton's ankles and Lily had knocked a bottle of champagne off the counter.

Fittingly, everything in Paxton's room was as shiny and white as his heritage; the massive leather sofa, the marble floor, the shag pile rug, the wallpaper. Other than that, it had the same vibe as his dorm room in Freshers; The Bloodhound Gang's Greatest Hits drifted out into the hallway, the same aroma of spilt alcohol and he had draped the same old flag with his family's coat of arms (a unicorn spearing a Frenchman on its horn) above the (also shiny white) fireplace. I opened the door quietly and saw Paxton hunched over his phone at the 'breakfast bar' that was only ever used for drinking. I took off my clunky sandals and tiptoed up behind him.

"Who you texting?!" I ask, grabbing his shoulders.

The words 'Harriet Benson' were quickly swiped off his screen. "Oh, it's nothing," he said, putting his phone down on the bar. It immediately started dinging, the message 'Harriet Benson: WE NEED TO TALK!!!' flashing up before he could turn his phone over.

"Come on, Paxton, what is going on there?" I demanded, hopping onto the stool next to his.

"Harriet and I are having an affair," said Paxton with a dramatic sip of his martini.

"How? You're not even in the same country," I said, mouthing the words 'White Wine' to a passing Lorando, making sure to mime a big glass with my hands.

"It's an affaire de cœur. Or at least that is what Harriet calls it. I think giving it a fancy French name makes her feel better about Whatsapping each other dirty pictures at 3am," Paxton said with a grin almost as wide as the martini glass at his lips.

"Oh God," I said, feeling slightly ill. "I did not need to know that. Wait, is that why you've looked permanently jet-lagged recently?"

"Pretty much."

"And here I was thinking it was from all the stress and hard work," I said as Lorando hurried by, pressing a glass into my hand.

"Well, there is that too. Harriet gets really turned on when I talk about my successful business. The kinky vixen."

I swallowed a sip of wine but it almost immediately hurled itself back out at that statement.

"There's also the time difference thing. It's been very stressful, being in highly charged international sexual congress during one of the great crises of our time," Paxton said.

I looked around. Why was no one else here yet? How much more of this did I have to hear? In fact, how much more of this could I even *withstand* hearing?

"Y'know Sam, it feels good to get this all off my chest. You're one of my oldest friends and I am so glad you are here. That's one of the reasons Harriet wants to come out here," he said, his phone now vibrating like a possessed dildo.

"Is that her? Wait, she wants to come out here and see you...me...us?"

"It is. She says she can't spend another week at the cabin with Allan. They got stuck there when the Baby Botch hit the UK. She wants to leave him and bring the kid out here, but all those international travel rules are making things difficult. They won't even let my private helicopter land in a nearby farm to pick her up, for Chrissake!"

"Wow, are you sure you're ready to shack up with her, you, the eternal bachelor?"

"Oh, it's not like that. Sure, I will get to see...my son, but she really just wants a change of scene," Paxton said, trailing his fingers along a row of mini-cacti lining the bar.

"Wow, for someone so...experienced...I didn't think you could be so naive," I said as he flinched at a prick.

"Ouch! You're casting aspersions, Samantha Chambers."

"It's not an aspersion if it's true! Harriet has never just wanted 'a change of scene'. She only went on that holiday to Malaga in Third Year because there was a rumour that George Clooney had a yacht there and a predilection for college co-eds."

"Yeah, right. My Harriet would never do something like that," Paxton said, waving me off with an olive speared on a stick.

"*Your* Harriet?!" I said, white wine catching the back of my throat.

"Yeah, like *your* Hatton!" Paxton shot back, his perfect little expensive dentist teeth glinting at me.

"It's not like that!" I said through gritted teeth.

"Yeah right, and I'm going to take a vow of abstinence and live in a Tibetan monastery!"

"Ok, well maybe it is a bit like that," I relented. "But it just wouldn't end well. Again. It's not like, I can't believe I am saying this, you and Harriet?!"

"That's true, nothing *can* compete with our love," Paxton said matter-of-factly.

"Yeah, it really is...something else," I agreed. "I don't know, it's just like we missed our time? He's already married and has a kid."

"Sounds pretty like Harriet and me!" said Paxton, giving me an encouraging nudge.

I was both a bit insulted and comforted. I patted Paxton's hand and he gave mine a tight squeeze. Maybe it would all work out, I thought. Just as soon as I had entertained that thought, a cold wash of reality came over me and I snatched mine away.

"It's nothing like you and Harriet! The kid is yours - I'm pretty sure I didn't give birth to Annie. I think I would remember that. Plus, Annie thinks I am even less cool than her actual parents."

"Oh, that's not true!" said Hatton, swinging into the seat beside me. "Only yesterday, Annie said you were 'nowhere near as bad' as she thought you would be."

"Oh er, well," I spluttered, my face going red.

"What are you guys talking about? I only caught the end of the conversation," Hatton asked innocently while Paxton giggled devilishly.

"The Baby Botch," Paxton swooped in to my rescue; my suffering must have ceased to amuse him. "It's tough getting the kids to listen to the restrictions when they think they know everything."

"That's true," Hatton said. "I told Annie the other day to be careful because anyone could get it - and she said anyone who isn't ancient. You want to know what her definition of ancient was? 25!"

We all shuddered, but I was also sighing with relief that Hatton had bought Paxton's story.

"What's the latest on the Baby Botch, anyway?" I asked. "Didn't you have a video call with the Health Department this morning, Paxton?" I trained my eyes on him, carefully avoiding eye contact with Hatton. We still hadn't spoken about the whole hand-holding thing and I thought it would be best to avoid all contact, physical or otherwise, to prevent a repeat indiscretion. I needn't have bothered though because Hatton appeared preoccupied with his stool, luckily the chair kind.

"Why won't this bloody thing work?" he vented, frantically pumping the lever that should have made it go up or down.

"Hey, don't worry, I will get Lorando to take a look at it. Just swap it for the one next to it," Paxton said, spinning around on his own chair.

"But it's my chair. I always sit in it. Why should I let Lorando look at it when I am perfectly capable of fixing it?" Hatton ranted. "I played a carpenter once!"

"Really? When?" I asked.

"I was the Baby Jesus in a nativity but he grew up to be a carpenter, didn't he?" Hatton snapped as the seat sunk to the floor. "It should be instinctual."

Paxton and I shared a worried look. "Hey buddy, we will leave you to it. You show that chair who's boss! Sam, walk with me," said Paxton, leading me cautiously away from Hatton, like we had accidentally stumbled into the lion enclosure at the zoo.

We went out on the balcony, leaving Hatton trying to beat some sense into the chair. Paxton produced a fat cigar from his jacket pocket and clamped it between his teeth.

"What's up with him?" I whispered as he lit the cigar. Paxton blew out a waft of smoke that smelt like an old leather shoe recovered from a septic tank.

"Eh, don't get too bent out of shape about this, but Electra was in the Daily Mail sidebar of shame today cavorting with her cheerleading coach."

"Oh," I said, suddenly becoming very interested in the pornographic mermaids that were carved into the balcony.

"Don't worry, he still has the hots for you," said Paxton, rubbing a mermaid nipple. "Hey, maybe if we rub them then it will bring us good luck! Like that Greyfriars Bobby statue back in Edinburgh."

"I'm not worried," I said, feeling my eyelid begin to twitch. "Like I was saying, it's a stupid idea. Never gonna happen."

"As Trotsky said when they shipped him to Siberia, "PASS THE VODKA!"

June was in the house.

"Hatton - what did that chair ever do to you?!" Paxton and I turned round to see June shooing Hatton away from the stool. She put her bottle of vodka on the bar and bent down to inspect it, all the while waving Hatton away with one hand.

Hatton skulked away and came to join us on the balcony. June unscrewed the vodka bottle with her teeth, spat the lid onto the bar and took a gulp. Then she got to work pulling and prodding various bits of the chair.

"She says she used to have one just like it," explained Hatton. "I thought I would leave her to it."

"I better go and call Lorando to wipe down the bar," said Paxton. "She has probably just spat Baby Botch all over it, the vodka-soaked lush."

Paxton disappeared in a stinky plume of cigar smoke. When it eventually cleared, it was just me and Hatton on the balcony.

"So...how are things?" I ventured.

"What?" said Hatton, checking on June's progress with the chair like an anxious father.

"How are things?"

No response, he was nibbling nervously on a nail and flinching every time the seat went up or down. I huffed, but then I remembered my journalistic training - make the headline sensational to catch attention.

"So I hear your wife is banging someone else on the front page of the Daily Mail?"

Hatton's eyes snapped away from the chair and clamped on to me. "Excuse me?"

"That's why you're in this mood, isn't it? No one can be that obsessed with a chair," I said, feeling far more irritated by the situation than I should. Of course someone as alluring and sensual as Electra, the woman who once didn't get the part of Aphrodite because she was too pretty, could inspire these feelings in a man. Not someone like me, I don't drive men to distraction. I drove Paxton to the airport once, that's about it.

"No, it's not," Hatton said, fixing me with a stare. I hadn't seen this look before, like Mr McGregor about to finally blow little Peter Rabbit's brains out. "It's..." he said, trailing off, waiting for me to fill in an answer I didn't know, to tempt me out of my burrow. He knew me well - the silence smoked me out.

"You know, I don't care if you're upset. I'm upset by most of the Daily Mail, and my wife isn't in it messing around with someone else," I said, now just needling him, like Peter Rabbit deliberately chewing up a crop just to get a reaction out of the gardener.

Hatton had switched to serenity though, watching the sun slowly drown offshore. "I'm really not bothered," he said and I believed him.

"Well...well...why aren't you bothered then?" I said, missing the fight already. At least I had something to be angry *against*.

"It's not strictly true, I'm bothered about not being bothered, actually," he said.

"Oh?" I said, feeling like I was a somersault behind him in the mental gymnastics. "Wh...why are you bothered...about not being bothered?"

He looked at me as if to say 'the answer is obvious'. It wasn't to me, but I preferred this more antagonistic approach rather than looking out into the distance like he was a romantic lead in a film I would never watch.

"I don't get it," I said, firmly folding my arms, but I couldn't quite look at him now because it felt like his eyes were pinning me between the pornographic mermaids whenever I looked up.

"Ugh, you really don't have a clue. I'm going to have to say it, aren't I? I couldn't care less what she is up to because all I can think about is you," he said, stooping down into my line of vision, speaking matter-of-factly, like it was a medical diagnosis he had come to terms with. Then he smiled and I also found myself smiling against my better judgement.

"OK, so I occasionally think about what on earth I am going to do with Annie too. She told me she loves Jesus the other day. I didn't see Christianity coming as part of the teenage rebellion."

I laughed. "Jesus is a boy in her class!"

"Oh, thank God. Or Jesus. Someone up there, anyway."

"It's fixed!" shouted June. "Get your arse back in here, Hatton."

We both turned with a start. I began to walk in but Hatton caught my arm. "I can't do a whole summer of this. Please tell me it's not just me. I'm not sure I can survive the embarrassment of having a bigger crush than my hormonal teenager does and the person not even liking me back."

It felt strange to have that much power over someone. Previously the greatest influence I had exerted was a guest spot as a wine critic in the Beath Enquirer; but this mostly felt like a mixture of relief and the sort of happiness I think people on the right doses of their medication experience.

"It's not just you," I said, a smile squirming out across my face.

"Oh, what a relief!" Hatton said, letting go of my arm and laughing like he had been given the all-clear about some health condition.

"Although, I think I spend a lot of time thinking about not trying to think about you. I guess it's a bit like you being bothered about not being bothered?"

"That's good enough for me," said Hatton, wiping his forehead. "I meant that to be a metaphorical wipe, but it turns out I am sweating like Paxton at a paternity test."

"You heard about that?!"

"He keeps asking me what I would do if I suddenly found out I had a love-child then showing me pictures of a random kid, so yes."

"GUYS! Come on! This vodka won't drink itself!" shouted June.

"What about an actual, proper, date tomorrow night?" whispered Hatton as we walked back in.

"OMG are you, like, asking me out?" I twittered back under my hand.

"Yeah, I am," Hatton said in a way that sounded very grown-up and matter-of-fact but also very sexy at the same time.

Paxton thrust a couple of glasses into our hands and it was all over, until tomorrow night, I told myself.

I took a seat next to Aubrey and James, who had arrived in the interim. Hatton sat in his (favourite) chair next to me. "Thanks June, you've done a great job," he said, even though he sunk several inches when he sat in it.

"Lorando has agreed to do a cheeky tasting of some local wine for us," Paxton told us. "The glasses you have in front of you are filled with the finest Belkitan wine!"

"This has to be illegal, we aren't allowed this many people drinking together in the bar!" I said, immediately regretting it. BE COOL, I told myself.

"Sam makes a good point. This is actually punishable by three years in jail at the moment, but it's not much different to how we live at the moment, so, who cares?" said Paxton, downing his glass. We all nodded, shrugged, and followed suit. "I promise to use my toilet to make the booze when we are all in the penitentiary!" vowed Paxton. Lucky us.

Paxton's declaration elicited some applause, no doubt fuelled by the half-empty bottle of vodka on the kitchen counter. Lorando propped open Paxton's door with a crate of wine and we cheered more. He waved off the applause and nudged the crate in, shutting the door behind him.

"Lorando, my good man, what's up first?" Paxton asked.

Lorando heaved the box into his arms and staggered over to the counter. He dropped it down with a clatter and retrieved a bottle from within. "This is a bottle of Karkalo, a red wine found only in Belkita," Lorando said, humbly displaying the rustic clay container to us. "It has notes of Sunny D and petrol and is responsible for 75% of teenage pregnancies on the island."

"How appetising," I said, bringing it cautiously to my lips. "What contraception do you recommend pairing it with?"

"Sam, this is Belkitan culture! Do you think you could maybe be, I don't know, less culturally imperialist in your outlook?" Aubrey gasped, looking apologetically at Lorando, her easily offended eyes saying 'sorry for the bigoted Brit'. Hot shame flashed over me, I had just thought I was being funny. Was I a massive racist?

A message popped up on my phone.

Hatton: Don't worry, she gets like this when she drinks vodka

"I'm sure there is a fascinating story behind the name 'Karkalo'," said Aubrey, pressing on. "The Belkitan people are so smiley and friendly," she said, pausing for a sip while I suppressed the urge to call out the fact 'smiley and friendly' are rich racists on holiday terms. "Karkalo must have a very lyrical and romantic meaning."

Now I turned and looked apologetically at Lorando, because I knew there was no stopping the Aubrey train once it left its station, even though it usually ended up at the wrong destination and ran everyone over on its mission to enlighten them.

Lorando looked hesitant, his eyes darting back and forth between an eager Aubrey and the wine he was pouring. "The name comes from a Belkitan legend," he said with an obliging smile.

"I knew it! How romantic!" said Aubrey, clapping her hands together before resting her chin on them like a child at story time. "Tell us more, Lorando!"

"Oh no, I really shouldn't," Lorando said with a bashful shuffle. "You are all very important people, you don't want to hear a silly little story from Belkita!"

"Lorando, don't be ridiculous! You might not know this, but cultural exchange is incredibly important. I have learnt so much from June's traditional Thai tales."

June nodded eagerly, but I saw a distorted smirk projected through the wine glass she used to cover her mouth. Ever since June had realised how simultaneously gullible and woke Aubrey was, she had been feeding her increasingly outlandish tales about life in Thailand, including that her local village worshipped a chicken called David.

Aubrey grinned encouragingly at Lorando, who smiled back, but much more warily.

"Well, if you insist. After all, there is a traditional Belkitan saying, 'A man cannot deny a woman his fat tuna if she asks twice."

"Is that euphemistic? I really hope it is," I said, losing patience with this pantomime.

"Sam, please!" glowered Aubrey.

"It's ok, I really don't mind, we joke about it too," said Lorando.

"Let the man speak his truth!" continued Aubrey. I heard a hacking sound next to me, it was Hatton, who had snorted the red wine out his nose. He was dabbing it vigorously with a napkin. I would have thought it was a nosebleed if it wasn't for the spluttering and the fact the napkin was now stained the exact same shade as his half-empty glass.

"Sorry, Lorando. I didn't mean to stomp on the history of Belkita with my WASP witterings," I said sincerely, because I would never *really* want to offend Lorando or any of the other good people of Belkita - just Aubrey when she was on a white saviour crusade.

"Do not apologise, Sam. I know you are a storyteller, so I hope you will appreciate this tale." Lorando poured himself a large measure of the red wine, looked nervously at Aubrey and necked it.

"So, the story of Karkalo, aka Baby Blood!" he said, smacking his lips together. "It concerns our island neighbours, the Fuctifanos. They are-"

Aubrey squealed and said, "Oh, the Fuctifanos! It was a Scots sailor sent ashore to establish first contact who gave them that name. Alas, he could not understand the language, so when asked by his comrades what the island was called, he shrugged his shoulders. But then, a wave of inspiration hit him and he said," Aubrey now took a dramatic breath "Fuctifano', he pronounced. Must be Gaelic or something."

Now Aubrey was interrupted by a squeak of laughter from June, which set me off, because we knew the real story. "I'm sorry, Aubrey," she said. "But every Scottish person knows that the sailor was *really* saying 'Fucked if I know' when he was asked what the island was called. Classic colonialism."

"They have another name for themselves, but I can't remember what it is," Aubrey said, blush burning her cheeks. "Anyway, wonderful people."

"Well, we hate them," said Lorando, apparently emboldened by the wine.

"Excuse me?" said Aubrey, smiling pleasantly but chafing with the intolerance.

"Our two nations have a deep dislike of one another," clarified Lorando, a seriousness coming over his face.

Aubrey blushed again, embarrassed on behalf of white saviours everywhere.

"I do not want to offend your refined sensibilities, Ms Markowitz, but there has been much trouble and strife down the ages between our two nations," Lorando continued gravely. "And the story of the Baby's Blood is no exception."

"I am so here for this," I said under my breath as Hatton passed me a contraband bowl of nuts - communal food had also been outlawed.

"But the Belkitans are always so sunny and friendly..." said Aubrey, doubtfully.

"Yes, but 'vengeance' is also enshrined in our national constitution. We are a complicated people," explained Lorando. "Where was I? Well, the Fuctifano had yet again invaded our brave island country."

"I was an extra in a film about one of those wars...Didn't Belkita invade them a lot too?" asked Hatton.

"Oh, we only ever defended our home country against the threat they posed across the sea with a few strategic military operations."

Hatton nudged me and showed me his phone, which was open on a Wikipedia page:

Belkitan War Crimes in Belkita, 1475-present day.

I suppressed a snort.

By now the whole table was listening intently to Lorando. "Anyway, our proud nation was once again attacked by the Fuctifanos. Our people sought refuge on this very spot! The main fort used to be here."

Everyone looked around in amazement at Paxton's standard-issue White Man Who Has Watched American Psycho Too Many Times suite as if they could see angry medieval men wielding swords at each other.

"How fascinating! So much history!" Aubrey told us. The subtext was, you're all a bunch of knuckle draggers who wouldn't know history if it clubbed you over the head and dragged you back to its cave.

"But it was not a safe refuge," Lorando continued, solemnly shaking his head. A pantomime gasp from Aubrey prompted the rest of us.

"The Fuctifanos invaded the fort and told us the brave Belkitans could live, on one condition."

"What was that?" asked Aubrey. "Did they traffic the women? Or tear babes from their mothers' bosoms to raise as child soldiers! You know, the Fuctifano have really gone down in my estimation."

"No, they said we must pay a tax for every child under 2 on the island."

Everyone exchanged looks that were all a variant of 'What? No rape and murder? Just a tax? Bit boring, no?'

"So, of course, the natural reaction was to catapult all the newborns at the enemy. If the drawings in our school textbooks are anything to go by, it was very messy. But at least they were not used to finance the Fuctifano reign of terror. And that's why the wine is called Baby's Blood. The end." Lorando picked up the bottle and studiously topped up everyone's glasses, but a few people, including Aubrey, pushed theirs away.

"It does seem a little...extreme," said Hatton, observing his own glass warily.

"Well, it's not personally how I would handle the situation either," admitted Lorando. "Ask the Belkitan Revenue Service - I always pay my taxes! And Baby's Blood is known to make people do crazy things. What's crazier than catapulting your offspring at an invading army?"

Aubrey gazed at Lorando in bewilderment, wondering who had given permission for her noble savages to go wild.

"Don't look so scandalised, Aubrey!" I took great delight in saying. "I mean, Catholics like to pretend wine is the blood of the Messiah when they drink it. Isn't that cannibalism? What's a bit of misplaced infanticide at the end of the day?"

"The Catholic Church *does* have a lot to answer for. The things Sinead told me when we were living together!" said Aubrey.

"O'Connor?" I asked Hatton.

"Yep," he confirmed.

"Lorando, I am so sorry. It was wrong of me to apply my perceptions of morality to your culture. I will compose a tweet owning my error of judgement and asking for your forgiveness," said Aubrey, picking her phone up off the table.

"There's no need! I don't even have Twitter," said Lorando.

"Oh, that doesn't matter," said Aubrey with a good-natured smile.

CHAPTER

32

"What will we do?" asked Hatton.

"What *can* we do?" I replied, staring at the glittering chandelier above the lobby, which had grown faded and yellow in my mind from seeing it every day.

"Tito's? Again?" Hatton said unenthusiastically.

"No, everyone will be there. Plus that's what we do every night."

"What about a walk around the garden?"

"I have walked Brutus around that bloody garden every day for the last 40 days. No."

"Well, I'm out of ideas. What do *you* want to do?" said Hatton, smiling awkwardly at one of the kids in his class passing by.

"What I really want to do…"

"Yes?"

"I want to get a haircut. A fringe to be exact. But it's not exactly a *date*, is it?"

"It could be! I'm an excellent hairdresser!" Hatton said, looking genuinely excited.

"Really?"

"I picked up some tips when I was in Bad Boy Barbers."

"What was that? Gay porn?"

"No! It was about how hairdressing lifted one boy from South Central LA out of a life of crime. I was hopefully miscast. Obviously," Hatton said, scrolling through his phone to show a photo of him in the early '00s dressed as a poor white imitation of Nelly in baggy jeans, basketball shirt and bandana. "BUT I did learn a thing or two about hairdressing. Can you keep a secret?" he asked, leaning in just close enough for the girl on reception to raise her eyebrows in a combination of disapproval and jealousy. I leaned into Hatton's ear, more to annoy her than anything else.

"No," I breathed. "It was actually me who told the Americans what cave Osama was hiding in."

"Well, I will tell you anyway; I haven't been to a barber in 15 years," Hatton said, still leaning in close, like he was telling me what the safe word for the evening in his dungeon would be. I pretended to be scandalised but also totally up for it, placing my fingertips over my open mouth. The receptionist's eyes darted back to her screen, her eyes quivering like outraged poached eggs.

"It's because I hate small talk," Hatton said, leaning back out. "I was over the moon when I learnt how to do a short back and sides on that film. It's in all my contracts that the hairstylist can't touch me. They probably think it's because I'm an aloof arsehole, but it's actually because I freeze and temporarily go blind if someone asks me if I am going somewhere nice on my holidays."

"Lol, that question is a bit redundant when we can't even leave the property," I said.

"Let's go back to my room. Or should I say, my salon?" said Hatton, already starting to climb the staircase.

The receptionist's eggy eyes looked like they would fall out in moral outrage at any moment; a 'salon', she had never heard it called *that* before, the cleaners would surely have their work cut out cleaning up the bodily fluids tomorrow morning.

"Come on, what's the worst that could happen?" Hatton asked, beckoning me up the stairs.

"A mullet? Scissor to the eye? Septicaemia?"

"Hey, you would suit an eyepatch. Plus, whatever I do will be better than your current hairstyle. What do you call it? Bedraggled llama?" he said, tugging at my (unintentionally) messy ponytail.

"Joke's on you, I consider llamas to be proud and intelligent beasts," I said, smoothing down my hair. Jeez, I really did need a haircut. Hopefully Hatton had sheers.

"Llamas are also very stubborn. I should know, I had to work with one on a TV show a few years ago and it spat in my face every time I got near it. Not to give you any ideas."

If only the receptionist could hear us now, I thought. We were now at the top of the staircase, but she was still watching us while drawing on a map for another customer. Maybe she could lip read and thought llamas, scissors and saliva were all part of our sick evening.

As we walked along the corridor, Hatton rummaged in his pockets, I presumed looking for the key fob to enter his room. Was this Toaster redux, I wondered? Could he actually cut hair? Did I really care at this point?

"Here it is!" he said, producing a fancy-looking Swiss Army knife from his pocket. It triggered a fuzzy memory of Hatton in a black turtleneck wielding one, surrounded by snowcapped mountains in an advert.

"It was a freebie from an ad campaign I did," he confirmed. "It can do practically anything. It even gets WiFi." A blue LED light flickered on its side.

I forced a smile. God, why did men get like this about gadgets? Had he forgotten the scantily dressed spectre of sex looming over our entire relationship? I had already zoned out, if I had to listen to anymore then I would just go back to my room with a different type of gadget and do it myself.

"...and it even has a compass!" he babbled. I nodded absently and he noticed. "But, er, why I was gonna show you this is that it has a really good pair of hair scissors. Here, look," he said, a pair of tiny silver clippers glinting in the hall light.

"Oooh, ok!" I said, relieved, even though I would never get that 90 seconds of prattling on about a pocket knife back.

Hatton fiddled awkwardly with it, trying to pop the scissors back in. "Oh! Sorry, I should have checked, are you ok doing it in my room? That came out wrong. I mean, my place or yours? That came out even worse!" Sweat beads were forming on his forehead. If he was 20 years younger, they would probably be carting him off to the hospital with a suspected case of Baby Botch.

"Yours," I said definitively. He looked surprised.

"Brutus hates scissors," I explained. "There's a reason he has been barred from every dog groomer in Edinburgh."

"Are you sure? I had to wrestle an Alsatian in an episode of Afghan Hounds...If you would feel more comfortable at yours..."

"Why would I feel more comfortable with the ever-present danger of you being savaged by a crazed 3-kilo dog and accidentally stab me in the eye in the process?" I asked, feeling a dubious frown crease my forehead. The lines were well-worn, like an old leather bag, but vintage is only good on your shoulder, not your face. At least a fringe would hide the epidermal accordion on my bag face.

"How considerate," said Hatton, tapping his keycard to the door. I followed him in, the room looking much the same as last time I was here, only without the giant clothes mound on the bed, plus there weren't as many lights on now. A hot flush came over me.

"Do you not turn the AC on in here?"

Hatton looked at me strangely. "I always keep it running."

I wiped my forehead and mumbled, "Oh yeah, I can feel it now," even though I really couldn't. I had been getting a lot of these lately; only a few days beforehand I had suddenly developed underarm sweat patches the size and shape of Sardinia while Annie did her presentation on latinx authors. She seemed to be slowly coming to terms with her identity, her blonde highlights were growing out and revealing her dark roots, but she didn't seem to care.

"Are you having second thoughts?" asked Hatton as I looked in the mirror to see I was still looking red and sweaty. I made a mental note to Google early menopause when I got back to my room.

"No!"

"Because it's ok if you are. A...fringe is a big commitment. You should only let someone, er, cut your fringe, if you really want to do it."

Ok, so we were not talking about the hair anymore. He better still actually cut my fringe but I was also eager to find out exactly what it was an innuendo for too, I thought. I wondered how to communicate that, and decided on a sort of unflappable newsreader voice, the one they use when reading a meticulous list of what a politician has been accused of doing in a men's public bathroom at 3am. It would show that I wanted to get down to business in both senses! I cleared my throat and adopted the clipped tone: "I want you to cut my fringe."

Alas, it came out more like a licentious Alexa than neutral newsreader, but Hatton still got my drift: "Right, let me put the big light on so I can see what I'm doing. I mean, to your hair!"

"Great," I said, sitting on the edge of the bed.

Hatton nodded and flicked on a light to illuminate his unlikely hair studio. I flinched when I thought I saw someone else sitting at the bedside bureau. A second look was somehow calming and more alarming, it was a lifesize dummy with BoxingBuddy3000 written on it.

"Do you put creepy wigs on that thing and practice your craft?" I asked, trying not to look directly into its pupilless eyes.

"He had a full head of hair when I started," he joked, aiming an elbow at its shiny bald dome. He laughed but turned around anxiously as the BoxingBuddy bobbed about from the impact. "He's for boxing practice... just to be clear. I'm surprised you didn't see him last time you were here, but he was probably covered in a mound of clothes during my breakdown."

"But he stuck with you during that particularly difficult episode. It must be love," I said, picking up its limp arm to stroke him.

"Yeah, well, I *am* in an open marriage," he said, and we looked at each other awkwardly, verging on guiltily. "If I can't explore my sexuality with a man-made rubber dummy now, when can I?" Hatton snapped around, beginning to fiddle with his bedside lamp. My eyes wandered around the room, first to an electronic photo frame on the dresser, which was scrolling through photos of Annie throughout the ages - somehow she still managed to look sullen as a three-year-old dressed up as Hannah Montana.

From there, my gaze roamed past the standard issue Belkita beach scene framed on the wall to his own regulation uniform of black tshirt and lounge pants, like a costume in a trailer, hanging in the open closet.

"This should be bright enough," he said, manouevring the reading light over the bed. "Take a seat." An apologetic hand motioned towards the top of the bed. "The light's welded into the wall or something. Sorry, I checked."

"No problem," I shrugged, even though I envisioned many problems.

I walked around the bed, trying to look nonchalant, which was made harder by catching my shin on the bedframe so badly that Hatton did a sympathy wince. Why was there a magnetic field between shins and bed legs?! I limped forward as casually as possible.

"Are you ok?" he asked, catching my elbow with a smile that just about made me forget my own name as well as the pain.

"Yeah! It's the bed that you should be worried about," I said, flopping down into the light and onto a surprisingly supple mattress.

"How come you got the good bed? It's so comfy, I might never leave" I said, squeezing the taut but bouncy surface; it was like someone had made a bed out of a Chippendale's butt cheeks.

"Be my guest! I mean, make yourself at home. Jesus, I need to stop talking - I sound like I'm one bathrobe away from Weinstein.

"It's ok!" I laughed, then I thought, why were scanty bathrobes wasted on the Weinsteins of this world when Hatton could be parading around in one in an entirely consensual encounter right now? Oh yeah, because we were both incredibly awkward people.

"Right, let's get this over and done with," he said, producing the Swiss Army knife from his pocket. Unusual choice of words, I thought; 'let's get this over and done with' was the sort of phrase you associate with a root canal or skin tag removal, not the art of seduction.

"All good! Right, hold still," he said, positioning my head. But maybe he took a bit too long. Was that lingering? And if so, was it in a romantic way, or in horror at the sun damage from when I fell asleep on the balcony last week?

"Is this still enough?" I mumbled, trying to throw my voice out my closed mouth.

"Yes, yes, fine," he said, snatching his hand away. I heard him wipe them on his trousers, probably ridding himself of the normal people cooties.

Hatton brushed a handful of hair over my eyes, not that I could see beforehand because I had already firmly screwed my eyes shut. I could just feel all the follicles moving forward gently but individually, kind of like a head massage. I smiled.

Next I heard the jangle of Hatton's pocket and the slide of metal on metal as he tested the scissors. Then he slid his fingers along the hair just above my browline.

"OK?" he said, something catching in his throat. Maybe he had crisps earlier.

"OK," I said. Hatton cleared his throat again when the fingers of his other hand touched my temple. Then my stupid mind immediately debated whether it really was a packet of crisps having that effect on his voice, especially when I knew he only ate them in times of extreme stress, like his wife leaving him or 9/11.

The scissors began to slice through the hair and I felt it fall down my face. I actually kind of liked that it was irritating my skin because it gave me something else to fixate on. There was a satisfying crunchy clip as the scissors cut through my hair, like a scythe through hay (I would assume, the last time I went to a farm was when I was six and even then I only saw some chickens).

"So...going anywhere nice on your holidays?" joked Hatton. "You know what I was thinking about the other day? That hotel in Copenhagen where we used to have drinks."

I opened one eye. His back was turned, brushing hair into one of those tiny hotel bins.

"Yeah. We had some good times there," I said, wondering where he was going with this.

"We should go back there when things go back to normal," he said. I could feel he was now evening up hair in the middle of my head, but his hands weren't as steady as before.

"Urgh!" I said, spiky strands of hair somehow falling *up* my nostrils.

Hatton stepped back as I rubbed my nose and face free of prickly hairs.

"Fine! I'm sorry I misunderstood! There's no need to say 'urgh!' about the whole thing!"

"What do you mean, you drama queen? I got hair up my nose!" I let out a massive sneeze.

"Oh..." Hatton waited for any sneeze aftershocks to clear. "Let me see," he said, bringing his face close enough to spot the hair sprinkled across my face like the world's itchiest woolly jumper. I stopped fidgeting as he wiped his fingers across my cheeks. This was *surely* an intimate gesture on his part, right? His own eyes were concentrating on a particularly stubborn patch of clippings that were clinging to my lower jaw.

"What did you mean you misunderstood?" I asked, trying to distract myself from the fact I was wondering if this is what it felt like to have a beard you could stroke and how fetching his own stubble was in comparison to mine.

"Oh, nothing. Look down," he said. I shot my eyes passed his face and looked at my thighs, the ones that I hastily reminded myself were too chunky for famous people to like. He blew on my eyelids and I felt the hair stuck to them as well as my metaphorical pants fly off.

"You must have meant something," I said, suddenly bold enough to look him in the eye. Mine weren't as piercing as his, but I had still found a chink in the armour, his eyes flitting down to his hands, which absentmindedly flicked the scissors open and shut.

"Oh, just, I thought you said 'urgh' at the thought of going to Copenhagen with me."

At least we had as being as neurotic as each other in common.

"If I objected to going anywhere with you, would I be in your hotel room right now? *Literally* in your bed?" I wasn't sure where this side of me was coming from, but it was bound to give me something to write about.

Hatton looked up slowly from the scissors, which had ground to a halt. I tried to add a wink to lighten the mood, but it only got more hair in my eye, like one of those avalanche aftershocks. My hands shot up to my eye, but Hatton's were there first. He wiped away a scratchy tear streaming down my face.

A few hard blinks and I managed to clear it, but his hands were still there. I had an impulse to mirror him, and I found my hands on his cheeks too. They were spiky with hair too, but it was stubble, which was far more normal than God knows what was going on on my face. We leaned closer and I wondered if we might velcro together. He opened his mouth to speak, but nothing came out for a couple of seconds, then: "Are you sure you-"

Yes, I was sure, so I pulled his mouth towards mine and kissed him. For a brief moment, I worried he was going to say, 'Are you sure you want a fringe?' again and I had misread our entire relationship. I shouldn't have, though. He laid me down on the bed slowly, like we were tipping back on a reclining chair. The Swiss Army knife was chucked on the floor with a dull thud as it hit the rug. He used the hand he had been holding it in to pull me close as we rolled towards the centre of the bed. I reached down for his belt buckle just as he tried to pull my top over my head and elbow got caught somewhere inside my shirt.

"OH MY GOD!" came a scream from the doorway. It sounded like... James? I pulled my top back down, one sleeve still flopping armless at my side. Seeing James in the doorway pulling at his hair, I did a stealth body roll off Hatton. James shrieked, "IT'S JUST SO WRONG!"

"That's just so offensive, James!" I said as Hatton fumbled with his belt buckle.

"Damn right it's offensive!" James bellowed, whirling round and pointing at his hair; it now fell over his temples in a scraggly mullet. "I have mutilated myself!" Trembling hands pulled a clump of the mullet off his scalp. "I just wanted a fringe! How hard could it be, I thought. As it turns out, pretty fucking difficult!"

"Don't panic James," offered Hatton weakly, beginning to get off the bed then realising this was not the time to approach James with a throbbing erection.

"Don't panic?! Don't panic?! If I was capable of that, I wouldn't have freaked when I cut a few strands a bit short AND DONE THIS TO MYSELF!" James jabbed his finger at his reflection in the mirror. His eyes caught mine in the glass and narrowed in on me. "How come *you* have a fringe and it looks so good?"

"Er...Hatton did it," I said, smoothing down my bed hair.

"I knew it! That's why I came round here. Hatton, mate, you said you were good at haircuts, right? UNDO THIS ABOMINATION!" James said, trembling like a chihuahua with a neurological disorder.

"Um, actually, I wasn't quite finished doing Sam yet," said Hatton, both of us trying not to smirk.

"You can do her later. I need you to do me right now."

I snorted.

"Honestly, you can be so immature," tutted James. "You don't deserve that fringe. You eat bread and don't even lift."

"James!" said Hatton, now pulling at his own hair. "Enough! It's late. I'm not some sort of performing seal."

"Exactly. You could never handle the scissors with flippers, for starters," I said, kicking my feet up onto the bed.

Hatton turned with a look that said 'you're not helping'

"Look, mate, go to bed. Sleep on it," Hatton said, steering James towards the door. "First of all, it might flatten down whatever that is." He patted a curly chunk on James' temple. "And it won't seem so bad in the morning. *And* I promise to fix it first thing, ok?"

"You promise?" James said, lingering at the door.

"Yes," said Hatton with a reassuring smile. Then he slammed the door in James' face.

"...I'll come by first thing tomorrow, ok?" said James through the door.

Hatton's upper lip twitched. "See you then, James," he called, then his voice dropped. "Where were we?"

"Somewhere around here?" I said, rolling to the centre of the bed.

Hatton did an enthusiastic roll onto the bed that I presumed he had learnt while fending off Alsatians at some point in his career. Then he carefully moved me underneath him and slowly wiped a hair off my eyelid.

"See you guys tomorrow," James mewled, like a cat wanting fed at 3am.

"BYE!" Hatton shouted. We lay frozen for a few seconds, the only noise the thud of our simultaneously annoyed and horny heartbeats.

"Do you think he's gone?" I asked quietly.

"Well," said Hatton, kissing my eyelid, "if he's not," he kissed my cheek, "then he's in for one hell of a show," he moved to kiss me on the mouth but I got to him first.

I presume/hope James went away after that, because if he didn't, he truly did get one hell of an (audio) show and is probably a bit of a pervert.

CHAPTER

33

It was 3am when I woke up for a pee. It took me a few seconds to work out where I was; the decor was so similar to my own room but something was different...I gradually remembered the details of the night before and the fact Hatton had a much nicer bed than me. I turned over to see him drooling on the pillow next to me but somehow still managing to look gorgeous while doing it. So *that* had happened. Again.

3am is probably the worst time of day to think about anything. You are alone with just your thoughts and the darkness. I walked to the bathroom and switched on the light. The reflection in the mirror told me that I was still a distinctly average looking naked woman and Hatton was still married, the ring next to the sink reminded me naggingly.

I plonked myself on the toilet with a sigh and unlocked my phone (of course I had brought it with me).

Sam: I've done something stupid...

June: Oh God, me too.

A picture of June with a very uneven fringe appeared on the screen. Her mouth was open in a scream and the photo was taken from under her chin, which made her look like a horrified frog.

June: I'm in the depths of Reddit trying to fix it.

I pulled out my phone and snapped a photo of my fringe.

June: UGH YOU TOO?!

June: Why does yours look so good?!

June: Is that men's deodorant in the background?

June: Are you naked?!

June: So I zoomed in and it's that fancy deodorant they sell in Jenkins Department Store that smells of sandalwood and the promise of a hot young Communist manacled to my bed. I smelled Hatton's jacket after a few vodkas last week AND THAT'S HOW HE SMELLS TOO.

June: OMG you are in Hatton's loo naked at 3am?!?!?! I.am.so.proud.

I was about to launch into a dissection of the night's activities when there was a knock at Hatton's door.

"Dad?"

I put down my phone and hastily wrapped myself in one of the hotel bathrobes hanging beside the shower.

"Dad! Wake up!" shouted Annie between snivels.

I poked my head round the bathroom door to see Hatton slowly getting out of bed and muttering to himself.

He caught sight of me as he pulled on his pyjama bottoms. I mouthed 'what should I do?' and he looked around the room as if he would suddenly discover a secret passageway.

Now Annie was banging on the door.

"I'm coming!" he shouted, panicked. I pointed wordlessly back into the bathroom to signal I would hide in there and he gave a relieved thumbs up.

He gave me a silent kiss as he ran to the door, whispered 'sorry' and I tiptoed into the empty bath to hide there. I timed pulling the shower curtain shut with the door opening.

I heard a muffled "What's wrong?" followed by a wail full of teenage anguish. I winced as it bounced off the tiled bedroom floor and ricocheted into the bathroom.

"Did I hear something?" asked Annie, now quite composed.

"Yes, probably you screaming," said Hatton. "Now come in and tell me what's happened." He sounded very paternal, he normally just sounded bemused by his daughter. That was good, I supposed. I imagined him putting a protective arm around her shoulder and leading her over to the table and chair by the bed.

There was relative silence for a minute or two so I began squinting at the mosaic-style bathroom tiles until I saw different pictures, like the wall one of those optical illusion images that if you stare hard enough at you see a sailboat or Elton John. I wondered if I looked intensely enough at the wall then I would see Jesus (1.0) and feel compelled to join a nunnery. That would solve a lot of my problems. No luck, I only saw a falling Jenga tower.

"He said what?" said Hatton, his voice rising. I shuffled up in the bath and pressed my ear to the tiles to hear better.

"That he needs to date a white girl to capture the American tween market. And it didn't matter if I was an 'adopted coconut', appearances are what count," Annie was still sobbing, but she sounded angry too now.

"Wh...wh...what's an adopted coconut?" asked Hatton, who sounded bemused again. I was glad he asked, because I thought I had misheard through the wall.

"That I'm brown on the outside but white on the inside because I was raised by you and mum," sniffed Annie, but it wasn't pathetic now, it sounded more like a bull before it charges.

"I'm going to kill Jesus," pronounced Hatton.

What a little twat Jesus was I thought, leaning back in the bath. I mean, sure, reject Annie for being desperate, moody or a general pain in the arse, but not for her ethnicity! I had to stop myself from getting out the bath to go and commiserate.

"No Dad, don't. He's not worth it. It's not like he is a straight Lil Nas X."

"Well, what can I do?" asked Hatton, the indulgent way you might ask a child with a sore throat which flavour ice cream they want. In my head, he was holding her one free hand while she blew her nose on the sleeve of the other.

"Can I stay here tonight? The last thing I want to do is sleep in the same room as Melody the Aryan poster child tonight. Plus she keeps saying "I'll get you Mickey, you damn mouse" in her sleep. It creeps me out."

"Of course!" said Hatton, while I silently screamed "WHAT?!" Then he seemed to remember there was the slight problem of a woman who wasn't Annie's mother in the bathroom. "We don't want you having nightmares like Melody, though. Why don't we go and see if we can get a couple of hot chocolates from the machine in the lobby first? We always used to do that when you were little."

"No, we didn't," Annie said, matter-of-factly.

"Maybe you were too young to remember."

"Maybe it didn't happen," replied Annie. I heard their footsteps come by the bathroom door and tensed superfluously, the same way I did when trying to park a car.

"Let's ask Parthenope the Plant, she has our whole family history now," said Hatton and they both laughed.

I relaxed a little as the door clicked open, then I heard, "Actually, I will meet you down there. I am just going to wash my face so I don't look so red and blotchy."

"NO!" shouted Hatton, just as I heard the bathroom door twist open.

"Ugh Dad, why are you being weird about the bathroom? Did you not flush the toilet again?"

"No! I ALWAYS FLUSH THE TOILET," he said, projecting his voice like he was in Shakespeare's Globe.

"Ok, cool story," said Annie. She must have barged past him and into the bathroom because I heard the clunk of her platform trainers on the tiles. A waft of air fluttered the shower curtain but not enough to reveal me. In my mind's eye, Hatton held his breath like he was about to dive off the famous Belkitan cliffs we hadn't been allowed to visit, then poked his head around the door. There was a deep sigh as he saw the coast was clear and said, "Fine, wash up. I will meet you by the machine...Annie."

"Thanks, Dad. See you soon."

I heard Hatton's steps slowly, reluctantly retreat out the bathroom, shuffle along the corridor and the front door close like a death knell. Soon his footsteps petered out in the corridor. Annie was still in the bathroom, just inches away.

I held my breath like I was underwater, even though I was in an empty bath. I occupied my oxygen-starved brain by watching Annie's silhouette through the shower curtain. She was bent over the sink, her long hair falling forward like a different type of curtain, one of those big heavy ones usually tied back with a sash. An arm reached out from behind the hair curtain and grabbed a towel from the side of the sink. Then there was the sound of water streaming into the basin, followed by dabbing as Annie moved the flannel to her face.

"I know you're in there, by the way," she said casually, throwing the face cloth on the floor. I froze for a few seconds, hoping she was having a cheeky seance.

The shower curtain swished open to reveal me huddled in a hotel dressing gown in the bathtub, like an overgrown spider who had made herself comfortable. Annie stood over the bath, her arms folded.

"Well, explain yourself," she said, her foot tapping on the floor.

I raided my mind for innocent answers, but came up short; I didn't think alien abduction or moonlighting as a plumber were going to cut it.

"Look at you!" Annie said, bursting into laughter. "This is too much. I wish I could put this on TikTok without ruining my own life by association."

"Yeah, well, my heart bleeds for you," I said, scrambling out of the tub whilst trying to maintain what little dignity I had left.

Annie shrugged and turned to the mirror to examine her reflection. "I don't really care, by the way. And not in the same way I don't really care about Jesus anymore. Like, I don't care if he dies in a fiery bus crash, but I just don't care that you're...whatever it is with my Dad. You guys think you're keeping it on the DL but it's SO obvious. It makes me cringe, but apart from that, it's meh."

"Really?" I said, tugging my robe tighter.

"Yeah, I mean, I don't think my parents have been happy for years, really. Dad would spend months away shooting shit films and mum says it's fine because she gets to spend more time with her new buff yogi," she said, brushing her hair with her fingers. "I'm just pleased they have finally caught on, to be honest. It was getting a bit awkward for me."

"Your parents aren't splitting up," I said, sitting down on the edge of the bath and pulling at the robe.

"Oh God, they're not poly, are they? I don't need two mommies."

"No! At least, I don't think so. Look, Annie, it's really not my place...you should talk to your Dad. But we're not together. Not really."

"One more time with feeling, eh Sam? My Dad was more convincing when he played Yentl on Saturday Night Live," Annie smirked, heading out the bathroom.

I stuck my tongue out at her as she left, laughing. The front door slammed behind her and I repeated, "We're not together. Not really," my words echoing off the cold tiles.

CHAPTER

34

"I was on YouTube until 3am trying to sort this out," said June, pointing to her fringe with her free hand. The other one was gripping a cup of coffee. Dark eye circles poked out from her new hairdo as we ate breakfast on Tito's balcony.

"Well, I think it looks good!" I said, pouring myself some more orange juice and shaking my own fringe out of my eyes.

"Sounds like you were busy too last night! Come on, give me all the details! Well, maybe not all of them. You can gloss over any bits that involve squelching or sex swings."

"What are you two degenerates talking about?" said James, plonking down a tray of muesli and boiled eggs next to June. He self-consciously tugged at his fringe, which was looking much better.

"Not you too!" laughed June. James shrugged bashfully. "What came over us all last night?"

"Boredom?" I offered.

"Ha! You were far from bored last night, I bet!" June scoffed.

I was worried James would pick up on her comment, but he was more interested in the food, his muscular jaw chomping on his muesli.

"Did Hatton manage to fix your hair then, James?" I asked.

"Oh yeah! It was really nice of him. He came round to my room at 6.30 this morning and did a great job. Look how even he managed to cut it!" James said, leaning closer to us. "Pretty good considering I was hyperventilating the whole time."

"Nice," I said, playing with a strand of my own fringe.

"I am sorry for interrupting last night, but my hair was a disaster, you have to admit that," said James, shovelling more muesli into his mouth.

"What did you interrupt, James?" June asked with mock-innocence.

"Oh, Sam and Hatton were in bed when I turned up having my fringe meltdown at half past midnight."

"Oh really?" asked June, pretending to be shocked. I had hoped he hadn't noticed that and was now trying to piece together a perfectly reasonable excuse. We are ardent environmentalists using body heat instead of those crappy storage heaters in the hotel room cupboards? It was too early for subterfuge.

"What's the big deal, June? I didn't have you down as a prude," said James, stripping a boiled egg of its shell.

"Wh-I'm not!!" spluttered June. Being called a prude was almost as bad as being called a Tory in June's books.

"Then what's the problem? They are consenting adults. Sam is clearly punching, but good on her, I suppose." This was the most shocking part of the conversation, a half-compliment from James. "If Hatton likes that...

carbohydrate look about your face. " I was relieved, at least there were some constants in life. "And, as far as I know, no animals or children are involved in their bedroom activities, it's all good," said James before biting into the egg.

"So you knew that Sam and Hatton are having a thing?" asked June as I sank down deeper into my seat.

"Doesn't everyone?" said James. "Is it meant to be a big secret? Someone needs to tell that Jesus boy, then. I had to confiscate a pornographic drawing of them he did in our PT session yesterday."

"Oh, Jesus," I groaned.

"Is it something I said?" James asked June while I cradled my carb-face in my hands.

"They keep insisting that they aren't really together. Hatton's in an open marriage, which I approve of, by the way. Free love should be the currency of the sexual economy," June said as she topped up her coffee and loaded three sachets of sugar into her cup.

"Can we please stop talking about this? It's my sex life and even I am grossed out right now," I complained, suddenly feeling itchy all over. "It's like I told Annie last night, we aren't really together."

"Yeah right, and I'm not really into health and fitness," fired James.

"Wait, what was Annie doing there?" asked June, putting her coffee down.

"Long story," I muttered.

"Damn right it's a long story, Sam. And there's more to it than you're letting on, we know that. And, when I say 'we', I mean everyone on the internet. Have you not seen some of the photos on Instagram? I keep tagging you in the comments," June said, taking her phone out the pocket of her denim jacket.

"I just thought you were sending me more memes about depression and Communism," I moaned.

"Sam! I can't believe you would ignore notifications from me! Your comrade!"

"Yeah, yeah, I'm sorry, don't send me to the gulag," I said, scrolling through my notifications. I clicked on one from June to reveal a photo of me and Hatton at the beach bar a couple of months ago. It wasn't like we were having sex on the table or anything, but even I had to admit, there was a definite...air of something, even in the grainy photo.

The comments only made matters worse: 'Is it bad I kind of want them to get together?' 'SHATTON <3 <3' (could they not have chosen a more flattering nickname?) 'nah SAMON' (at least someone agreed about that) then a lot of comments in Danish that I couldn't quite understand but certainly had a lot of aubergine and splash emojis.

"See?" said June.

"Are people so bored during this pandemic that *my* life has become gossip worthy?" I moaned.

"Yes," June nodded. "For God's sake, we had some sort of synchronised haircut breakdown last night, it's doing crazy things to us all."

"OK, well my crazy thing is a summer fling then. It will all be over come September. Hatton will go back to his gorgeous wife and I will go back to my carbohydrates," I said, shoving a slice of toast in my mouth, mostly to annoy him.

"Come on, Sam. You don't get over things that easily. You still haven't forgiven the Marvellous Mahal takeaway for when they screwed up your order a year ago," June said, raising old and ugly feelings of betrayal and injustice.

"That's completely different," I said, the bitter taste of cold Korma in my mouth. "You'll see," I said, pushing my chair out with a deafening scrape. Nose in the air, I walked away.

I didn't need to look back to know that June and James would be watching for a crack in my armour, but my nose skyward nose meant I just missed bumping into Hatton on his way to breakfast.

"Good morning!" he said, catching me around the waist.

"Good morning!" I said as business-like as I could.

"So, about last night…"

"Yes! It's a summer fling, isn't it?" I cut in. "It's probably the best way to treat the whole thing. A few more weeks of," a flashback of the night before distracted me. "A few more weeks of this and then you go your way, and I go mine?"

Hatton let me go and nodded. "If that's what you want?"

"It's exactly what I want. I'm just that sort of person. That's who I am. With that in mind, my room, 7.30?"

"I will be there," Hatton said. He looked a bit bewildered, but not entirely upset at the prospect.

"Ok, good," I said, striding off to my first lesson of the day. On the way, I pulled out my phone to send a very important message to June and James.

Sam: SEE?!

CHAPTER

35

I saw Hatton before then, though. The postman delivered around 2pm and it was one of the most thrilling times in the day; you would get your hands on whatever you had impulsively purchased out of sheer boredom on Amazon the night before.

I was eagerly anticipating the arrival of a corkscrew-cum-bookmark that had seemed like a good idea after three glasses of wine. And it still seemed like a good idea a whole 18 hours later, which was better than the purchase of matching sailor costumes for Lily and Brutus. It wasn't due to poor quality or anything like that, it was the injuries I sustained trying to wrestle them into the costumes that made them regrettable.

As I approached the staff pigeon holes in the lobby, I saw Hatton was ahead of me tearing into a jiffy bag.

"What have you got there?" I asked. He didn't reply, he just continued to look at it all misty eyed.

"This plant has come all the way from Central America and I can't even go to the next town over. It's funny. And depressing," he said, enviously studying the beaten package.

I couldn't really blame him, I had found myself getting nostalgic for Beath Buses earlier; they were never on time and the bus drivers treated their routes like jazz improv, but at least you were going somewhere.

"What sort of plant is it?" I asked as he produced a small zip-loc bag from the parcel. It was full of dirt and I was beginning to suspect he had been duped.

"It's the one we named Parthenope after - Regulus Parthenopus," he said, presenting the bag of dirt to me as if it was a beautiful bouquet.

"Um, are you sure it's a plant?" I said, squinting at the bag.

"Of course it's a plant!" he said, appalled. "You know, I played a horticulturalist in the rom-com You Can't Make Her Think-"

"Here we go..." I sighed.

"*And* I learnt a lot about the exotic plant trade!" he persevered. "The seed in this 'dirt' as you so elegantly called it, will grow into a rare and beautiful plant."

He carefully poured the contents into a pot. We both looked into it. "Still looks like dirt to me..."

"It's not! You need to-" our noses collided as we peered into its dark recesses. We snapped back at the sting of the pain and the memory of our Glasgow Kiss.

Both of us pinched our noses and looked away. As we turned back, I rubbed my nose and Hatton shook it off.

"You need to *trust* it is there, is what I was about to say," Hatton sniffed. "The seed will reveal itself in its own time."

Just then the human former Parthenope popped up between us. "What's this? Oh, a seed!" she said.

"You can see it?" asked Hatton, poking through the soil.

I couldn't help it - I said, "Come on now, Hatton, the seed will reveal itself in its own time!"

"How droll," he said, looking up from the pot.

"What is it?" asked Annie.

"It's the Regulus Parthenopus, you know, the plant we named you after," said Hatton, offering the pot to her.

"Ugh, don't remind me," huffed Annie. "Besides, I've changed my name now."

"I know, but I thought it might be fun for us to grow it together, like when you were little," Hatton said hopefully. Annie gave him a look that made me want to dissolve into the wall.

"Or not," mumbled Hatton, laying the pot down on the table.

"Well, I'm glad we sorted that out, I'm going to meet Melody for lunch," said Annie, turning on her heel.

Hatton nodded and continued to glumly poke at the 'plant'. "I guess I will go and stick it in a pot in my room, then."

Annie swivelled round. "No you won't! Your room's too dark. It needs sun, otherwise it will die!' She waved her dad off like he was a locust and took the bag away.

"Oh, right, sorry, I forgot," Hatton said meekly.

"I didn't! I had to care for that plant all by myself when you went off to Afghanistan for five months! It's a lot of responsibility for a six year old," she said, cradling the pot. *"And* it was pretty traumatising because it took me three months to work out that people were talking about the plant when they said 'Parthenope looks dead!"

"I didn't know that," said Hatton, watching his daughter hold the package to her chest.

"Oh, er, look at the time!" I said feebly. "I promised I would...help... June...drink a bottle of wine?" I said, grabbing my corkscrew packet and heading away.

"You might as well go with her," said Annie, her attention fixed firmly on the plant. "I can handle this."

"Oh, ok," Hatton said with a strange mix of confusion and obligingness, the kind you have on the first day of a new job. Normally I would have loved to have a drink with him, but it was too sad to watch him shuffle away from father-daughter bonding.

We made our way out of the room, Hatton turning back to watch Annie walk away with little Parthenopus. "So, we're going to help June drink wine? I would have thought she was quite proficient in that."

He might have been the parent in the situation but he looked like a small child who needed a hug. I sighed and put an arm around his shoulder, throwing in a reassuring squeeze. He smiled and squeezed my hand back. It was nice.

"You know, Annie is quite proficient at taking care of plants, but I still think she could use a helping hand."

"You think so?" he said. Hatton's hand fell from mine and into his own, clasping almost prayer-like.

"Yeah! Go and ask her how you can help," I whispered, clicking the door back open.

"Ok," he said bashfully. "Thanks, Sam." He ran after his baby botanist. They were just out of earshot, but I could almost hear her sigh when she saw him, but then she relented and pulled him away by the hand.

Hatton stumbled after her, turning back just once to mouth 'Progress!'

CHAPTER

36

"Sam, what's the most spectacular way that I can kill myself?" asked Paxton, swiftly draining a martini glass.

"I don't know Paxton, something involving a rocket? You must have Elon Musk's number."

"Call Elon," Paxton said while noting it down on a napkin.

I had been trying to work on a new chapter in Tito's bar when Paxton had collapsed in a chair beside me a few moments earlier.

"Come on, Paxton. Don't be like this. I haven't seen you get this worked up since your parents suggest you marry a nice girl from the country club."

"School inspector. Here. In a week."

"OK, well, it can't be that bad. There must be some sort of checklist of criteria we have to meet," I said, thinking about how I had monumentally shat over my last employer's attempt to pass an inspection. I made a mental note to write that scene down later. I had been doing quite well at piecing my story together recently, and exploding porridge was a crowd pleaser. However, I resolved to be better for Paxton.

"This is the checklist!" Paxton said, his phone infinity scrolling through a dense pdf. "Why have I put off reading it for five months, Sam?! Why?!"

Paxton had put off reading it for five months because he was the sort of person who only ever started revising for an exam the night before with a fistful of Adderall in one hand and a highlighter in the other, but I felt reminding of him of this at this precise moment might not be well-received.

"Bring it to the staff meeting tomorrow. We will work something out." I said, doing my best 'please don't jump' smile.

Paxton nodded to himself. "Alright, I suppose the working day is almost over, after all."

"It's 2.30pm..."

"Is it that late already? Shall we get something refreshing - maybe a G&T?" he said, waving Lorando over.

"Paxton!" I said firmly. "I'm working. And you need to rest. And work out what is in that document. Go to your room."

"Jeez Mom, ok!" he huffed.

I glared.

"Alright! Alright! I'm only joking, though you would be a total MILF," he said, skedaddling from the table.

"I'm not a MILF!" I shouted after him, just as Lorando arrived at the table to take an order.

"I'm not!" I informed him. "Don't MILFs have to be older, Lorando?" I asked.

"Erm, I am afraid that I am not familiar with the exact parameters associated with pornographic naming conventions, Ms Chambers," he explained nervously. "But I do make very good Sex on the Beach, can I interest you?"

I raised an eyebrow.

"In a cocktail, that is!" Lorando blushed.

"Maybe later, thanks Lorando," I said, getting back to work.

Paxton shamboled into the staff meeting five minutes' late, his hair standing on end. He was clutching the crumpled inspection handbook like it was a Bible he was using to ward off Satan. However, if you have made it this far in the story, you will know it was far too late for that intervention when it came to Paxton.

June was scribbling furiously and I leaned over to get a better look. "It's private and confidential!" she said, hunching over her desk. "I promised Lorando...I promised *someone* I would keep it a secret."

"Sly," I said, rocking my chair back to the ground, just catching the words 'Strike Plan' flash across the paper. June was apparently finally fulfilling her destiny as a unioniser and communist agitator. "Man the barricades, comrade," I said under my breath.

"It's not funny, Sam! Lorando showed me where all the local staff have to stay last night. They are all sharing this crappy, run-down villa at the edge of the garden. It's terrible. Paxton should be ashamed. We have to take action." June fell quiet as Paxton flashed a Kennedy-esque smile at her.

"Hey everyone, thanks for coming, sorry I'm late. I'm not sure why, it's just the way I am," said Paxton with a laugh that felt a little tinny. No one laughed, we all had other things on our mind. The silence was broken by Hatton making an even later entrance. I craned round to see him sitting on a desk at the back of the room...staring at me(?) What was this? High school? And why was I still looking back when Paxton was trying to explain a 12 point framework of teacher assessment to us?

"Earth to Sam!" said Paxton with a fake laugh. "Come on, I need you to focus, the inspector will be sitting in at your end of term reading."

"Ok, there's some decent stuff in there. Koala has actually got a pretty good sci-fi piece about mutant cannabis plants coming along. Annie has this really interesting piece from the perspective of a plant and Melody has a really blah but perfectly acceptable poem about flowers."

"But what about Jesus?" Paxton asked, chewing a nail. "He's the loose cannon."

"Yeah, his is a sort of Marquis de Sade meets Alan Titchmarsh freak show," I said apologetically. "I'm sorry, I did my best. But I think he is going to be like this until he gets fixed. It was the same with Brutus."

On cue, Brutus ran past the window, pausing with a 'Never forgive, never forget' look in his eyes.

Paxton flicked through his papers. "James, what say you take Jesus for a personal training session while the reading is happening? Tell him you have an exercise plan to make sure he is super buff once the Baby Botch is over."

"Riri," said James, folding his arms.

"What does Rihanna have to do with this?" asked Paxton, tacking bits of paper to the whiteboard with that wild-eyed look of the guy in the It's Always Sunny in Philadelphia meme.

"Riri!" repeated James. "It's the Belkitan word for no. Lorando taught me it last night when the bar staff were practising protest songs."

"Shut up!" said June, kicking James' chair.

She needn't have bothered though, because Paxton was still writing 'JAMES PT SESSION' in the diary pinned to the board, despite his objections.

"Reserve me a hammer or scythe, June," James said under his breath.

"Noted," June nodded as she continued to write.

"I'm sure glad that's sorted," Paxton said. "Now, June, try not to be too...you, ok?"

"What do you mean? Thai? Should I dye my hair blonde and borrow Sam's foundation made especially for white people and ghosts with acne?"

"No! I am no racist! I think you are super hot, actually, but, that's really not what this is about. Just try not to undermine capitalism *too* much when you're speaking with the inspector, ok? Also, I want your class to do the musical they have put together, the one about the Russian Revolution. Now, they can keep in the Boney M number about Rasputin, but I draw the line a 'He Had it Coming' from Chicago after the Romanovs are executed."

"Fine," sighed June. "It comes for us all in the end, anyway."

"What was that?" asked Paxton, writing '7PM - MUSICAL' on the board.

"I said it's fine," replied June with a sharp smile.

"Hatton, my man! Can you show the inspector some stunt moves in the gym?"

"I am sure I can do that," said Hatton, still at the back of the room. I very deliberately did not turn around.

"Great, now, that just leaves Aubrey. I want you to do the 'teacher interview' with the inspector at 3pm."

"Oh, gosh! What will he ask me? I don't know what to say!" said Aubrey, nervously thumbing an essay.

"It will be a cinch, Aubs. All you have to do is tell him what a great boss you think I am, how organised the school is and how all the staff here have a great work-life balance."

"Everyone, apart from the ones who live in a dilapidated shack," muttered June.

"Sure! That sounds great!" said Aubrey, a grin on her face.

Paxton nodded eagerly to himself and kept repeating 'Everything's coming up Paxton' while we all grew increasingly uncomfortable.

"Can we go now? I promised I would phone Electra at 9.45," groaned Hatton, leaning against the door.

Well, that was absolutely fine, I thought. Phoning his wife is a perfectly normal thing to do that he definitely doesn't have to explain to me. Because we have agreed this is just a summer fling and he is in a terribly bohemian relationship with one of the most fresh-faced, subtly plastic-surgeried 45 year olds you could ever meet. Why did I feel this weird, greedy ball bouncing about my chest then?

"Yes! Come on, Paxton, we all have things to do!" I said, trying to think of something if Paxton dared to ask what I had planned. I would say writing, I decided, even though I could never write in the mornings because I find them disgusting.

"That's what I like to see! A bunch of go-getters! Off you go, the drinks will be on me tonight at Tito's. I might even get you one of those plates of nachos if I remember," said Paxton, clapping his hands. I wondered what rating he would have got in an Empowered Employee inspection. Probably First-Class, they always thought all sins could be absolved with a cheese-based rewards - and they weren't entirely wrong.

"Oh goodie," I said, passing through the door Hatton was holding open. He followed behind, leaving June to catch the door with her fingers.

"Oi mate! You should be glad I think chivalry is a tool of the oppressor!" she shouted, wrenching it back open for James.

"Are you alright?" asked Hatton, grating at my side, like a label not cut off properly.

"I will be, once you get off my case," I said, scratching the crook of my arm. A rash had raised. The last time I had got one of these was when Sandra the CEO had threatened to fire me for a quote that appeared in the newspaper five years before I started my employment.

"What's that?" he asked, taking my arm clinically, but also like a sexy doctor on a TV show.

"I have a rash, ok? It's probably because I don't eat enough yoghurt, or eat too much yoghurt, or had a slice of bread last week. Ask James, he's always got a reason why I am hideous," I said, pulling my arm away forcefully to camouflage the reluctance. I decided striding off was the best course of action, even though I felt light-headed now. I got annoyed at myself. Who was I? An Austen character, only less middle class and the inability to pull off an empire dress?

"I'm worried about you, you don't seem right," said Hatton, following me across the reception.

"I'm fine," I replied, which is something that people are not fine ever say. Why was he so insistent with his questioning? I asked myself, setting it like an essay question as I scratched at my arm on the way to class. Here are the reasons I came up with:

- He expected me to collapse in a melodramatic ball of despair at the mere thought of him phoning his wife and didn't get the desired reaction

- He thought he could gaslight me into actually collapsing in a melodramatic ball of despair. I would show him!

"Just take care of yourself, alright?" he said as I walked away.

"Yeah, yeah," I said as I entered my classroom. The kids were already there, apart from Annie. Jesus was leaning back on his chair, doodling on Melody's notebook, who was giggling and making a crap attempt to shoo him away.

Meanwhile, Koala was on the phone, asking his lawyer, "What law says I *have* to go back to my parents after this?"

Annie breezed in a few seconds later. "Sorrynotsorry I'm late," said Annie, leaving a streak of mud down the door as she closed it behind her.

"That's ok, it must have taken a while to...dig your way here?" I said, watching her produce a wipe from her Koolux bag to clean her dirty hands with. She tried to pick it out carefully, but still ended up frowning at the smudges she left on the satchel.

"Parthenope needed some extra TLC. It was a big day for her," she explained.

"Have you started talking about yourself in the third person? Hang on, I thought you wanted to be called Annie now anyway?" asked a confused Jesus.

"I do! Parthenope is the plant I'm growing with my Dad," she said with a sweet smile, even thought she was balling up the wipe with a white knuckle.

"My parents are always trying to get me to grow plants with them," groaned Koala. "Terrible, isn't it?"

"It's actually fun," shrugged Annie. Everyone turned to look at her in surprise. "Kind of," she clarified.

This seemed to satisfy her classmates, who turned back to the front of the class.

I slowly became aware that they were all looking at me as I unpacked my bag. "What's up with you lot?" I asked with a hostility that was really meant for Hatton. I felt bad about that, but not enough to stop scowling at them.

"Are you ok, Sam?" asked Annie. "You look a bit more, I don't know, skin disease-y than usual."

"Urgh, what's it with your family asking me that today?" I said, scratching my arm.

"Retreat! Retreat!" Jesus stage-whispered at Annie. She held a hand up to block her view of him.

"I have a pill for that," said Annie, pointing at the rash, cautiously, like she might catch a disease.

"Of course you do," I muttered.

"I used to break out in hives before my rhythmic gymnastic competitions when I was four. It still happens sometimes when I'm stressed out, so I have a prescription for stuff that calms it down. You can come by my room if you want some."

"Taking drugs from my students. What a fantastic way to get struck off," I said, passing round an extract we would be working on that day.

"You can't just brush off attempts to help you with sarky remarks!" Annie said, swiping a sheet out my hand.

"Physician, heal thyself," I replied.

"I read in one of my journals today that they think a rash is actually a sign of the Baby Botch," said Koala, taking the sheet of paper from my hand like it was a biohazard before thoroughly slathering his own in hand sanitiser.

"Ha! Good one," said Jesus, keeping his eyes on Melody as I lay the handout on his desk. "She is *waaay* too old to get that."

"Excuse me! I'm only 29. And 11 months."

"Yes, they reckon even older people can get it," confirmed Koala.

"*Older* people? You make it sound like I am about to draw my pension," I said, catching my reflection in the window glass. Jeez, I really didn't look great. Red, blotchy, sweaty. I mean, all those things weren't unusual for me, but the scale was now quite industrial.

"Yeah, that's a bit cruel Koala. You know pensions are a sore point for millennials; they will have to work until they die," said Annie. There was acid on her tongue, but there was concern in her eyes.

"She's probably just menopausal," offered Jesus. "When is it that women's ovaries stop working, again?"

"Right, ok. I have had enough of you all. I was going to let you all 'prepare' for the inspector visit next week. By that, I was going to take all of you to Tito's for nachos. But you've fucked it now, so today's lesson is going to be narrative voice. You will be taking on the character of a woke millennial. I want you all to log in to the Daily Mail and comment on every article about how much you love Meghan Markle and illegal immigrants. I expect you all to get into at least one comment war."

"Noooo," came the collective groan.

"I stan Meg but they are all just so racist and *old* on there. It's like having an argument with one of the Nazis who escaped to South America," whined Annie.

"Well, that's what you get for being little arses to me," I shrugged. "Go on, download the Daily Mail app on your phones. I will be coming round and checking you're all doing the assignment."

More sighs of protest went round the room as they reluctantly pulled their phones out. There was a knock at the door and I saw Hatton's face peeking through the glass. All the students looked to the back of the room then back to me, before stifling giggles and peering at their phones as if they were incredibly eager to get started. Even Annie, the perennially embarrassed, followed suit. I thought about ignoring him, but he knocked again and looked even more worried than the kids did. Someone actually caring if you live or die is a pretty low prerequisite for a 'relationship', but I was kind of touched by it. Plus, the sooner I spoke to him, the sooner he would go away.

"I will be five minutes. When I come back, I want all of you to have at least told some gammon man that Meghan is better than Kate Middleton and that Brexit was a bad idea, ok?"

I walked as smally and apologetically as I could out the room, opening the door just enough for me to get out and closing it sharply behind me. Hatton had been standing right next to the door and wasn't giving me any room, either. I decided to put this on a mental list of things not to like about him, which would definitely make it easier when he went back to his wife.

"What's up? Aren't you meant to be on a phone call?" I whispered, glancing down at my phone - 9.47am.

"That doesn't matter," Hatton said, rifling through a trouser pocket. "I brought you something." He held out a small jar, I took it and read the label: 'Taxi-Derm: Fast acting! Works on fine lines, post-operative scarring and severe burns' There was also a picture of a runover raccoon applying the cream while a taxi sped away in the background.

"Thanks...I guess?"

"Oh, ignore the description. You don't need it for any of that."

"Really? Because your daughter and her classmates have just so kindly reminded me how old and haggard I am," I said, opening the jar to reveal a thick white paste. I dabbed a little on my finger and rubbed it on the back of my hand. It smelled like the vets.

"It's really good for all skin complaints. It might help your arm, here," he said, taking a dollop from the open jar and rubbing it into the crook of my elbow. It did feel very soothing, I had to admit. I was also a bit turned on, which wasn't ideal.

Luckily, the moment was soon ruined: "I got horrendous thrush from a leotard I had to wear in a superhero film a few years ago. This cleared it right up," he informed me.

"Lovely. I am having a cream for genital complaints rubbed into my arm eczema. And they say romance is dead," I said, almost as cold as the cream on my arm, but I knew romance was alive and well because I was still somehow thinking 'Oh what a charming and sweet gesture this is, deep down'.

"Well, true romance isn't all secret sex and will-they-won't-they moments. It's actually caring enough about someone that you will touch their weird skin complaints and not even mind that it looks a bit contagious," he said, drawing small circles in the cream on my arm. I tried to pull it away, but he had a good grip, despite the slipperiness of the ointment. "And I think you might want to rub cream in my weird skin complaints too, not just a summer fling, if you are honest."

I nodded, half-reluctant, half-relieved. "But not the thrush, that sounds like a step too far."

"It was pretty bad," he admitted. "Why don't we sneak down to the beach tonight? We will take some wine and we will just talk. Annie told me about a secret pathway through the gardens that the kids use. Let's set them loads of homework to make sure we are alone." Hatton said, waving to the class, which were all watching us, not doing their Daily Mail exercise. "There's no privacy here. I didn't flush the toilet at the usual 7.53 this AM so James asked me if I was constipated at breakfast. Then recommended all the things I should eat to relieve myself."

I laughed and rolled my eyes.

"I'm not constipated, by the way," Hatton blurted. "I just slept in."

"Wow, I am really seeing different sides to you today. Bowel obstructions, penis thrush...It's going to be a hot date tonight!"

"Hey, I'm hot under the collar just thinking of your dermatological issues," he said.

"What time shall we get together, then? 8ish?"

"Oh, damn, I forgot. Can we reschedule? I have to talk to the plant then."

Talk to the plant? Was he that desperate to not spend time with me? Was he so uncreative that it was the best lie he could come up with? Both made my heart sink.

"That's the worst excuse I've ever heard! Even worse than 'I'm washing my hair," I scoffed.

"No, I really am!" he spluttered. "See..." he scrolled through his phone. "The carbon dioxide is good for the plant."

I still wasn't convinced. He rolled his eyes. "Tell the class you need to step out for five minutes, I have got something to show you."

I sighed and turned back to the class. Jesus was singing the Thong Song to a bemused but captive audience, so this definitely bought me a few minutes.

I nodded and Hatton held his phone in front of m. I pretended I needed to scooch closer to see better. Alas, he seemed oblivious. "Watch this!" he said, bending around me to press play.

On the screen, Annie was sitting next to the plant, her head resting on her arms. She was talking while looking up at the plant, but the audio was too crappy to make out what she was saying.

"What are you two talking about today, then?" Now it was Hatton's voice coming from the phone. Annie looked up with a start. "Oh my God, are you filming this?" she laughed, with uncharacteristic good humour. Hatton was laughing on the video too.

"Whatever, I like talking to her. She's a good listener. Plus, I'm helping trees grow. I'm saving the environment but I also don't have to go full-Greta Thunberg. No offense, Greta, if you ever see this. I thought it was so cool when you smiled at me that one time in Stockholm!" she gushed.

"Greta Thunberg is never going to see this! Now, what are you talking about?"

"Childhood memories," said Annie, more to the plant than her dad.

"Yeah?" asked Hatton as the camera came to rest in front of Annie and the plant - he must have sat down.

"Yeah. I was just telling her about my first day at Aunt Alicia's."

"It's a fancy kindergarten," Hatton explained as he showed me the video. "She had to go on a waiting list practically before the first lizard crawled out of the primordial ooze."

"Ah," I whispered back. "The struggles of the rich and famous." That earned me a dig in the ribs.

"Pay attention!" he said to me. His teeth were gritted but he was laughing and so was I.

I coughed and turned my attention back to the screen, where Annie was mid-story.

"...while you and Mum were talking to Aunt Alicia, I wandered over to the arts and crafts area. I used to love gluing glitter to things!"

"She's not lying," Hatton confirmed to me. "She glued glitter to my hair as I slept once. It was a very...bold look at the BAFTAs."

"Sh!" I said. I must have heard the glitter glue and the BAFTAs story from Hatton a hundred times whilst sitting next to him on talkshows. I concentrated on Annie's words:

"...so then Sapphire McGinty sat next to me," she continued. Annie said 'Sapphire McGinty' the way a war hero grandpa might say 'so then Himmler pulled up a seat next to me in the Nuremberg canteen'.

Next to me, Hatton sighed dramatically. Sapphire McGinty was obviously the pantomime villain of the piece.

"Isn't she the daughter of...what's-his-name...starts with an 'R'...Rowan McGinty, is it?" I asked. Hatton nodded darkly.

"Sapphire asked who my mummy and daddy were and I pointed across the room to you both," explained Annie. "Then she LAUGHED at me and said you couldn't be my parents because I didn't look like you." Hatton was shaking his head in the footage - I could tell by the way the screen moved from side to side.

"So I told her I was adopted. Actually, I think I said 'adomted', but you know what I mean."

"We were always very honest with her about that," Hatton explained to me.

Back on screen, Annie was telling the plant, "But I said it wasn't true! We did look alike! I have the same nose as my Dad *and* the same mole on my cheek as my Mum!"

I glanced away from the screen to Hatton's profile. She was right - their noses were very similar. Looking back at the screen, I noticed that Annie did indeed have a mole where her mother also famously had one.

"Sapphire said I looked nothing like either of you because you weren't my real parents! Do you remember that, Dad?" Now her eyes were focussed on Hatton holding the phone.

"Of course I do!" he said on the video. "You came over to us crying. What a horrible kid. I went right up to her and told her Santa doesn't exist after that. Funny, she looked exactly like *her* Dad when he lost out on that Brit Award."

"Nice one," I said.

"Thanks, Dad," said Annie, a smile stretching out from behind a leaf. Now the plant was in focus and I could have sworn it had grown since the start of the video.

Hatton closed the video with a proud smile. "See, things are going well," he said.

"Yeah, you two are definitely bonding."

"Er, I meant the plant! Did you not think it had grown by the end of the video?" he said, a blush advancing across his cheeks.

"Of course," I nodded seriously. I couldn't deny I had, but the emotional growth was definitely more remarkable.

"Anyway, I really should get going. Today we are going to tell Parthenope - the plant - what we wanted to be when we grew up." Hatton slipped the phone back into his trouser pocket and got up.

"I'm sure Annie, I mean, *Parthenope,* will enjoy that," I said.

He raised his eyebrows and turned to leave. "What are you up to latert? Fancy telling me about your first day at school? The beach at 10pm?"

"Isn't there an ailing yucca plant you need to minister to or something?" I asked.

"No, I would just like to hear about it," he said, so nakedly I felt I should hand him a fig leaf.

"Ha!" I said, crossing my arms as if my nipples were on show. "You say that, but the last time I had that conversation with a guy, it became all about him. Ask June."

"I think I can keep my ego in check for an evening," he said. Normally I would never believe a white middle-aged man who said that, but there was something about him that persuaded me. "I want to know about you."

If the fig leaf wasn't metaphorical, it would have floated off by now.

"Ok," I said. I wanted to follow up with 'it's a date' but then I would have to kill myself for being as trite as a teen rom-com.

CHAPTER

37

It turned out quite well not seeing Hatton that night because I was craving some alone time.

It was 7pm, which meant all the teachers were in the bar. Apart from me. I had stayed in my classroom. As much as I liked everyone else, I was starting to feel allergic to them. Whenever I turned round, there was June, or Hatton, or Paxton, or the kids. There was nowhere to collect my thoughts, let alone write them down. As tempting as it was to begin the nightly assault on the walls of boredom by lobbing glasses of wine at it, I wanted peace and quiet more.

I kept the lights off in the classroom lest I attract Paxton, an alcoholic moth who would surely fly straight in to tempt me to the brights lights of the bar. Whenever I heard a voice or footsteps, I froze, just in case they stopped by and interrupted the beautiful solitude that I hadn't felt in months.

When I heard a stampede of steps coming down the corridor, I shrunk behind my screen. No luck, they tumbled straight through the door. I reluctantly put my head above the parapet of the laptop glow.

"Don't leave me alone with her!" gasped Jesus. He slammed the door shut with one hand and held his shirt together with another.

"With who? What happened to your shirt?" I asked, not sure it was really in my interest to be privy to either bit of information.

Jesus was distracted by something on the other side of the glass and darted to the side like a plucky but petrified lizard being pursued by an eagle on a David Attenborough programme.

Melody appeared in the doorway, scanning the room. "Have you seen Jesus?" she asked, opening the door as he quivered unseen on the other side of it.

"Which one? Christ or your boyfriend?"

"My boyfriend," said a frustrated Melody. Jesus shook his head silently at me.

"In that case, no, but I'm pretty sure I saw Christ on my toast this morning," I laughed. Melody did not.

"Right. Well, if you see him, not Christ, the other one, tell him I am looking for him," she said, prowling off. "Jesus!"

Jesus stood still against the wall until her footsteps couldn't be heard anymore. "Is she gone?" he mouthed.

I nodded yes and he collapsed forward into a seat. He laid his head down on the table with a thunk. It was really quite alarming, considering he was normally risking a head injury, leaning back with at most two chair legs on the ground.

"What's wrong, Jesus?" I asked, pulling up a chair to take his confession.

"Melody wants us to do it behind the bins," Jesus said, screwing up his face.

"The bins? Really?" I said. "Is that her kink? I don't want to know," I said, raising a hand just as Jesus started to answer. "All of this is very inappropriate. This doesn't seem like a pastoral care issue, more like something you should address to the local council, they are the ones responsible for the bins." I got up, desperate to end yet another unfortunately sexual conversation with Jesus.

"Don't send me back out there," he said, grabbing my arm. "It's not the bins that bother me," Jesus looked around again. "It's...it's the sex."

"Jeez, Jesus, I don't want to know. You can't keep talking to me like this!" I said, pulling my hand back.

"Sam, please listen to me!" Jesus said, pushing his chair back. "I don't want to have sex with you! I don't want to have sex with Melody. I don't want to have sex with *anyone*." He shoved his hands deep into the pockets of his baggy jeans.

"OK..." I said. Even if Paxton had provided teacher training, I doubt it would have covered this specific scenario.

"I am asexual," Jesus said lowly. He cleared his throat. "It feels good to say that, but my manager told me I can't tell anyone who matters, so you better keep it quiet."

"I am both flattered and offended. But Jesus, why doesn't your manager want you to tell anyone? You must be knackered from acting like a horndog 24/7."

"But that's it! I have sponsorship deals from dating apps, I am always cast as the young Latin lover, that's my entire USP. If I don't have that, what am I?"

"What you really are?" I offered.

"Exactly, I'm screwed. Except I'm not, obviously." A tiny smile insinuated its way back onto Jesus' face.

It was funny, but I was trying not to be such a mean hag, so I didn't laugh. I just smiled. "Your secret is safe with me." I put a hand on his shoulder, relieved it wouldn't result in a come-on for a change. "It's your secret."

"Thank you," he said, collapsing back into the seat, this time with relief.

"It's up to you when you tell everyone," I said, slinging my bag over my shoulder.

"When?" scoffed Jesus. "I'm *never* going to reveal it to anyone else. Ever."

His assured delivery made me think of the way I had told people Hatton and I absolutely were not together a few months beforehand.

"That's your decision, I respect that. But, oh Jesus, just remember, we all reveal stuff about ourselves, even if we don't want to. People notice things. Like how you hug someone goodbye at the airport or order a drink at the bar."

"Say what?" asked Jesus, his nose wrinkling in confusion.

"Or how you hide in a classroom from your girlfriend when she wants to have sex behind a bin," I said, snapping back to reality.

"Fair enough. It would be nice not to feel weighed down by this massive secret all the time," he shrugged. "But can I just stay in here a little longer?"

"Of course," I said, smiling. "I will leave you to it."

So *this* was the real Jesus. Jesus 1.0 having a thing with Mary Magdalene had always been one of my favourite conspiracy theories, but I might have to reconsider even that at this point.

I was thus weighing up Western history when Melody reappeared in the doorway. Her hoodie was up and there was something of the grim reaper about her - if he had done a line of athleisure for Zara.

"Melody! You gave me a fright!" I said. My heart was banging about in my chest like a loose washing machine drum. It didn't feel quite right, but when did anything these days?

She sniffed the air. "He *was* here, wasn't he?"

"Um, yes," I said, my heart now picking up pace. "But, Melody, I really think it's a good idea to give him a bit of space, ok?"

She looked at me darkly from underneath the hoodie.

"Could you not do that? I don't have time for any more teenage angst," I said, hastily gathering my last few bits and bobs.

"He told you about the bins, didn't he? Amn't I just awful?" she said with delight.

"Um, it's really not for me to judge," I smiled passively. "I am sure it's all just a big misunderstanding!"

She let out guttural moan, the sort people hear in horror films before something starts following them in the woods. "Everyone just thinks I'm nicey nice Melody. Well, I'm not. And I'm sick and tired of pretending. I have smoked 20 a day since I was 11 and I want to have sex behind bins. One time I decked Mickey Mouse with a tyre iron at Disney Land. But no one ever suspects you when you look like this," she said, waving (what I only now noticed were) yellow stained fingers across her Girl Next Door face. "Part of me wants to get caught, just to get the acknowledgement. They say some serial killers get like that in the end." A steely film came over her eyes. She lit a cigarette, inhaled deeply and blew out a wall of smoke. "Not that I would ever actually kill someone. Not on purpose, anyway."

"Right..." I said. I felt like I should be recording this conversation for an upcoming Netflix documentary about her life and crimes.

"Can you not just give me some lines or a detention?" she pleaded, the cigarette quivering between her fingers.

"Melody, you're an adult. I can't punish you. At least not without a body for the Disney thing."

Now her eyes had a murderous glint. I reminded myself that she had said she would never kill - at least not on purpose. The second part gave me pause, to put it mildly.

"Look Melody," I improvised, my eyes darting around the room. They latched onto the pristine tables, cleaned every day to prevent the Botch. "Why don't you vandalise a desk and then clean it off?"

Melody's eyes brightened to their usual 'the light is on but nobody's home'. "Great," she said, whipping out a pen like the flip of a knife.

CHAPTER

38

After that, I fled to my room for some peace and quiet. The less I knew about Melody at this point, the more entertaining the inevitable true crime podcast about her would be. To be fair to Daddy's Little Dementor, I was glad for a little time away from *everyone*. I was always skeptical about self-care but now I knew I needed some.

After I had firmly bolted the door behind me, I slipped out of my skirt and walked around my room in my pants, because who honestly puts on trousers in their living quarters unless there is a food delivery guy at the door? I wandered over to the hotel room table, which I normally used to store those salty crisps you only ever eat on holiday.

The crisps were particularly crunchy and I felt a trail of crumbs sprinkling down my front. I dusted myself down and that's when I noticed it:

My bikini line was out of control. It looked like one of those jungles NGO volunteers wade through while complaining about how it would be cut down for palm oil on the news. Send those crooks my way, I thought, this needs slashed and burned.

I had already decided I would wear a cute bikini from Primark-but-didn't-look-like-it-was-from-Primark down to the beach that night. I had gathered from my rudimentary experience of men that most didn't care if you had a singing muppet for a merkin as long as a vagina lurked underneath and Hatton didn't seem any different. However, it mattered to me. I was starting to look and feel like a sheep that needed to be shorn, but bikini waxes had been outlawed because the Belkitan government thought they encouraged young people to have sex and the scientific jury was still out on if it could be sexually transmitted.

It had to be done, though. It was more merciful this way, like putting a small fluffy animal out of its misery after it had been hit by a car. What to do, though? June had done some beauty therapy courses back in the day, so I messaged her. Screw self-care alone time!

Sam: Help! I have a bikini wax emergency! Come to my room with a vat of wax and an iron will, comrade?

June: I'm not going anywhere near your nether regions, mate! I have bigger fannies to take on! Like Capitalism. Operation Overthrow starts tonight...

Sam: Operation Overthrow?

June: The staff are going on strike! DO NOT tell Paxton!!

Sam: Jesus

June: It has nothing to do with that sex pervert.

I closed our chat and did a rather frantic Google, clicking on the first DIY Brazilian Bikini Wax link that came up. The first tip was 'Make sure you are using the right type of wax, as if I might be standing here with a giant candle that I was about to drip all over my crotch. The second tip was PREPARE YOURSELF. What was this, Judgement Day? Would the quality of my wax job determine whether or not I could enter the Kingdom of Heaven?

Wavering, I scrolled down half-heartedly, but my heart stopped for a second when I read this: 'Do not be alarmed if you cannot remove the wax when all other methods have failed. Simply relax and call an ambulance.'

"Hell, no!" I shouted, throwing my phone on the bed. I would just have to pretend that my bushy undercarriage was some sort of fashion statement. The image of me being found by paramedics, spreadeagled on my bed, covered in wax was just too mortifying. At least body hair seemed to be back in vogue; Annie had actually called me a 'prisoner of the oppressor' when she caught a glimpse of my shaved underarm in class one day.

There was a knock at the door, then June shouting, "IT'S BRAZILIAN TIME!" I winced, held a pillow over my crotch and shuffled to the door.

When I opened it, she handed me a pack of wax strips. They had a pair of disembodied lady legs in the front that looked as smooth and rubbery as Barbie's.

"Are you alright?" she said, pulling a menacing balaclava over her face. "You look all red and blotchy like that time we did the fun run for kids with cancer."

"Yeah, I'm fine. Why does everyone keep asking me that?"

"They have probably just never seen anyone go that shade of gammon who isn't middle-aged, male, and annoyed about Travellers camping in a field in the next county over. Anyway! I have to go help Lorando," June said, her eyes darting back and forth in the balaclava. "Good night and good luck! Quick tip - don't listen to Google and make sure you stretch your skin as tight as possible before ripping the hair out!"

June darted down the corridor, leaving me to stare helplessly at the waxing strips. Maybe it was her words or the thrill of her communist fervour, but I felt emboldened to at least try and do a wax now.

"Any other tips?" I called down the corridor.

"Wine and anti-inflammatories!" she replied before disappearing round a corner.

'Wine and anti-inflammatories' I repeated to myself, pulling a bottle of the local Karkalo out of the mini-bar. If it was strong enough to send one of the local pagan gods to the moon powered solely by the stuff, then surely it would help me navigate my way around my own vagina. What's more, James, goaded by June, had drunk an entire box of it at a party and complained of being unable to feel his nose, boding well for the pain relief.

Knowing prevention was better than cure, I headed over to Annie's room to see if she had any of those pills to take any of the remaining edges off. I just wouldn't mention I was preparing my pubis for some action with her dad, there was no need to muddy the waters with these finer details at this point. If asked to elaborate, I would just point to the rash on my arm, which was creeping up my bicep again anyway.

I knocked on her door, something she hated because it was so 'old-fashioned'. There was a grunt and she reluctantly opened the door.

"Urgh, it's you. How many times have I told you to just use the app for the hotel doors?" she said, pointing to the digital doorbell beside me. "That way I can delete your request and ignore you."

"That Swiss finishing school really paid off, didn't it?" stepping passed her and into her lair.

An outraged Annie slammed the door behind me, presumably to prevent the social death of being associated with me in public. "What do you want?" she asked.

"Drugs," I replied, heading straight for her bathroom, which I noticed was a lot nicer than mine. Bulbs bedazzled a glowing mirror worthy of a beauty YouTuber. There was a rainshower so big it could have qualified as its own weather system, and, of course, a medical cabinet any chemist would have been proud of.

"You look like you are on them!" said Annie, following behind. "You are even sweatier than usual," she said, lingering in the doorway to keep her distance.

"It's not that bad. I am just glistening in all those bright bulbs," I said, shielding my eyes. "Anyway, look at my rash!" I said, holding it out for her.

"No thanks!" she said, stepping back into the hallway. "It's on the far left of the cabinet. Keep it. Just don't come back to my room in this state again."

I pulled open the medicine cabinet, but it felt more like stepping into the backroom of a pharmacy. A wall of subdued medical labels stared back at me, presumably aping the effects they had on the patient; almost all of them were white with an incomprehensible name printed on the front. I was going to have to consult the pharmacist herself.

"Annie?"

"What?" she asked, her eyes shooting death stares into the bathroom mirror, which bounced off and straight into mine. I didn't budge, having built up a tolerance of her disgust over the last few months.

"You're going to have to help me here," I said, pointing at her apothecary.

Annie looked at me pityingly. "Take this," she said, plucking a pack of pills out the cupboard. "Now go away. I can't look at you any more. It's too tragic. Like some roadkill that isn't quite dead yet lurching about the motorway."

I was tempted to say, 'When did you see my vagina?' but managed to restrain myself. Actually, I was more just distracted by how itchy my arm was.

"What are you laughing away to yourself about, you absolute weirdo?" Annie moaned, pushing me towards the door with her remote control.

"Aren't you worried you will get old people germs from that?" I asked as I was prodded back into the corridor.

"Ha! I never use this thing," she said, brandishing the remote. "Who the hell actually *watches* TV?! Anyway, I have had enough of your cheek, young lady, get out of here!"

"Young?" I asked, raising an eyebrow.

"Oh, sorry!" Annie said with genuine repentance. "I misspoke. What should I have said...have fun doing whatever disgusting old people intercourse that you do with my Dad? Or break a leg? Nah, break a hip is probably more appropriate for your age bracket." Then she slammed the door with youthful zeal.

What kind of microcosm was I living in where I got drugs off my pupil so that I could give myself a bikini wax to prepare for sex with her father and she was aware of the entire situation? I popped a pill and looked at the pill packet as if it might have the answer - perhaps it was one of the adverse effects?

CHAPTER

39

I sat on my bed and poured a glass of Karkalo. It was the colour of an old blood transfusion bag and had a syrupy thickness to it. A whiff of it proved why it was banned from sale outside Belkita; it was so strong it could probably bench more than James.

I picked up the pills and read the back of the label - one pill every 4-6 hours. So, in self-medicating terms, gulping down two plus half a bottle of Karkalo should just about do it. I took a swig of the wine, which was surprisingly pleasant, despite the health warnings on the label; it tasted a bit like a boiled sweet your gran would eat. I popped one of the pills in, which tasted of nothing, which boded well, because that is exactly what it was meant to make you feel.

I lay back on the bed and waited for the mixture to take effect. Sipping on the Karkalo, I scrolled through my social media. June's Instagram story was suspiciously absent, but then again, she was engaging in an industrial conspiracy. James had posted an artful shot of 'Protein Banana Bread', a hulking specimen lurching out of its tin, and I can't even talk about the bread. This was the third bread he had whipped up this week, having previously created a 'Slimming Sourdough' and a 'Peanut Butter Whey Cornbread Surprise'. Hatton had posted a boomerang of the waves on the beach that we were going to meet at in - oh dear God - an hour?!

After a brief moment of panic, I felt fine again; there was no need to get into a tailspin, I had plenty of time if I just kept calm. I had either had an emotional growth spurt or the wine and tablets were working. Figuring it was probably the latter, I grabbed the box of wax strips, topped up my glass of Karkalo and discarded my pants. Remembering June's advice to pull the skin tight, I selected a portion of skin close to my upper thigh, stretched it and applied strip number one. It was a highly unerotic experience to go through to feel sexy, like restraining a turkey with alopecia. As the wax affixed itself to me, the realisation that there was no going back seeped in. I would have to pull it off to get rid of it, even if it removed not only the hair but other chunks of body matter along the way. There was no turning back, much like writing a book, or quitting your job, or having a weird thing with Hatton, or coming to Belkita. I had done it to myself, like I always did.

Other people probably thought of unicorns to distract from the pain in these situations, but of course I was distracting myself with an existential crisis as I finally summoned the courage to rip the wax off. Anyway, the pain, like the unfortunately racistly named Chinese Burn, was immediately relieved by the realisation that my pubic area was still intact. All that had been moved was a bunch of hair stuck in the wax, looking like a smashed bug on a windshield; I had feared something more like a disarticulated badger dragged behind a tractor for six miles. Encouraged by these positive results, I pressed on. Of course, I must give thanks to Karkalo at this point for making the whole thing possible, celebratory sips marked each time I came away unscathed.

As a pile of strips Formerly Known As My Pubes built up, I paused to inspect my work. So it wasn't quite salon quality and my skin had the same hue as a ginger left out in the sun, but I was impressed. Maybe it was a side effect of the Karkalo and drugs, but I didn't think it was too bad. Buoyed by the results, I moved on with newfound confidence to the next challenge - what is politely described in beauty salons as 'the back', or, in more unrefined circles, 'lady butt hair'. It's one of these things that we pretend don't exist, like The Illuminati or celebrity paedophile rings. However, it's just as hard to root out as the Illuminati. Thankfully, anyone with lady butt hair is too old to be bothered by a paedophile sex ring, so it's a lot harder to draw unsavoury comparisons with them.

I reached down at an awkward angle, marvelling at the flexibility Brutus and Lily possess to clean their own fluffy arseholes. I was only at about belly button level and could already feel a twinge in my lower back. I snapped up and took a glug of Karkalo straight out the bottle before plunging on. Slap! went the first wax strip onto the inside of my unsuspecting butt cheek. I waddled over to the remaining wax strips, akin to an ostrich realising it has food poisoning. I fell back on the bed, momentary relief giving way to discomfort as I became aware that there was something alien down there. Was this how those nutcases who claimed to have been molested by aliens started? One misplaced wax strip slowly driving them insane? I rolled over and reached back to extract it, but my back twinged again, this time a sharper pain. It must have been bad if I could still feel it after three quarters of a bottle of Karkalo and some pain medication probably only consumed by pill-popping teenagers and elephants post-surgery. I gritted my teeth and made another attempt to extricate it, but I still couldn't get a decent grip.

Now the panic was setting in and it was bad; the sort of panic when you can't open a public toilet door and start to imagine your embarrassing rescue. What was the point of all this personal grooming if I was going to look like a papier-mâché project? Which emergency service was it most appropriate/least mortifying to call in such a situation?

My reaching for the strip descended into a manic scrabble. As distressed as I was, I was also exhausted. This demon wax strip was obviously not to be trifled with. I knew when to respect a worthy adversary, so retreated to a seated position when my back spasm subsided.

In a moment of decisiveness that I suspect was fuelled by the evil spirit of Karkalo having some interaction with equine-worthy medication, I resolved to just strap on my bikini bottoms as is and head over to the beach anyway. The seawater would loosen the wax, I reasoned. Maybe I could just rip it off in the water completely unnoticed! Even I thought I was full of false confidence at this point, but I brushed aside this aside, along with other inconvenient facts like you are not meant to bathe for at least 24 hours after a bikini wax - this was always in capitals on the disclaimer the beauty therapist made you sign. Well, I was the James Dean of pubic topiary, I told myself as I threw a floaty beach kimono on over the top of my bikini. I really should have realised I was further gone than I thought when it dawned on me that I was wearing the garment back to front with my butt hanging out like I was running away from the asylum in my hospital gown.

How could Hatton resist? I wondered as I chobbled down the corridor, the wax strip poking out between my bikini pants and backwards gown.

CHAPTER

40

When I reached the beach, I realised that I was not entirely removed from self-doubt. I sat down on some rocks, behind one that was just big enough so that Hatton couldn't see me. I had spied him walking along the water's edge, a bottle of wine in one hand and two glasses in the other, or at least I thought I had. Maybe it was a hallucination, it did sound like wishful thinking to me.

On the one hand, the Karkalo-pill combo told me that I was hot shit, even if I did have wax hanging out of my butt cheeks. On the other hand, the same voice that follows every woman around like a lifelong playground bully was piping up again: This man has kissed some of the world's most beautiful women. He has been married to one of them for 15 years. And here I was, an average-looking woman on a good day hiding behind a rock with failed DIY pubic deforestation.

Then the Karkalo crept back in. *He* had invited *me* here. I could spend the rest of my life trying to figure out why, but I didn't hold out much hope of ever finding the answer.

I hoisted myself up, using one of the rocks for support and strode towards Hatton, ready to offer my partially deforested body to him. He caught sight of me, but didn't look pleased. He looked concerned, or at least I thought he did, everything was quite fuzzy now. I was also sweating so much that I kept having to wipe drops of it out of my eyes.

"Are you ok?" he asked, not a bead of sweat on him, his clothes on the right way round, stubble in all the right places, no wax strips hanging off his arse. It was true, I thought, Hollywood people are different. How could he not be reacting to how hot it was?!

"I'm great!" I said with a shrug, which made the kimono fall off my shoulders.

"Are you sure? The rash looks nasty," he said, pointing to the exposed redness on my arm. I pulled the kimono back up over my shoulder. The gown felt wet, like I had already been swimming.

"Let me take a look at it," Hatton said, catching the sleeve of my robe. He withdrew his hand, rubbing his fingers together when he realised how wet it was.

"Let's go for a swim!" I said, reasoning that it would be less obvious what a sweaty mess I was when I was submerged almost completely in water. I sprinted off towards the dark waves.

"Hey, come back!" Hatton called as the cold water hit my feet, sending icy waves of relief up my body. Nonetheless, I dunked my body under because temporary madness and night swimming would be easier to explain than the sweaty swine of a woman I was. I had once read in an article that Electra didn't sweat because she had meditated with a yogi who specialised in expelling all negative emotions from the body; it was better Hatton wasn't exposed to the horror of reality like the buddha leaving his palace for the first time. If he was, I would probably end up as an unpleasant chapter in his autobiography about how sleeping with the human version of a corpulent slippery seal made him realise how much he loved his beautiful bone-dry wife.

Forgetting this was all a self-destructive inner monologue, I floated on my back, gave a hearty seal bark and clapped my hands together like flippers. Hatton, who was wading in now, looked at me like this was the start of a donkey show in Tijuana that he had accidentally stumbled into.

"It makes sense if you're in my head," I said, standing up in the water and tapping my skull. Hatton's look changed, from cautious and hard to something softer. I felt reassured, maybe everyone else *was* right if I too could notice the attraction after three quarters of a bottle of Karkalo and pain meds. I ran my hands over my bikini top to make sure everything was still in place; I didn't want to expose myself, *not yet*, anyway.

"You're a strange one. But that's why I like you," he said, flicking water at me.

"Oooh! OMG! Hatton Finch *likes* me!" I squealed in my best sing-song voice.

"Don't be childish, it makes me feel even older than I am," he said, side-stepping a wave in his Aztec-patterned board shorts. They would look good floating off into infinity later on, I thought.

"Says the guy splashing the girl he likes. What is this? A trip to the local leisure centre?"

Halted by the banter, he stopped and looked down. I thought that maybe I had been too harsh on him. After all, he looked like anything but a kid, the spread of golden-grey hair starting on his chest and leading down into the water.

I walked towards him, worried that I had torpedoed my chances with one stupid joke. Worried not that I had offended him, but that he was so insecure about his age that he couldn't take it. Soon I was in close range of him, but he was still looking into the dark water with a sulky expression on his face.

"You can't *seriously* be upset about-"

His arms scooped down into the water and I was hit by a massive splash. As I wiped it out my eyes, I could hear Hatton laughing hysterically.

"I can't believe you just did that," I said, parting my fringe like a water-logged curtain. Was this how it felt to be a popular girl in a municipal swimming pool circa 2003?

"What are you going to do about it?" said Hatton, stretching out his arm in a way that I was sure had been carefully choreographed by an A-list director to show off his abdominal muscles. He walked towards me with a swagger, but because he was wading through water, there was a definite Victorian-lady-in-a-bustle vibe to proceedings. I tried not to laugh, but I couldn't help it. He flicked water at me again with a quick flick of the wrist. A nice, tanned, slightly veiny wrist. "What are you going to do about it?" he repeated, this time with a definite smile that said, 'you can do whatever you want'.

So I tickled him. It seemed inkeeping with our adolescent approach so far. At first I grabbed the wrists that had caught my attention, then his strong but slippery arms, lodging my hands in his armpits. He wriggled away, but without commitment. In fact, with each stroke we seemed to come closer together, until our arms were about each other, waists and mouths dangerously close, too close to insert a witty comment between us. It felt like we were not fighting against all the reasons that we shouldn't be together anymore, but against whatever had kept us apart for so long.

Then I felt really hot and these little swimming seahorses with lovehearts for eyes were bobbing on the waves behind Hatton. On a rocky outcrop, Paxton was perched, only he was a merman, with a tail and a bikini top made out of shells. It was unnerving, but it weirdly suited him too. He was pointing and laughing at us. June popped up beside him, but she had the body of the crab from the Little Mermaid and was clapping her pincers together excitedly.

"Can you see that too?" I asked, holding on to Hatton's shoulders to steady myself.

"See what?" he said, breathing heavily. Was it lust or annoyance? Probably both.

"The sex seahorses!" I exclaimed, poking at one floating above his head. "And why has Paxton got a tail? And when did June become a crab?"

Hatton was nodding, but not as if he understood what I was talking about. He scooped me up and said, "Ok, let's get you inside. I don't think you're well, Sam," in a practical but tender way that made me glad we were in the sea because otherwise I would have some explaining to do about the puddle underneath me. Then panic hit me; we were almost back on dry land, poor Hatton would probably collapse when confronted with my full weight.

"I'm sorry I'm like a rhino compared to probably everyone else you've shagged," I mumbled into his neck. He laughed and kissed my forehead, instead of his arms just snapping off, which was a pleasant surprise. "Not only are you sick," he said, putting me down gently on the sand, "you're clearly crazy." He looked at me with a smile, but I could see worry in his eyes. How bad was I? I wondered, suddenly scared as he moved away from me.

"Don't leave me, Hatton," I said, unsure of exactly how I meant that.

"I was just getting my phone," he said, popping back up beside me. "I'm just going to phone an ambulance. You're very hot, you know," he said, putting his hand to my forehead.

"Thank you," I said, winking. He moved his hand from my face and grabbed one of mine, dialling with the other.

He laughed a little but he was concentrating on the phone. I started to feel very sleepy and everything went as blurry as frosted glass. I heard the words "as soon as you can", "rapid pulse" and "fever", but I was more concerned about something else.

"I waxed my own vagina for this and I'm not even going to have sex tonight," I grumbled, watching merman Paxton mockingly wave my rogue waxstrip before diving underwater.

That's the last thing I remember before everything went black.

CHAPTER

41

The first thing I saw when I opened my eyes again was Hatton. He smiled encouragingly at me and the crinkles created on his cheeks almost made up for the offensive public toilet blue and baby vomit yellow of the room around us.

"Hello, Sleeping Beauty," he said, planting a kiss on my hand.

I wanted to fire something back about how I was a child of the '90s and identified much more with Mulan than the heteronormative Sleeping Beauty, but my mouth was dry and my tongue slow. I made do with twitching my lips.

A person in white coat hovered into view above me. It slowly dawned on me where I was; they were writing things down on a chart; the public toilet blue scrubs to match the walls, a white coat for some dignity.

"Hospital?" I asked, realising nowhere could contain quite as many depressing hues, except perhaps a call centre.

The doctor and Hatton nodded. The doctor, grimly, Hatton with relief. The doctor walked off scribbling and Hatton did some weird half-hug, like we were at our first underage disco. I side-eyed him, at least I could still do that.

"Sorry, I didn't want to hurt you after what happened," he responded.

"What happened?" I asked, like I had blacked out from too much Karkalo. *Had* I blacked out from too much Karkalo?

"You had a bad case of the Baby Botch," he said.

I laughed, even though it made all my insides feel like they were being pulled out with a coat hanger. Hopefully a nurse would show up with some drugs soon, I thought.

"Come on! Baby Botch! I'm way too old for that.

"You would think!" Hatton said, stretching back and smiling in the same ugly brown chair in hospital rooms and teacher lounges across the world.

"But I'm almost 30," I said sceptically, eyeing Hatton like he was a cold caller trying to sell me double glazing and I was a pensioner who had just seen an episode of Watchdog about this very ruse.

"Yes, well, I don't think the Botch got the memo," he said, adjusting a pillow that was sliding down the back of me. "It's a mindless virus, not a creep banned from playgrounds for trying to groom under-18s on the internet."

The doctor reappeared. I could get a better look at her now. She had dark curly hair piled high above her purple-rimmed glasses and winged eyeliner with the perfect flick, of which I was very jealous.

"Will you tell her she had the Botch?" asked Hatton, exasperated. He sat on the edge of the bed and put a hand with a wedding ring on it round my shoulder. I wasn't sure how I felt about that, but suspected I was on so many drugs that it would be a while before I had an authentic emotion again.

"Yes, Ms. Chambers, you had what is commonly known as Baby Botulism. It causes a severe fever and loss of inhibition due to brain swelling."

"Oh, so I wasn't a complete state because of the Karkalo and the drugs?"

"Well, the alcohol probably didn't help matters, but the drugs you were brought in with are a brand name for baby aspirin, did you know that?"

"Annie lied to me!"

"We used to tell her it had all these magic healing properties when she was a kid," sniggered Hatton.

"I don't get it," I said. "I'm almost-"

"30, we know," sighed Hatton, getting up off the bed.

The doctor smiled. "Well, you must look young for your age, at least to the Botch. Joking aside, it's not unheard of for people in their late 20s to get it," she explained, writing down something on the chart. "And you did have a bad case; we have had you sedated for three days and pumped full of antibiotics to fight it. You are lucky this gentleman found you when he did," the doctor said, her eyebrows, a work of beautiful facial calligraphy, wiggling suggestively.

The doctor produced a tablet (the electronic kind) from a pocket. "A possible symptom we are currently researching is long-term irritability before admission. Is that something you have noticed at all?"

"Yes!" said Hatton.

The medic tapped away on her screen and I glared at Hatton.

"What! It's true! Remember when you got annoyed at that waitress who thought we were together? And June keeps slagging you off about having a go at some poor salesgirl at the airport. Plus you have been just about as moody as the teeangers you teach."

"That is true, actually," I conceded, weakly. "I just thought that I was sliding into Karenhood."

"Karen-hood?" asked the doctor, looking up from her screen. "I'm not familiar with that condition, what is it?"

Just then June burst through the door, followed by James, who had a protesting hospital orderly over one shoulder. Bringing up the rear was Annie, who sloped in as James held his victim at arms' length.

"I told them they could not come in, Dr Voluna!" shouted the orderly, his feet kicking the air.

"Ms. Chambers," said the well-groomed Dr Voluna, "Are you comfortable with these people being here?"

"Of course, they are my friends," I said. Annie shuddered. "Except for Annie. She just came in to check if the rumours of my death were true. As you can see, she's bitterly disappointed."

Annie rolled her eyes and made a gagging noise that I have only ever heard Lily do before a hairball. "Isn't she still contagious or whatever?" asked Annie, loitering by the door frame.

"Oh no," said Dr Voluna. "Baby Botch is no longer infectious once the symptoms have set in. If Ms. Chambers continues to make good progress, she may be able to go home tomorrow."

"I cannot believe she had that," said Annie, shuffling into the room. "She's, like, 30!"

"Yes, we have established that, thank you," murmured Dr Voluna. "She has the classic rash that presents in late-stage Baby Botch. My guess is that you ignored the other symptoms, because, it's a theme we keep returning to, you are 30. Did you have a fever? Blurred vision?"

"Yes," I said as June put me in some sort of loving headlock. "But I just wrote it off." The last bit was muffled against June's chest.

"Please, she is still in a fragile state," the doctor said, commanding June away with a point of the finger. June prowled off, like a lioness sizing up the latest addition to the pack. "I was just explaining to Ms Chambers how lucky she was that Mr Finch stumbled upon her in the romantic darkness of the beach on Wednesday night."

June bit her lip and did a fist pump that said 'Go on my son'. James was trying to suppress a laugh and failing miserably. Tears were forming in the corner of his eyes. Hatton was making one last attempt at an Academy Award, innocently smiling at Dr Voluna. Annie looked as if someone had shown her the Two Girls, One Cup video in slow motion. I looked into Dr Voluna's well-framed eyes and gave her a shrug to say, "Well, wouldn't you?"

Dr Voluna rolled her own shoulders in a way that said "fair play." "Anyway," she continued, "We should be able to release you tomorrow. I think that is enough visitors for now. If you can all head out, please, except for Mr Finch."

"Why does he get to stay?" pouted Annie, like she actually wanted to be there.

"Sam's parents can't get here because of travel restrictions, and since I brought Sam in, I am classed as her emergency contact while in Belkita. Sam has a *lot* to catch up on."

"True dat," said June, followed by a cackle. "But I'm her best friend in the entire world, can I not just have five minutes to catch up with her?"

"If she feels up to it," said Dr Voluna.

"Yes, I do!" I said.

"See?" June said, giving Dr Voluna a thin smile.

"I will take Annie back to the hotel and be back in an hour or so," Hatton said. "Come on, munchie." Annie cringed at the nickname as they left the room, James following behind, asking the doctor about the effect of avocados on muscle mass.

I watched them all file out and turned back to June. Big ugly tears had made her usually subtle eyeliner stain down her face like an '80s metal band member.

"You're never allowed to get ill again, you know," she said.

"June," I said, trying to shuffle out of bed to comfort her, but finding myself too entrenched in the pillows and bedsheets.

"I mean it! It's all your fault, you know," she said, dabbing her eye with a pinkie finger.

"What is?"

"I found religion. Me, a card-carrying socialist atheist!"

"Really?" I said, a giggle escaping from my mouth.

"Unfortunately." June wiped a smudge of black onto her sleeve. "I prayed to the Buddha for the first time since I was a kid for you to get better, or at least come back as a puppy I could adopt. I felt so dirty."

Now I was crying, but with laughter.

"It's not funny!" she said, beginning to giggle herself. "I almost dropped my placard on Lorando when he told me you had been taken to hospital."

"Oh, yes, the workers' rights protest. How did that go?"

"Paxton caved to all our demands," she said, wiping her shoulder. "I think it helped that we were protesting in the car park just as the inspector arrived. And I broadcasted the whole thing live on YouTube - shares in his family business nose-dived!"

"Oh God! The inspection! I completely forgot about that! How did it go?"

"Well, half the staff were on strike and Hatton ran through the car park carrying you whilst you screamed about the Little Mermaid and taking drugs off the students. That was all within 15 minutes of him getting there."

"So, better than expected?"

"Ha! Exactly. I think Paxton only had two or three heart attacks." June got up and walked over to the blinds, carefully bending one.

My brain was still foggy, but I was slowly piecing everything together. "Wait, does that mean I'm on YouTube screaming about being the Little Mermaid with a wax strip hanging out of my ass?" I shrunk back into the bed like a hermit crab back into its shell.

"Well, of course," said June. I let out a dehydrated groan. "Don't be upset, there are some really good auto-tuned remixes of the whole thing online! It's done wonders for your profile." June sounded a little half-hearted, her eyes trailing along the hospital corridor.

"That's Paxton now. I better go. Things are still a bit weird since I led a worker's revolt against him." June tiptoed back and gave me a kiss on the forehead. "I will go out the window, less awkward that way," she said, hoisting the window open. "What is this? Three floors up? Totally manageable." June grabbed onto the drainpipe running down the side of the building. "See you at the hotel, comrade!" she said with a salute as she shimmied out of sight.

Just then, the door to my room swung open and Paxton slid in like he was about to tap dance in a musical. "She lives! Thank Satan and all his little helpers! Selling my soul to him actually worked!"

"Don't be ridiculous Paxton, the Devil doesn't accept damaged goods like that," I said.

Paxton laughed heartily. "Thank God they didn't have to amputate your acid tongue. How are you doing? I came down as soon as Hatton messaged me to say you had come round."

"I'm OK, I think. I'm not really sure, to be honest," I said, feeling my own brow.

"Well, you look a lot better than when I last saw ya. You had seaweed in your hair, your boob had popped out of your bikini top and you had a wax strip stuck to your ass," he laughed.

"Oh God," I mumbled. "I would be embarrassed but I don't know if I have any shame left at this point. Let's change the subject, how was the inspection?"

"Well, let's just say I too would be embarrassed but I definitely don't have any shame left at this point."

"That bad?"

"Oh, yeah. Between the protest and my semi-naked, delirious member of staff being carried around by her shirtless colleague while it was broadcast to the world, it wasn't a great start."

"I'm sorry!"

"Ah, forget about it. It was pretty spectacular. I loved it, really," Paxton said, sitting down in the standard-issue chair and kicking his feet up onto the bed. "It made me realise, I am not the working kind. I'm much better at spending money than making money."

"You do have a unique skillset," I conceded.

"I know, right?! That's what I told the inspector. I said, look, pal, pass me or fail me, I don't give a shit. Let's get martinis."

"And what did he make of that?"

"Well," scoffed Paxton, "Apparently I am not 'thought leader material', 'really quite dangerous' and 'not fit to be in charge of an electric scooter, let alone a school'. Some people have no sense of fun."

"Haters gonna hate," I confirmed.

"Whaddyagonnado, eh?" Paxton shrugged, like he had been told his parcel had been delivered to a neighbour, not like his entire business had imploded in front of him. "Anyway, have I got a surprise for you!" Paxton scampered back out into the corridor and I braced myself; Paxton's surprises were usually not pleasant, like the time he decided to 'surprise' me on the morning of my final exam with a 5am bedside serenade of Club Tropicana on his way back from a night out.

Paxton re-entered the room holding someone's hand. I recognised it immediately; it was Harriet's hand, no doubt about it. She was the only person I knew who painted her nails 'Primrose Pink'. I recognised the shade because it had been discontinued in our Third Year and she dragged me on a hysterical odyssey to buy every remaining bottle in Northern Scotland.

Sure enough, Harriet emerged, towing Caspar behind her.

"Samantha! I came as soon as I heard the news!" she said, handing Caspar to Paxton, who held the boy naturally but nervously. "Keep him away from her, I don't want him getting the Botch," she said, shooing Paxton out the room.

"Come on, little fella, let's go and get a snack from the hospital shop," Paxton said, like they were your average father and son in a Macaulay Culkin film, not the baby daddy with his unconventional threesome sprog.

Harriet waited until Paxton and Caspar were out of earshot before asking, "How ARE you, darling? It must have been awful."

"Well, actually, I'm-"

"I have left Allan, you know! I had to get out. Those ridiculous travel restrictions though. I had to tell them at the Border that you were my sister and in deep distress. Just play along if anyone asks, there's a good girl," Harriet said, whipping out a lace fan and wafting her curls.

"Well, this is quite shocking," I said, hoping a nurse would arrive with some drugs to knock me out soon, or I would at least have a seizure to save me from this conversation.

"It's a scandal, isn't it? There's more, though," Harriet said, a blush rising on her cream cheeks.

"Oh?" I said, practicing my best 'I have no idea what you are talking about' face.

"Steel yourself," instructed Harriet, grabbing my wrist.

"Consider myself steeled."

"Paxton, Paxton is, he is Caspar's father," Harriet released my wrist and collapsed back in the chair.

"No," I said. I too was lethargic to muster fake shock.

"Yes. I am dreadfully sorry I never told you. We have kept the whole thing very hush-hush."

"Hm." I drummed my fingers on the bed.

"This Baby Botch makes you reconsider what you want out of life, and I have realised it is Paxton. And for us to bury that silly hatchet about your writing. I simply won't leave until you say we are best friends again, just like the old days," Harriet seized my hands again, before quickly dropping them and dousing her own in hand sanitiser.

"Well, Harriet, I would-"

"It's settled then!" she declared. "I better go and find Paxton. I love him, but I am not sure I trust him not to leave our son in a strip club."

"They only went to the shop!"

"This is Paxton we are talking about."

"Good point," I admitted.

Harriet gave a chuckle that was pure Home Counties and turned to walk out the door, but bumped into Hatton.

"Oh hello, pardon me," she said, turning back to give me a sly smile.

"Er, hello," said Hatton, looking confused.

"Oh, I am Harriet...Benson for now," Harriet said, extending a limp hand for Hatton to take.

"Uhuh," he said, shaking her hand but looking at me.

"Sam's best friend," she clarified.

"Isn't that June?" Hatton asked, adding a good-natured laugh as an addendum.

"Oh, you card!" guffawed Harriet, hanging on to Hatton's bicep for apparent support. "You must be that Hatton fellow she is always on Estonian TV shows with."

"Danish," said Hatton, taking his hand back.

"No thank you, I couldn't possibly have a pastry. I have been worried sick," said Harriet.

"No, they're Danish TV shows, not Estonian," he said, nodding politely as he moved passed her and into the room.

"Oh yes. Well, close enough," said Harriet with a girlish shrug.

"Yes, only about 700 miles out," Hatton said to himself as he sat down in the chair.

"Well, you two look very good together. Even if Samantha is the colour of death and you clearly haven't changed your shirt in two days, at least it's designer," Harriet said, her eyes scanning us with an Interpol intensity. "Yes, Samantha, I much prefer him to the last one," she said, her polished teeth glinting in a smile as she shut the door behind her.

"Well, that was an experience," said Hatton. "I thought you were joking when you said she was like that."

"Oh no, Harriet is many things, but not a joke. More like a warning," I said.

"What did she mean, I much prefer him to the last one?" Hatton asked, leaning on the armrest with a smile that confirmed he knew exactly what she meant.

"You'll have to read the book, just like everyone else," I said, folding my arms.

"Of course I have read it. You know that. I am intrigued about who the dashing male lead will be in the second book."

"Oh really?"

"Yes, and whether they manage to overcome disease, errant spouses and their own stupidity and end up together," he said, stroking his chin.

"I've been wondering about that too," I admitted.

"Any ideas?" he asked.

I was running out of ideas, but I didn't want to admit that. "You will have to buy the book, just like everyone else," I teased.

"What if I decide to wait until the film comes out?" he fired back, getting up to leave.

"Oh come on, everyone knows the films are never as good as the books," I said, catching his arm as he walked around the bed.

"Yeah, yeah. Well, I brought your pen and notepad from the hotel," he said, taking them out his back pocket and casually tossing them on the bed. "I want you to write down exactly what you want," he said, leaning against the wall so he was at my eye level. It was disconcertingly intimate. "Whatever it is, I will do it." It sounded like a dare. "Leave Electra. Hire one of those planes with a banner that says 'HF 4 SC'. Shave my head and become a monk. Never speak of this again."

"Are those the only options?"

He smiled and stood back up. "You're the writer. Use your imagination."

CHAPTER

42

Hatton,

I have never actually written to you before, apart from the odd text message. It's strange, because I feel like I am writing to you every time I put pen to paper. Every time I left Denmark, I would make a mental note of all the dumpster fire incidents in my life so that I could tell you. Now you're there all the time and I write down everything that has happened like it's some sort of record we can look back on in years to come.

That alone suggests I want this to continue, which I do. I never thought I would say this, but Harriet was right, the Baby Botch makes you reconsider things. I used to think you were this sort of beautiful parakeet I could only watch in a pet shop window, but, with the best will in the world, I have realised you are just a common street pigeon just like me, deep down, behind your fancy feathers.

From living in Beath, I know that pigeons have a tendency to do a whole manner of disgusting things to each other, including cannibalism, death by pecking and sacrifice to their seagull overlords. I'm starting to think that this is a bad analogy. Maybe we are more like the two swans that come and nest in the nice bit of Beath by the newbuild flats. Or maybe

I'm just an ugly duckling. Anyway, everyone loves the swans, the locals ran a 'Save Our Swans' campaign at the same time as their 'Heave-ho the Hobos' protest, but I digress. The more important thing is that the swans apparently mate for life. I am not suggesting we do anything as drastic as that, but, I guess, as I'm writing this I realise that I love you and writing it down isn't enough, I'm going to have to tell you in person.

Sam x

CHAPTER

43

The next morning I was given the all-clear by Dr Voluna. I messaged June and Hatton the good news. June got back right away.

June: YASSSS! I'm organising a party for you tonight!

Sam: Oh God. Why?

June: Have you forgotten you are 30 on Sunday? Everyone is flying out on Friday though.

Sam: Please. Don't. Really, I don't mind.

June: Too late. I have already bought enough vodka to kill Yeltsin. Again.

I closed the chat and hovered over Hatton's, but there were no new messages.

I was hoping I could have had the love conversation in private on the way back to the hotel, but I was sure there would be plenty of time before the party started.

June arrived about an hour later, and not a moment too soon. I had only been conscious in the hospital for a little over a day, but I was already over the smell of chemicals and illness, plus the horrendous interior design. She came in carrying a 'With Sympathy' helium balloon.

"What's that for?" I asked as she handed it to me in the hospital corridor.

"It's all they had in the gift shop. And it kind of works, you are turning 30, after all."

"In the words of Morrissey, that joke isn't funny anymore," I said, reluctantly taking the balloon from her.

"Come on, the cultural obsession with youth is at least comical," June said, taking my bag from me and leading the way down the hall. "It's all a load of donkey bollocks, anyway. Look at me, I am 41 and only just entering my prime," she said, adopting a shrill Miss Jean Brodie brogue.

"Oh really?" I asked, following behind her as she skipped ahead.

"Yes, I had some great news the other day! The Mayor of Beath died!" she said like she had been told Cuba had annexed the United States.

"That old guy? The one who used to dress up as Santa Claus and turn on the Christmas lights?"

"The very one!" confirmed June as she danced out into the hot air of the carpark.

"Isn't that sad?"

"Well, maybe. For his like, 5 kids and 19 grandchildren, or whatever it said in the obituary. BUT, it's great news for me. It means I can run in the by-election and become the first Socialist Mayor of Beath!" June said, shaking with excitement so much that she only just managed to open the car door.

"You're going to enter politics?" I asked, stepping into the passenger side.

"Yes," said June in the key of 'duh'.

"I just thought I would double check. I suspected I was having another one of my hallucinations, but you're not a crab, so I wasn't sure," I said, strapping myself in as June fired up the rusty engine.

"Come on, Sam, you know it makes sense!"

"June, it's never a good sign when you have to quote Del Boy Trotter to justify your political ambitions," I replied, rubbing my sweaty temples.

"I won't have you knocking Only Fools and Horses! It's how I learnt English in the '90s. It's a fantastic cautionary tale about capitalism too," said June, manoeuvring the car out of the parking space. The vehicle was so knackered she it was like she was heaving the car herself with every turn of the wheel. "Plus," she said, exhaling heavily, "She who dares, wins!"

I turned to the burnt yellow Belkita fields coming closer to us. Maybe June would be a good politician, I thought. She genuinely cared about people and would freely admit to any sexual indiscretions without the bat of an eyelid, which was a refreshing approach. Plus, she was popular in Beath, everyone knew who she was and she was always donating X amount of her profits to local drug rehab facilities and dog sanctuaries, Beath's two main industries.

"You know what, June? Good for you. I think you will be a great Mayor."

"Thanks, I think you will be a great campaign manager," she replied, grabbing my hand with the passion of Thelma & Louise before they drive off the cliff.

"A what?"

"You have such a way with words, you would be perfect!"

I chafed under the praise and dread of a mayoral campaign. I had to admit though: "She who dares, wins, would be a good slogan, though..."

"That's my girl!" said June, shaking my shoulder with a hand that really should have been on the wheel. "Now that's sorted, what's going on with you and Hatton? Are you guys in? Out? Doing the hokey cokey and turning around?"

"I think we're...on," I said, my heart beating faster as the hotel came into view. I touched my jacket pocket, checking the letter was still there in case I chickened out and couldn't tell him.

"Ugh, finally," said June.

"I need to speak to him when we get back to the hotel," I said as the building crept closer, like a cloud across a spotless sky. "I don't know, I feel nervous though. He said he would do whatever I want-"

"Are we going to find him naked, chained to a radiator with a bottle of baby oil?" asked June as the van tripped over the speedbump at the carpark entrance.

"No!" I said, rolling my eyes. "I just have a feeling that something is going to go wrong."

"Why?"

"Because it always does."

A welcome committee had formed at the hotel entrance. Paxton was waving with one hand, the other arm around Harriet, who was in turn smearing Caspar in suntan lotion so that he looked like a friendly ghost. Lorando stood shoulder to shoulder with Paxton, giving me a thumbs up. James was clapping forcefully, his arm muscles wriggling in approval. Aubrey was next to him in gym gear, waving at us with Jane Fonda vigour. The kids from my class were standing in a line holding a homemade 'WELCOME BACK SAM' banner, Melody smiling pleasantly, Jesus blowing kisses at our van and Koala and Annie with a certain reluctant embarrassment, Annie looking even more pained than usual.

Hatton wasn't there, though. Maybe he *was* chained to a radiator somewhere. I looked around the carpark for a sign of him. After a full circuit of the grounds, my eyes returned to the hotel entrance. Out came Hatton, but he looked like he was a thousand miles away, clapping absentmindedly and looking off towards the sea. I didn't know why, but it soon became clear, because someone else joined him on the steps: Electra.

"Well this just got interesting," said June through a ventriloquist-tight smile. "She must have arrived while I was picking you up, the sneaky minx. Want me to take her out?"

"No, it's fine," I said, crumpling up the letter in my jacket pocket. The truth was that it was not fine in the slightest. I felt really grubby now that Electra was an actual person in my world and not just an abstract obstacle, like an exaggerated but unseen character in a sitcom or a wife in a Brontë novel.

We got out of the van and I fixed a smile to my own face as we approached the group.

"Sam! I am so glad you are better!" trilled Aubrey, breaking away from the group. "I tried to come to the hospital and visit you, but they said that visiting hours were over!"

"That's ok, Aubrey. When did you come by?" I had heard that the over-25s were now allowed outside to exercise again on Belkita.

"I went for a midnight run and it was on my route. The receptionist spoke to me like I was totally removed from reality. The cheek!"

"Oh, yeah," I said, watching Electra, who had linked arms with Hatton and was deep in conversation, but he still seemed in the shallows of it, his eyes darting around the group. They caught mine and I gave Aubrey a hug and turned towards my pupils.

"That's very sweet of you, guys," I said, stepping back to take in the banner.

"Don't mention it. Really," said Annie.

"I drew the penis in the top left corner," said Jesus.

"Of course you did," I said, looking over to see a graffito penis that had a big red 'X' through it.

"I crossed it out," said Koala in a huff. "You have the artistic skill of a sex-crazed caveman."

"Well, it was still a nice surprise," I said.

"Not as much of a surprise as my Mum turning up," said Annie. It was hard to tell if she was more embarrassed by her mum, me, Hatton, or all three.

I nodded and screwed the letter into an even smaller ball in my pocket.

"You must be the Sam who has been keeping my husband out of trouble!"

Electra and Hatton were now standing behind me, looking like an advert for Viagra; a good-looking middle aged man with a beaming, age-appropriate Venus on his arm.

"That's me!" I said, feeling myself wilt like a reluctant penis. She was even more beautiful in person than on screen, whereas I was just about passable with an Instagram filter.

"I can't thank you enough for keeping him company in Denmark," she said with a Princess Di smile. Dear God, was I Camilla Parker-Bowles?! "It can get lonely when you have to travel for work the whole time, can't it?" The question was addressed to us both.

"Um, I suppose," said Hatton when she squeezed his arm. I made a vague noise of agreement, though I think it came out a little strangled.

"Anyway, I am so glad you two have had each other," she said. James said "HAH!" behind us. Hatton and I twitched in unison. Electra turned to Hatton blithely. "Darling, let's head back to the room. I need to freshen up after the flight and you need a shave! Lovely to finally meet you, Sam," she said, already leading him away.

Alone, I realised everyone else had been watching the exchange from the way they snapped from silence to chatter.

"So, what about this party, then?" I said, striding over to June, who was now in an animated conversation with Harriet.

"I have taken the liberty of assigning a masked ball theme," declared Harriet.

"The theme *was* enough vodka to kill Boris Yeltsin," seethed June.

"Quite," said Harriet. "Anyway, the closest thing I could find to Venetian masks in Belkita was novelty rubber monstrosities in," Harriet paused, as if about to be sick, "Big Daddy's Joke Shoppe, but they will have to do." She put down Casper and picked up a bulging plastic bag at her feet as if it pained her, not because of the weight, but because of the contents.

"Here, you have this one," she said, handing a T-Rex mask to James.

"Why?" he said, holding it at arms length like Harriet had just handed him a decapitated head.

"Because I said so," said Harriet, bemused by the descent. "Sam, here's one for you," she said, passing me a chicken mask, complete with beady dead eyes and a big red wobbly thing on top of its head.

Now it was my turn to whine "Why?"

"Because you're turning 30, it's your last chance to be a spring chicken!" Harriet laughed at her own joke.

"Also I think Sam is going to chicken out of doing something," said June, elbowing me in the side.

Harriet continued rummaging undisturbed. "Who should we give these parrott masks to?" she asked, retrieving two brightly coloured bird heads from the bag.

"Definitely Hatton and Electra," I muttered.

"Gosh, yes. They are such a beautiful couple, aren't they?" said Aubrey, who was now peering into the bag too. "Like a couple of little lovebirds!"

"Exactly," I said, wringing my mask in my hands.

"I will take them. My room is just down the corridor from theirs. Oh, and I will take that unicorn mask for myself too!" Aubrey said, gathering them all in her arms.

"I suppose you can have this one, June," said Harriet with a titter, withdrawing a BDSM latex mask from the bag.

"Oh, if only I had known! I wouldn't have left my one in Edinburgh! Thank you, Harriet," she said, snatching it off her. Harriet's lip curled.

"And what will you two be wearing?" I asked, glancing between Harriet and Paxton.

"Well, I never travel without my own set of Venetian masks!" Harriet said, like it was a mini-bag of toiletries. She dipped a hand into the tote bag on her shoulder and produced two ornate eye masks with long flowing ribbon ties, each a deep red with gilt edging.

"What a silly question," I said to myself.

"Come on, Sam, let's go and get ready," June said, leading me away. Once we were out of earshot in the lobby, she said, "I can't believe she just turned up like that! You have to go and find him, now!"

"I haven't even seen my pets yet!"

"Brutus is humping things. Lily is looking on in disapproval. You haven't missed much. Now, go! Find out what the hell is going on!"

"Right, ok," I said, heading off in the direction of Hatton's room. I was just messaging him 'We need to talk' when I felt Harriet's pincer-like grip on my shoulder.

"And where do you think you are going?" she asked.

"Harriet, I really need to speak to-"

"Nonsense! You need to shower so that you don't smell of hospital. Be in the bar in 20 minutes to greet your guests. You can do as much talking as you like then. Now where's your room?"

"That way," I muttered, pointing in the opposite direction to the one I was moving in. Harriet steered me around with her claws.

"Off you trot, then," she said firmly.

In my room, I was greeted by a wolf-like howl from Brutus and a blink of acknowledgement from LIly. At least they would always be by my side, I thought, as Brutus tried to insert an enthusiastic tongue up my nostril and Lily prowled by, trailing her tail along my back. Harriet was right, I needed to shower, I thought, getting a whiff of the stale smell attached to me. I went into the bathroom and quickly disrobed, Brutus running off with my pants, as he was accustomed to do. It was easier just to let him do it, there was much wailing on both parts if you tried to take them off him before he lost interest.

People often said they had their best ideas in the shower, so I hoped something would come to me while I was under the spray. I even fiddled with the settings to see if a 'tropical rainshower' or 'turbowash' would give me a lightbulb moment. It was useless though, I was out of ideas. I would just have to try and stumble through the party until I could talk to Hatton and find out what was going on.

I was drying myself off when there was an insistent rat-a-tat-tat on my door.

"Samantha! Hurry up! The canapés will be circulating any moment now!" called Harriet through the door. There was a desperation in her voice, like she had just told me we must escape into the night because the Gestapo would arrive any second.

"I'm coming, I'm coming," I said, zipping the dress up my back. This was definitely my nicest dress, it wasn't even in a sale, had flowers on it, floaty sleeves and you couldn't just pull it over your head and go about your life. I slid my feet into a chunky pair of sandals, pulled my jacket back on, grabbed the chicken mask and headed for the door while Brutus looked on. I could almost hear him say: "Just keep moving, leave me and the pants in peace."

Harriet was still banging on the door so I marched out lest she come back with a battering ram. "You look nice," she said when I opened the door. "The sandals are a little orthopaedic, but it's not the end of the world. Put the chicken on!" Harriet tied her mask around her head and I slid my head into the rubber chicken. The eye holes were tiny and I only caught glimpses of Harriet striding down the corridor as I made my way behind, holding onto the wall for support in my sweaty rubber prison. Luckily, I had spent so much time in Tito's that I was drawn to it like a homing pigeon. The clinking of glasses, Mexican music and chatter also helped.

I heard a collective "weeeeeey" and a smattering of "Here comes the birthday girl!" when I rounded the last corner. From my impaired viewpoint, it seemed like Lorando had perhaps been a little creative with the number of people allowed in the bar under the relaxed Botch guidelines that the government had issued over the weekend as cases fell. It all felt a bit overwhelming, panic was definitely brewing in my chest. I pulled up my mask to see if James was there. If anyone could understand a full-on meltdown, it was him. I looked around but there was not a T-Rex insight.

"Happy Birthday, Sam!" said Lorando, approaching in a mask, one half the drama 'laughing face', the other the drama 'sad face'. He planted a kiss on each of my chicken cheeks. "Thanks Lorando. Have you seen James? I really need to speak to him."

"He's the T-Rex, isn't he?"

"Yes!"

"I saw him in the kitchen a few minutes ago," Lorando said with a smidgen of disapproval

"Great, thanks," I said, hurrying off in that direction.

"Samantha! Where are you going? We are just bringing the cake out!" shouted Harriet as I took off down the corridor.

I pulled open the heavy kitchen door and saw two legs sticking out the bottom of an open fridge door. A dinosaur head popped round the door, along with a hand holding a massive chicken leg.

"Oh, thank God you're here!" I said, shutting the door behind me and leaning on the kitchen island for support. "I'm freaking out and I think only you will understand."

James placed a reassuring-chicken-free hand on my shoulder and rubbed my arm. This was a much better response than I was expecting, maybe he was finally warming up to me!

"Ok, so don't take the piss, James-"

He immediately started to laugh. It irritated me, even though it was muffled by the mask.

"Ok, but-" he said.

"I said I don't want you to take the piss! Now shut up!"

He was silent. Perhaps I had finally earned a modicum of respect from him. "Here's the thing, right," I swallowed, my insides dropping down as if they were in a broken elevator hurtling towards the ground. "I have come to the realisation that I am in love with Hatton. Like completely and embarrassingly so."

This is when I expected James to interject with some withering one liner, but he didn't say a word, he didn't even seem to be moving.

"Are you not going to make some joke about this being a gender-bending version of Beauty and the Beast?" I asked and James raised his hand to interrupt. "You know what, I don't want to hear it," I said, doing a talk-to-the-hand gesture. "I just had to tell someone because I can't tell him. Ever."

He shrugged a 'why?'

"Oh come on, James! It would ruin his life! His bloody wife is here. They will probably get back together and live happily ever after and it will be too awkward for us to ever work together again. That's the best case scenario, imagine if I showed him this letter," I said, grabbing the ball of paper in my pocket and throwing it onto the countertop.

James picked it up and began to unravel it. "What would he say to that? It's a pigeon-based love letter! It doesn't even mention that I had an elaborate day dream the other day where we went shopping in IKEA together. We shared a plate of meatballs and had an argument about which bookcase to buy, for Christ's sake!"

I took a breath, halting my tirade to finally allow him to give some feedback. Still silent, he lifted a hand up to his mask. The hand looked familiar, but it wasn't James'. My stomach plunged down further, reaching its final destination somewhere around the Earth's core.

"Oh God. Oh no," I said, covering my face as Hatton revealed his. I started making a high-pitched sound, a cross between a fire alarm and a kettle.

"It's ok, it's ok," Hatton said, even though he looked very far from ok. "Just take a deep breath and we can talk about this."

I ripped off my mask. "WHYAREYOUDRESSEDLIKEJAMES?!" I hissed, pointing a shaking finger at the mask in his hand.

"He got all self-conscious that the T-Rex mask would draw attention to his short arms, so we swapped," he said, holding up the dino head.

"WHATAREYOUDOINGHERE?"

"You know I get hungry when I'm stressed. Well... Anyway, that doesn't matter right now, all that matters is what you just said. Did you mean it?"

I had never seen him look so serious, but now I was the one who was silent. It was like I had used up all my words. I couldn't find any, even though 'yes' would have sufficed.

"I wrote it down, didn't I?" I eventually spluttered.

"Yes, but I want to hear it too, the full audiovisual experience," he said, like a director frustrated with my performance.

"Why are you moving the romantic goalposts?" I said, half-laughing, half-seething. "Shall I see if I can get some lottery funding for a multimedia exhibition?"

"I just want all of you. Sometimes it feels like the last few months have been just one long hallucination. I just want confirmation that I am not in this alone," he said, grabbing a slice of pizza from the fridge and tearing a strip off with his teeth.

"Well, how could you be alone when you have your darling wife Electra here by your side?" I said with all the venom I had felt circulating through my system that day. It gave me some relief, but I also felt awful, not that I was going to show the second bit.

"I didn't ask her to come," he said, shaking his head.

"Oh well, she is here now. And you didn't even say anything," I barged past him and took a slice of cold pizza for myself. Arguing made me hungry.

"There wasn't time-"

"Oh, and thanks for the birthday wishes, by the way," I said, raising my pizza like it was a wine glass, then taking a massive bite.

"Well, happy bloody birthday," he said, gnawing on a pizza crust. "Will you be taking a celebratory flight on your broomstick to celebrate making it another turn around the sun without being burnt at the stake?"

"Ha! Well, I'm sure you will be very happy with your beautiful wife and her freshly steamed vagina, or whatever Gwyneth Paltrow has persuaded will help her achieve eternal youth this week. Just keep her away from virgins and altars," I said, screwing my remaining pizza into a ball and shoving it in my mouth.

"You know what, you might be turning 30, but you have got a lot of growing up to do. I can't believe I thought this would work."

I chewed furiously on my pizza ball so that I could follow up with "Neither can I!"

"Great, well, get back out there and have a nice birthday. Have a nice life," he said, going back to the fridge for more pizza.

I stomped off towards the door. "Yeah, yeah. Goodbye, Auf wiedersehen, au revoir, blen alee as they say in Belkita," I wrenched the door open and felt a waft of warm air from the corridor. "Oh and just FYI, I do love you, you stupid bastard!" Hatton popped his head round the fridge again, but he was looking past me. I turned to see what at:

Harriet was standing at the door with a birthday cake covered in candles. As was the rest of the party, including Electra, who looked like I had turned up the heat too high on her vagina steamer.

"Happy Birthday!" shouted Harriet, trying to salvage the situation. Everyone else was silent, apart from the odd nervous cough.

There was some yapping and Brutus broke through the crowd. I saw his fluffy tail weaving between the legs of the party goers, then I winced as his little snout poked through; Brutus was still carrying my dirty pants.

"You too, Brutus?" I said as I picked him up and quickly stuffed my pants in my pocket. "I think I will see myself out."

CHAPTER

44

A few weeks later, I was sitting in June's massage shop, now her campaign headquarters, photoshopping a red fist into the background of a poster. We had been on the campaign trail ever since we hastily returned from Belkita on the evening of the pizza and the pants.

My phone vibrated and I twitched with irritation. I was really in the zone with the design, but I knew I better answer it, in case it was important. June had been a hit with the media, because, well, she's June and journalists were always calling for a soundbite.

It wasn't a journalist, though. It was Paxton. I considered letting it ring out, but curiosity got the better of me. What hairbrained scheme was he up to now? Part of me wanted an update on his relationship with Harriet, even though another part of me felt a little physically ill at the thought of it.

"Sam! Old buddy, old pal! I haven't seen you since Belkita!"

"Tell her I haven't forgiven her for ruining my party," I heard Harriet say in the background.

"It was actually my party, but never mind," I said under my breath.

"Anyway, there's no need to get into all that now," Paxton said and I sighed with relief.

"What's up, Paxton?"

"Well, I have started my own podcast," he took the camera and gave me a view of a recording studio. "I converted my second kitchen. Pretty neat, huh? Anyway, the podcast is called That's Rich. People love it. It's just me talking about what it's like to be insanely wealthy."

"Yes! I have listened to an episode. It's very you, Paxton." In it, Paxton rattled around his wine cellar opening obscenely expensive champagnes and ended the recording with a stirring rendition of What is Love by Haddaway.

"Thank you! Anyway, I want to do my next episode on my political connections. Our next door neighbour used to be a big deal in Italian politics, so I have invited him to take part. Is June available next Thursday? It would be great to have her on."

I scrolled through her diary. "Hm...no. She has community consultations all day."

"Damn, Thursday is the only day he is available. Could you come on instead?"

"Me?" I laughed.

"Yup. You can talk about being a political fixer now."

"Paxton, I'm using the free version of Canva, I'm not exactly Machiavelli," I said, shifting the fist a little across the screen.

"Well, you can talk about being a writer, too, I don't care. How's the book going?"

"Well, it's going," I said. I had been writing down my account of Belkita when I wasn't being a 'political fixer', but I still didn't feel like I had a good ending to the story yet.

"Ok, well, think of something a bit more interesting to say before then. How does 4pm your time sound?"

"I can do that," I said, dropping it into the diary.

"See you then! Better go, Harriet and I are screening Mandarin tutors for Caspar and I need at least two Scotches before that is remotely bearable."

I saw Harriet loom back into view, her eyebrows shooting up her head so far that you would normally need a system of winches and pulleys to reach that height. Paxton said "Uhoh" with a devilish glee and hung up.

"Who was that?" asked June, emerging from a massage room, which now served as her personal office.

"Paxton. He wants me to go on his podcast next week," I said, throwing myself back into basic graphic design.

"Oh, really? You know who you should talk to?" said June, grabbing a few sheets from the printer beside me.

"Not this again," I sighed, rubbing my forehead.

"You guys had one stupid argument that ended with 'I love you', for Trotsky's sake!" she said, waving to a potential voter outside. "I should have made you stay and face the music, but what with the travel bans relaxing that week, my own damn political ambition got in the way. I regret that."

"There is no music to face. It's a silent disco all in your head," I said, beckoning June over to see a gossip article about Hatton and Electra hugging each other at an airport, which I looked at when my motivation was lagging; the hatred really stoked my graphic design skills.

"I have seen more sexual chemistry at a castrato convention," pronounced June, glancing at the screen.

I had thought that too, but presumed it was just the tangled wires of my emotions misfiring. I shook my head. "Whatever, I am too busy being the Peter Mandelson to your Tony Blair, without the Iraq War and all the other problematic stuff," I said, closing the browser window. "It's not Baby Botch Summer anymore, I haven't got time to wallow in romantic intrigue."

"Fine, spoilsport," said June, flopping down on her sofa. "What's my diary like tomorrow?"

"I have got you pulling a pint in a pub, classic politico move," I said.

"Ugh," whined June. "It's not that new one that sells £7 pints that the staff bring to you on electric scooters, is it?"

"No, you're going to Jock's," I told her. June's eyes brightened.

"The scuzziest local bar in town? Where everyone has a red nose and red eyes? Full of old codgers and prostitutes from 7am-midnight? Rumour has it they harboured an escaped orangutan as a bartender for three years in the '80s?"

"The very one. No other politicians dare to go there. It's going to look great on your TikTok and get all the waifs and strays of Beath to vote for you. God knows there is enough of them."

"Drinking in the dirtiest pub in town," said June, taking me in a bear hug. "You're the best friend a girl could ask for."

CHAPTER

45

As June's Campaign Manager, I went along to events like the pub photocall to document it for her social media and manage any press enquiries. However, that whole week I felt a bit distracted, I kept thinking about the podcast with Paxton and what it would be like to be back in the spotlight myself, and alone this time; the last interviews I had done were almost a year ago in Denmark and they were almost always with Hatton.

I had also been distracted by my phone, which seemed to ring with alarming regularity. A true millennial, I order everything online specifically so I don't have to have an anxiety attack and mispronounce my own name on the phone.

This was the exact scenario running through my head as I felt my phone buzz. I was walking Brutus down Beath Walk when it rang for the fourth time that day. I pulled it out of my pocket to see it was the same person who had already called three times - Koala. Why couldn't he just text like a normal person? I wondered as I resigned myself to answering.

"Hello, Kooler," I said. Turned out my fear didn't come true - I just mucked up his name instead. To be fair, I was clutching the phone between my ear and shoulder, bending down to poop scoop a poo Brutus had seen fit to do just as a herd of rush hour commuters piled towards us.

"Oh, hello, Sam. I have tried ringing a few times, but never got an answer. You do not even have your answer phone turned on, do you know that?"

I did, because I only ever got long rambling answer phone messages from June after she had eaten hash brownies and had a conspiracy theory about the New World Order.

"Oh, right. I will take a look into that," I said, tossing the poo bag on top of an overflowing bin. I made a mental note to tell June to tackle waste management in her manifesto. "How are you doing," I took a deep breath and steeled my tongue, "Koala?"

"I am moderately peeved, Sam," he said with a sniff. "I have just accepted a place at the Graham Bell University College in Edinburgh."

"Congratulations!"

"Well, thank you...they allocated me a room in Hewson Halls."

"Oh, the party halls! I hear they have their own police station there to deal with all the ragers," I said, as if I didn't have direct experience of it when I came home from St Fillan's for the holidays.

"Yes, it's an uncivilised cesspit, according to my research. I have told them that they can offer the room to someone more suited to it, perhaps an exchange student from Sodom or Gomorrah."

"What are you going to do instead?" I asked as I passed a construction site for yet more student halls, set to be the tallest building in Beath, towered above only by the local indignation at being invaded by posh students.

"Well, that is the reason I am calling you. I need some recommendations."

"Like where to live?"

"Precisely," he said. "What about Morton Haugh? I have seen a fantastic bungalow for sale there."

"Morton Haugh?" I laughed. "I suppose it's ok, if you like hanging out with old age pensioners, playing boules and being in bed by 9pm."

"It sounds ideal, doesn't it?" Koala said gleefully.

"Koala, don't you want to have a proper student experience?" I said with a tired sigh.

"I most certainly do not, thank you very much!"

"Koala, I'm just trying to look out for you! I don't want you to look back in a few years and regret not doing things."

"What I will regret is not signing this contract for the property in Morton Haugh!" he said as Brutus and I walked past the 'show flat' for the new student housing development. A group of students spilled out and I overheard "perfect for hotboxing" and "party til 5am". It was then that I realised Koala was right - he most certainly did not want the typical student experience.

"You're right, it sounds right up your street!" I said.

I was proud of Koala being true to himself, but I wasn't so enthused about how true to myself I was being. Despite all the distractions, I still managed to whip myself up into a spiral of overthinking before the recording with Paxton.

I felt the dread of going for a job interview, not the anticipation of speaking with an old friend. It didn't help that Lily and Brutus considered every video call an opportunity to stage an audition for WWE, usually with Lily throwing herself off a bookcase on the background on top of Brutus, the two of them whirling around the floor in a cartoonish ball of fluff.

"Forget about it, I will get someone to edit out the hissing," said Paxton as the fight carried on in the background. "And go get yourself a glass of wine and chill out, you look like Mark Zuckerberg about to give evidence."

"Ok," I said, slipping off screen to pour myself a glass of Prosecco, even though there didn't feel like much to celebrate. June had hosted a fundraiser the week before and had a few bottles leftover, so they were now stacked in my wine rack.

I returned with a large goblet of Prosecco and took a swig. The bubbles perked me up, but also reminded me of drinks with Hatton in Denmark. I got annoyed at myself for everything reminding me of him lately; at Jock's I had even found myself giggling at the clumsy flirtations of a punter who looked a bit like Hatton if he was 75, smoked 30 a day and drank vodka at 8am.

"When's this politician guy going to join the call?" I asked Paxton.

"Oh, he can't make it," Paxton said as a hand, presumably Harriet's (pink nail varnish), handed him a Whisky Sour. "Someone phoned him up claiming to be from the STI Clinic and told him someone from his last Bunga Bunga Party has rapacious gonorrhea and to get to the hospital before any appendages fell off."

"Paxton, what do you mean by 'someone'?" I said warily as Paxton wiggled his eyebrows over the cocktail.

"Oh, I mean me," he said with a hyena laugh.

"Paxton, what have you done?" I asked through gritted teeth, gripping my goblet of wine.

"Relax! I found an even better guest," he said, still laughing and I was pretty sure the joke was on me.

"Who is it?" I asked, a sense of unease coming over me. I flinched as Lily jumped onto the table. She sauntered across, making sure to show her butthole to the camera (it's obligatory for cats). I pushed her behind out the way to see Paxton still chuckling to himself. "Come on, tell me."

"Oh, just Hatton! I told him you asked for him personally," Paxton said, swirling the ice in his cocktail.

"But I didn't!" A prickly feeling I couldn't quite place came over me.

"He said he would be delighted to come along," continued Paxton.

"He did?" I asked.

"Yeah, sure, why not?" said Paxton, adjusting his earphones. "Who cares, it's going to be ratings gold. All your little Danish stans will break the internet just to hear it."

"Paxton, I'm going to take up baseball just so I can use your head for batting practice," I said, imagining knocking his head out the park.

"Don't look at me like that!" Paxton said coyly. "You know you love me really."

"You're just lucky that I don't want to leave Caspar without a father."

"Harriet would make an excellent rich widow though, wouldn't she?"

I nodded - she would. I could just imagine the collection of black designer veils weaved by Sicilian nuns that she would buy.

"Stop distracting me! You and Harriet aren't even engaged. The issue at hand is that you have orchestrated an incredibly awkward situation for me!" I caught sight of myself onscreen - never advisable on video calls - and found deep, Gordon Ramsay-like furrows had ploughed their way across my forehead.

"It's okay, you don't have to thank me right away, you can do it any time you like. And if you could say it with Glen Lough '78 Scotch, that would be fantastic."

I continued to scowl.

"You know, you could just log off, or demand that I find another guest. And I would, if you really wanted me to, but you don't, so here we are," Paxton said, taking another sip of his cocktail. I was surprised by the perceptiveness of his comment, because it was all true, but also because of the remarkable clarity for someone who openly admitted drinking absinthe in the bath to unwind. In the morning.

"Touché," I said, reluctantly raising my glass to him.

"You should have a couple of minutes before he logs on to really get yourself worked up. I, meanwhile, am gonna freshen up my cocktail," Paxton said, disappearing offscreen to the clink of ice.

I grabbed my phone and summoned June:

Sam: JUNE! HELP! PAXTON HAS DONE SOMETHING CRAZY!

June: Oh, so he told you?

Sam: You knew?

June: Of course I did. You didn't think he came up with it all by himself? He drinks absinthe in the shower in the morning, ffs!

I left her on read for a couple of minutes while I mostly said 'What am I going to do' over and over again in my head, interspersed with occasional cursings of Paxton and June. My phone buzzed and interrupted my incantations.

June: Ouch! Leaving me on read! I've got a meeting with some disgruntled pensioners to go to now...but you and Hatton have unfinished business. You know it makes sense!

CHAPTER

46

Paxton returned to the screen, his cocktail sloshing over the edge of the glass. "Oh, he's in the waiting room. What do you say, Sam? In the words of the holy trinity, Destiny's Child, are you ready for this jelly?"

I took a big gulp.

"Wow, I have never heard anyone gulp loud enough for the mic to pick it up before. Anyway, on with the show!" Paxton admitted Hatton to the call and I put myself on mute as I gulped again. I couldn't tell from the screen if he was looking at me or Paxton, but he had the same pleasant, professional smile that he trotted out for TV appearances. I put on the pleasantly glazed face I used when one of June's potential constituents started telling me about how outrageous it was that the rats were eating the pigeons in the park.

"Welcome to another episode of That's Rich with me, Paxton, the Hamptons' 12th Most Eligible Bachelor 2012! That's Rich is sponsored by Just Jeeves, the bicycling butler food delivery service - quote PAXTON to get 20% off membership to the exclusive club. A corrupt banana republic also sponsors the show because they mistakenly think I can use it to brainwash the 'Global Elite', whoever they are, but I digress. This week I am joined by my author pal, Sam Chambers, she's not rich but she can match me drink for drink, which is one of the prerequisites for coming on this show. I am also joined by Hatton Finch. He's definitely rich and ageing like a fine wine, don't you think, Sam?"

I gave Paxton the finger. Hatton was on mute but I could tell he was laughing. That was a good sign.

"Wow, listeners, you can't see that, but the delightful Sam just gave me the one-fingered salute. Now, my fans will know that I am a loquacious son of a gun, but I am gonna take a different approach this episode. I am going to sit back with this delightful whisky sour that Just Jeeves delivered the delicious whisky for in under 20 minutes and let Sam and Hatton do the talking.

Paxton put himself on mute and kicked his feet up on the table.

Hatton and I looked nervous, like pre-teens told they are going to have to touch a member of the opposite sex at a dance recital. As the silence dragged on until I had to say something.

"Um, so, how are you?" I asked. And gulped.

"You're on mute," said Hatton.

I quickly jabbed the microphone button and went a shade of red known as 'flustered lobster'. I always despised people who didn't realise they were on mute and now I was one of them. What had I become?!

"Um, sorry," I said, smoothing my hair back.

"It's alright, there's always one, isn't there?" Hatton said with a smile that pricked like a needle.

"I know, it's embarrassing, anyone listening would think I was the old fogie, not you," I said, smiling back. I saw Hatton's cheeks twitch as he took a drink from a flute beside him.

"Is that prosecco?" I asked.

"What else? Seemed appropriate," Hatton said, holding it up to the camera.

"Me too," I said, my goblet wobbling into view.

"Cheers," said Hatton and we clinked our glasses to the cameras.

"Remember when we used to drink this in Denmark?" I ventured, taking a sip.

"Of course I do," said Hatton and the Victorian lady inside me swooned.

"Um, anyway, when I was on mute, I was asking how you were doing?"

"Not bad, thanks. I am back in Denmark at the moment, actually. I got talking to one of the networks about an idea for a TV show and they went for it."

"Congratulations!" I said, genuinely pleased, but cautious. "It's not…"

"Another shitty show about Afghan Hounds? No. It even has artistic merit!"

"Well, I am really pleased for you," I said.

"You should be pleased for you too. It was Bae for Pay."

"It was what?" I spluttered on a sip of prosecco.

"They want to buy the rights to it. I told them you're the one they have to speak to about it, but I knew you would never approach them yourself, so..."

"Um, wow, Hatton, I don't know what to say," so I said the only thing that did come into my head. "How is Electra?" Bit of a mood-killer, but hey-ho. I caught sight of Paxton leaning close to his screen, shovelling popcorn into his mouth.

"She is well, thanks for asking. I saw her at the airport the other day. We were sending Annie off on her Gap Year. She is going to Guatemala, by the way, going to find out about her heritage, explore the country."

"That's great for Annie!" I said "And yes, I did see a photo of that online."

"Yeah, it was pretty emotional, our baby going off to explore the world all by herself. But that's the last time I saw Electra. We actually had a long talk after...that... in Belkita and it was what we both wanted."

"Oh, I'm sorry to hear that." But I also wasn't.

"Don't be, we both agreed that it was right for us. As the statement prepared by our agents says, we have 'joyously unmeshed'. We grew apart," he said with a casual acceptance. "Plus there was the issue of me being completely in love with you." Now I knew he was looking at me on the screen, there was no doubt about it.

"I imagine that could pose a problem," I said coolly, even though there was a studio audience whooping in my head. "Especially since I am completely in love with you too."

Hatton pumped a fist and Paxton, on mute, pulled his shirt over his head and ran around his room.

"What do you say you hop a flight to Denmark on your next day off and we can discuss these personal and professional matters in person over dinner?" asked Hatton, in a mock-officious tone.

"Funny you should say that," I smiled at him, "I know this great little cowboy place in Copenhagen..."

EPILOGUE

"Are you coming to the studio?" I asked Hatton, picking a copy of the script off the kitchen table.

"I will see you there," he said, taking a bite of toast, then kissing me, because we are those people in a long-term relationship who don't care about how gross crumb-filled kisses are anymore. Lily watched on from her cat tree in quiet revulsion. "Annie wants to video chat. She has tracked a cousin down in this rainforest town and wants me to meet him." Annie had been travelling around Central America for almost a year now, piecing together her adoption story. Hatton and I had even visited her for a few weeks and she was only embarrassed by us like three times.

"That's great! Well, say hi for me," I said, heading for the door.

"Will do," said Hatton, logging on to his laptop.

I put Brutus' lead on and walked him to the door. There was a smattering of mail there, I flicked through it until I found an envelope trimmed in lace addressed to me. I was already running late, so I threw the rest down on the mat, shouted "Byeeeeeeloveyou," and went on my way.

I heard Hatton echo it as I shut the door. Examining the envelope on the way down the stairs as Brutus bounded ahead, I realised the handwriting looked familiar. Where had I seen it before? Then it dawned on me - it had scrawled 'I LOVE WILLIES' across my head in First Year; the writing belonged to Harriet.

I reached the street, looking up briefly at the ubiquitous tinkle of bike bells that you hear on the streets of Copenhagen. It was a bright but brisk Spring day, so I walked quickly to warm up as I tore into the envelope, a tiny pearl popping out and skittering across the street. Brutus gave chase and I pulled him back, almost dropping the letter in the process. Everything back under control, I unfolded it and saw it wasn't exactly short of the jewels, though, it was positively spangled in them. Halting at a street crossing, I began to read:

You are cordially invited to the wedding of:
Ms Harriet Judith Benson
and
Mr Hillary Maxwell Blixen St Giles Paxton III
On
23rd September
Location to be revealed
R.S.V.P

Wow, so that was happening. I didn't even know they were engaged. I immediately got on the phone to Harriet to hear the gossip.

"Hello, Mrs Paxton-to-be!" she answered.

"Harriet! Congratulations! I didn't even know you guys were engaged!"

"Thank you, darling! I am so delighted! Paxton got me THE BIGGEST sapphire ring you have ever seen. We are keeping things a little hush-

hush though. Paxton doesn't want a big society wedding in the States and neither do I. I would have to have one of those hideous American bachelorette parties with his relations where we drink mimosas and wear sashes! So we are inviting a select group to a top-secret event."

"Well, I feel very honoured to be invited," I said.

"Oh, so you will come, then?" Harriet squealed.

"Of course! Hatton and I will be there, wherever it is," I said.

"Good! I want to invite who has played a part in our love story," she informed me and I tried not to audibly gag. "I wasn't sure which address was best for June. Has she moved into an official residence now that she has become Mayor?"

"Ha, no, she turned it over to a homeless charity. She is still in her flat, I can send you the address."

"That would be fantastic. I have invited everyone else, you, all the staff and students from Belkita, Allan (we are on good terms now), Dean…"

"Dean?!" I said, grinding to a halt in the middle of the road.

"Yes, he has already said he will come. That won't be a problem, will it?"

It would, actually…

ACKNOWLEDGEMENTS

First of all, I think it's important to acknowledge everyone who read Bae for Pay, if it hadn't been for you (and your demands for a sequel!) then I wouldn't have created Boo for Who? So, keep reading and I'll keep writing.

Once again, Sibyl Adam's editing has pushed me to create something bigger and better than before. Thanks to everyone who read the drafts, especially Catriona MacDonald, Marijke Cortenbach, Charlotte Reid and Nick Kelly for offering thoughts/memes that helped shape the final version.

My parents, Eva Barrett and Gordon Steel, along with my partner, Rob Burgess, have been unfailingly supportive and encouraging, even when I quit my job in the middle of writing this to follow a different path.

I also appreciate Iris and Titus agreeing not to sue me for basing the characters of Lily and Brutus very obviously upon them.